Cause for Alarm

Cause for Alarm

THE VOLUNTEER FIRE DEPARTMENT IN THE NINETEENTH-CENTURY CITY

Amy S. Greenberg

PRINCETON UNIVERSITY PRESS

PRINCETON, NEW JERSEY

Published by Princeton University Press, 41 William Street,
Princeton, New Jersey 08540
In the United Kingdom: Princeton University Press,
Chichester, West Sussex

Library of Congress Cataloging-in-Publication Data
Greenberg, Amy S., 1968–
Cause for alarm : the volunteer fire department in the
nineteenth-century city / Amy S. Greenberg.
p. cm.
Includes bibliographical references (p.) and index.
ISBN 0-691-01648-8 (cl : alk. paper)
1. Fire departments—Maryland—Baltimore—History—19th century.
2. Fire departments—Missouri—Saint Louis—History—19th century.
3. Fire departments—California—San Francisco—History—19th
century. I. Title.
TH9505.B2074 1998
363.37'09752'609034—dc21 97-43370

This book has been composed in Berkeley Book

Princeton University Press books are printed
on acid-free paper and meet the guidelines for
permanence and durability of the Committee
on Production Guidelines for Book Longevity
of the Council on Library Resources

http://pup.princeton.edu

Printed in the United States of America

1 3 5 7 9 10 8 6 4 2

CONTENTS

LIST OF TABLES, FIGURES, AND MAPS

ACKNOWLEDGMENTS

WITHOUT the support of friends, colleagues, and a remarkable number of generous acquaintances, I could never have completed this book. From Alexander von Hoffman, who originally suggested that I take a look at firemen, to conference panel audience members who challenged me with tough questions, numerous people have improved this project with their advice and suggestions. Jeffrey Scott Adler, Bernard Bailyn, James Baumohl, Donald Cannon, Robert Chandler, Richard John, Terrence McDonald, Kevin Mullen, Mary Ryan, and Pieter Spierenberg have provided important input at various stages of writing.

Steve Aron, Mark Carnes, Philip Ethington, Ellen Fitzpatrick, Alexis McCrossen, Eric Monkkonen, Jose Moya, William Pencak, Stephan Thernstrom, and Ronald Yanosky all read drafts of this project and deserve an extra thanks for bearing with my often stubborn resistance to their good suggestions. Also important has been the feedback and support of my colleagues at Penn State; Gary Cross, Gary Gallagher, Lori Ginzberg, Thavolia Glymph, Susan and Billy Jo Harris, Deryck Holdsworth, Caren Irr, Philip Jenkins, Sally McMurry, Jeffrey Nealon, Anne Rose, Francesca Royster, Londa Schiebinger, Robert and Marie Secor, Susan Squier, Claudia Swan, and Nan Woodruff, especially, have amazed me with their generosity. Because of them, Penn State has proven to be a wonderful environment in which to work, think, and survive.

Several institutions deserve ample thanks for their financial support of this project. The Office of Research and Graduate Study at Penn State, The Charles Warren Center for American History, The Mellon Foundation, and the Harvard Fellowships office provided me with the time and funds to conduct research and focus on my writing. Deborah Malmud at Princeton University Press deserves a special thanks for her enthusiasm and sense of humor.

Librarians at the Bancroft Library, Missouri Historical Society, Maryland Historical Society, Enoch Pratt Free Library, San Francisco Public Library, New York Public Library, Wells Fargo Archives, and Library of Congress have all facilitated my research, as has Dean Krimmel at the Peale Museum in Baltimore. Nik Huffman deserves credit for his creative cartographic work. I would also like to thank Robert Middlekauff, who convinced me that there was no more honorable field of investigation than history.

Without the love and support of several close friends I could not have started this book, let alone completed it. Leisurely dinner parties, afternoons wandering around, and long phone calls with Alexis McCrossen, Skye McGinnes, Kathy Newman, and Eileen Randall made the alienation of writing bearable. My brothers, Mike and Ken Greenberg, deserve special thanks for their unflagging support and willingness to laugh at me. My parents, Kenneth and Jane Lee Greenberg, have long stood as my models of well-read citizens, and I am in debt to them for giving me volumes of Suetonius, Shakespeare, and Cellini at an impressionable age. Jack Doyle, the late Ann Doyle, Mary Ann Greene, and Sheila Ward have also provided me with meaningful support over the years.

The most patient man in the world, William Gienapp, deserves a special thanks. A model adviser, he held his tongue where he knew advice would do no good. He read countless drafts of this project and proved willing to edit and re-edit my work. He offered his support and guidance at a difficult point in my graduate career, and proved both able and willing to encourage ideas dramatically different from his own. His aid in this project has been invaluable.

My final thanks is to Richard Doyle. He has been an active participant in my work, a crucial source of encouragement, criticism, enthusiasm, firefighting puns, and my best ideas. He has fanned my ambitions and tempered my cynicism. From the beginning he has believed in this project thoroughly. His love and example have made me a more rigorous thinker, and a better person.

Cause for Alarm

BEGINNING AT THE WAKE

It was no ordinary alarm that brought together San Francisco's volunteer firemen late one December evening in 1866. The manly firemen—the butchers and clerks, the merchants and politicians, the immigrants and the native born—donned their velvet- and leather-trimmed dress uniforms and gathered in equally elegant engine houses to solemnly mark the end of their volunteer careers. At midnight, December 2, 1866, firefighting in San Francisco became the work of men hired by the city, as the volunteers were officially replaced by a paid force. A large portion of the 775 volunteers joined together to celebrate the glorious history of their organization. They recounted elaborate parties held in their honor, all manner of races, visits to other cities, and parades at home. Most of all, they retold stories of fires—fires they had subdued through skill, bravery, machine, and will.[1]

At exactly midnight, the city's fire bell tolled solemnly, marking the end of an institution which, in the words of a commentator, "had so worthily upheld the best traditions of California manhood and patriotism during its long term of volunteer service." The firemen removed their hats and sat in contemplation until the bells silenced. Bands in some of the firehouses played solemn dirges. Finally, an alarm set by one of the former firemen brought all of the old volunteers out of their houses for one last race to a fire—a fire in which the volunteers burned themselves in effigy and voluntarily succumbed to their enemy. The proper burial of the defunct department was then sanctified, complete with lit candles and a stuffed fireman's "corpse" dressed in a fancy volunteer uniform. A merry wake in the early hours of the morning concluded the proceedings. The daily papers agreed that it was a noble display.[2]

San Francisco's volunteers had always been a stylish group, and this ceremony reflected their love of the dramatic as well as the great significance of the moment. These volunteers were well aware that theirs was one of the last great volunteer departments. Starting with Cincinnati in 1853, the volunteer fire departments of all large American cities had fallen, one after another, to the mechanical superiority and greater order of the paid municipal fire department. San Franciscans had watched as their brother volunteer firemen in Providence, Boston, New Orleans, St. Louis, Baltimore, Chicago, and even New York had been pushed aside, their institutions shamed and dismantled, their machinery removed, their houses leveled or taken over by paid firemen. Only Philadelphia's volunteer department tenuously held on longer than San Francisco's.[3]

San Franciscans heard or read about rituals of mourning by firemen in city after city. After what amounted to years of struggle between municipal government and volunteer department, volunteers marked their failure in dramatic ways. In 1853, Cincinnati's former firemen physically attacked the new steam engine that effectively replaced them. On the final day before a paid department's inauguration in 1856, the firemen of New Orleans festooned their engines with black crape and signs announcing the "death" of their companies and marched through the town to the tune of "The Girl I Left Behind Me."[4] In Baltimore in 1859 a team of volunteers tried to outrace a team of horses to a fire, in a last attempt to prove their superiority to new methods of fire prevention. In 1858 in St. Louis, firemen burned down their own firehouse.[5] What the San Francisco volunteers marked with their dirges and mock burial was not only the end of fifteen years of service to their community, of the growth of the city they protected and guarded, of friendship and community within the department. The firemen were also marking the end of an era in America.

Writing a Fireman's History

The historian is always forced to start a history from the end, even if she does not begin a narrative with a dramatic denouement, as I have here. It is difficult to counter the appearance of inevitability in a story which has already been written, but it is the historian's task to reintroduce contingency into events that have long since ossified. Because volunteer firefighting was once so closely connected with ideals of citizenship, honor, and masculinity, its history has proven particularly difficult to decode. In retrospect, transformations in firefighting in the nineteenth century seem trapped in an American narrative of technological and social progress. To urban residents in the first years of the second half of the nineteenth century, when these scenes of mourning and moments of urban reinvention occurred, the volunteer fire department was an anachronism, made obsolete by technology and the "progress of the age." Ten years after the funereal ceremonies of San Francisco's firemen, historians read the volunteer period as the natural predecessor to the paid department—its successes and failings important insofar as they contributed to the formation of the later system.[6]

Yet twenty years earlier, the volunteer fire department had had an aura of permanence. Americans honored their urban volunteer firemen and made investments in their organizations that indicated faith in their long-term survival and prosperity. Even ten years before the denouement, few individuals suggested that municipal departments would soon be the rule, not the exception.

The constant revision of the meaning of the volunteer fire department should highlight, and not obscure, the significance of this institution. Debate over the role played by the department in the social, cultural, and political development of the city did not end with the nineteenth century. The urban volunteer fire department has been subject to a wide variety of interpretations, all of which recognize that this institution was central to antebellum urban development, while almost all completely disagree over the meaning of the transformations it wrought.

In the late nineteenth and early twentieth centuries, these institutions were the subject of detailed, adoring, lengthy works of local history. The authors of these local histories were often aged volunteer firemen themselves, and they narrated the rise and fall of their departments within a larger narrative of the growth of the city. In the more ambitious works, like Edward Edwards's *History of the Volunteer Fire Department of St. Louis*, written in 1906, the glorious history of the fire department is cast within a story of American progress as well as the development of the specific metropolis. Boosterism, American Exceptionalism, and Victorian binding converge together to frame the volunteer firemen in a particularly dignified manner.[7]

Outstanding individual firemen figure largely in these accounts, as do the valor of the men as a group and their heroic activities. The more elaborate of these volumes generally contain a photograph. The surviving members of the department, captured at an anniversary celebration, stare back at the reader with somber expressions. Even when the photo is missing, the gaze of the aged volunteer remains. This is not objective history. The ugly side of fire department activities, the racist incidents, the arson, the incompetence at fires, the fighting—all are glossed over in these histories. If such low activities must be explained, the blame falls on "outsiders," men who may or may not have worn a fireman's uniform but were not, in the heroic definition of the author, truly firemen. If it is impossible to blame outsiders, these activities are cast within a paradigm of quick and total decline directly preceding and legitimating the introduction of paid forces. The volunteer fire department (meaning the orderly members of the department before disorderly members infected and destroyed the institution) is the sum of its heroism. In these histories, the volunteer fire department shines forth as the brightest example of the excellence and continuing promise of the city.[8]

In the 1950s and 1960s the volunteer fire department returned to the historiographical stage as a subject of study. Several Ph.D. writers, each looking at the department of a single city in detail, drew similar conclusions about the meaning and significance of volunteer firefighters. A consensus was reached by these historians, as well as the older generation, that the volunteer fire department was a particularly heroic institution. Here men from all walks of life worked together, in the words of Anthony B. Lampe in 1967, "out of a sense of duty, pride and concern for their fellow man when he was in trouble. The volunteer never expected a monetary reward or praise or fame for this work. The basic fact that someone needed his services motivated him to action."[9]

But the ramifications of volunteer firefighting to the history of the city were quite different in the reading of these historians than to the earlier generation. To these authors, the age of the volunteer fire department was nothing less than a "volunteer age." The volunteer age was an era of cooperation and urban spirit, sadly lost to the current era of rampant individualism. The narrative of these historians was clearly one of American and urban decline, but with the promise that by learning from the example of the volunteer firemen, a better future was possible. Citizens might not voluntarily join together to fight fires, but they might, like those noble firemen, take responsibility for one another, and for the health and growth of their communities.[10]

The third historiographical reinvention of the volunteer fire department occurred in the late 1960s and 1970s, when the methods and goals of the "new social history" offered a new rationale for examining voluntary associations. The "new social history" embraced quantitative methodology as a means of studying previously silent groups. Its practitioners looked closely at individual cities in order to reconfigure the history of the invisible and powerless in the annuals of America. Over one dozen dissertations were written about fire departments in cities near degree-granting institutions, most of which combined some quantitative methodology with details provided by the old celebratory histories of the turn-of-the-century period. These studies placed the significance of the volunteer fire department on its effect on local politics and on class and ethnic conflict, as well as within the social world of individual neighborhoods during that time.[11]

Out of these dissertations, many of which provided excellent accounts of fire department development in specific cities, came important works of social history. These accounts offered an analysis of the lives and the importance of the working class in the antebellum city. Using the dissertations of Stephen Ginzberg and Richard Calhoun in New York and Andrew Neilly in Philadelphia, social historians reread the volunteer fire department as a working-class institution. Middle-class membership became insignificant, even though fire companies were once largely middle class. Those members "turned their attention to entrepreneurship, they withdrew from the companies" in the 1830s. The volunteer fire company was then free to flower into what Sean Wilentz called "the premier workingmen's social clubs of the 1830s." As Bruce Laurie stated in a seminal article in the early 1970s, one reason why "fire companies provide fertile virgin ground for historical investigation" was because "studies of fire companies can reveal valuable information about the life-styles and leisure-time activities of various sectors of the working class."[12]

In a transformation that some of the firemen would have appreciated, violence, once the skeleton in the firefighting closet, was suddenly celebrated. Fights and rowdiness were read as evidence that these working-class firemen had their own value system, opposed to that of the urban middle class. In the implied definition of these historians, the volunteer fire department meant the *disorderly* members of the department, the exact opposite definition used in earlier accounts. In Wilentz's work, volunteer firemen became the upholders of a working-class republicanism who used the fire department to assert their value in a society that was learning to discount them. The volunteer firemen, in this narrative, were eventually brought down by their tenacious efforts to gain political power through their institutions, increasing ethnic rivalry between companies, and the disgust of middle-class observers who recognized that volunteer companies were inefficient and disorderly.[13]

The accounts of working-class fire departments in New York by Sean Wilentz and in Philadelphia by Bruce Laurie were part of compelling larger works on working-class history in these two cities. They continue to be widely read and have become the basis for the contemporary account of the urban volunteer fire department everywhere. They are compelling histories of firemen by historians interested in documenting the history of working men. These accounts have been extremely influential on later histories of these eastern metropolises, and on the histories of most American cities.[14]

Any account of an urban volunteer fire department has had to contend with the legacy of New York and Philadelphia, and specifically with Wilentz's and Laurie's accounts. Steven J. Ross's reading of Cincinnati's volunteer fire department is strikingly similar to the work of Wilentz. Ross relies primarily on Kathleen J. Kiefer's master's thesis on the Cincinnati department, and the questionable assertions of reformers at the time, to draw his picture of a political fire department opposed to "bourgeois intrusions" on their culture. The Cincinnati volunteers frightened manufacturers by their occasional attempts to "link their roles as workers to their activities as firemen," distrusted "increased capitalist manipulation of the courts," and mobilized votes. Ross finds that the volunteer fire companies of Cincinnati, the "city's most important multiethnic working-class social organizations . . . posed too many threats to the city's reigning capitalists to be tolerated."[15]

In *America Becomes Urban*, Eric Monkkonen bases his model of national changes in firefighting on Laurie's work on Philadelphia and an earlier work on New York. The firemen of these cities represent all American firemen in his account of American urbanization.[16] David R. Johnson's entry on "Police and Fire Protection" in *The Encyclopedia of American Social History* makes the same leap from New York to the nation. In an otherwise complex account of change in urban protection, his antebellum firefighters are a less sophisticated version of those same rowdy individuals who appear in the accounts of Wilentz, Laurie, and Ross. Once again the reader learns that by the 1830s, working-class volunteer firemen posed a threat to both the political and physical structure of the city. His assertion that "buildings frequently burned to the ground while the volunteers fought one another" is based on a single source on antebellum firefighting in New York City.[17]

When reintroduced into a wider narrative of urban or working-class history, the volunteer fireman too often becomes a caricature of the carefully drawn picture of the previously discussed historians. In an entry on "The City" in the same encyclopedia, the volunteer firefighter is distilled into a single crystalline image, conveyed in one Wilentz-inspired sentence: "Fire Protection was originally provided by middle-class volunteer fire companies, but by the 1830s they had become lower-class fraternal and athletic clubs, centers of ethnic, occupational or neighborhood gangs more interested in racing or in fighting than in quenching fires."[18] At the least, the paradigm of the working-class disorderly fire department has influenced what aspects of fire department history contemporary historians have focused on in their own investigations, and, at worst, it has forced the history of other city's departments into a mold that ill-fits them.

The past analyses of urban volunteer fire departments have made important contributions to the understanding of local history, the history of urbanization, and the formation of the working class in this country. Still, they have failed to account accurately for national changes in firefighting in the nineteenth century, and they have failed to chart transformations in the relationship between the fireman and his community.

This is the first academic work to take a comparative approach to the history of volunteer firefighting.[19] I examine in some detail the development and importance of volunteer fire departments in three regionally distinct cities: San Francisco, which was protected by a volunteer fire department from 1851 to 1866; St. Louis, which had a volunteer fire department from 1820 to 1858; and Baltimore, whose first volunteer fire company formed in the 1780s and was replaced by a paid municipal department in 1859. This study, like the turn-of-the-century accounts often written by aged firefighters, attempts to understand the urban volunteer fire departments from the inside out. I have focused on the individual experience of the fireman in several chapters in an attempt to reconstruct the importance of the volunteer fire department to the individual member. I have attempted to understand why a man would join a volunteer fire department, what it provided him with, and why he clung so tightly to his company.

Like the later studies of the volunteer fire department as symbol of the "volunteer age," I also examine the great love and adoration tendered to the firemen by urban citizens. I attempt to explain why, for many years, the firemen could do no wrong in the eyes of grateful city dwellers. I also investigate why this adoration stopped and attempt to explain what this change reveals about the firemen and their society.

And, like the historians of the working class, I attempt to understand the class and ethnic dynamic of the volunteer fire department, the political significance of these departments in their local context, and the transformations that occurred in their membership and activities.

I have been fortunate to have access to the sources of information utilized by each of these three groups, and have made use of them all. At different points in this study I offer evidence based on census records, city directories, maps, city documents, contemporary newspapers, old ledgers of the firemen, and firsthand accounts. I also make use of the cultural world of volunteer firefighting—the art, music, and theater created for or in response to the volunteer firemen. And of course I owe a huge debt to the dissertations, articles, and books written by past students of volunteer firefighting.

As the reader shall learn, my conclusions about the volunteer fire department differ radically from those of the three previous historiographical traditions. In a few words, New York was not San Francisco, or St. Louis, or even Baltimore, the cities of my study. By the 1830s, fire companies in these cities had not mutated into lower-class fraternal clubs or ethnic gangs primarily interested in races and fights. While some departments were violent from their beginnings, there was no clear national pattern of increasing violence among volunteer firemen anywhere but on the stage, where a fighting fireman reigned supreme. All three of these departments sustained memberships that were decidedly heterogeneous in both occupation and ethnicity until their final decade. In fact, some departments could be better described as white-collar clubs than working-man's clubs. But to describe any volunteer fire department in class terms is to misunderstand the internal logic of these organizations. The fireman did not identify either himself, or his organization, primarily by class, and his culture was distinct from that of both the working class and the emerging middle class, whatever his occupation. Firemen identified themselves as manly men, first and foremost, and viewed their membership as a masculine brotherhood, where strength, appearance, and bravery determined the ultimate value of an individual. Gender, and not class, is the key to understanding the internal order of the volunteer fire department.

Nor were these men truly volunteers. Indeed, as I show in chapter 1, these men, while generally working without a salary, received valuable payment for their services. They received fine firehouses and machinery, freedom from jury duty, and a public tribute that elevated their status in a republican-liberalist political culture, where heroic deeds largely determined a man's worth as a citizen. Like earlier historians and residents of antebellum cities, I too celebrate the heroic deeds of the volunteer fireman. But unlike earlier historians, I will not argue that firefighter heroism was a natural and clear reflection of the greater virtue of urban Americans in the past. Nor will I argue that firefighters were virtuous insofar as they upheld a working-class republicanism. On the contrary, I argue that a comparative account of volunteer fire departments illuminates a series of changes that transformed not only these fire departments, but urban America as a whole in the first half of the nineteenth century.

The Evolution of the Volunteer Fire Department

Any account of volunteer firefighting in the United States needs to start its history long before volunteer fire departments, or the United States, even existed. Monumental and destructive natural fires caused by lightning on this continent predate human settlement. Cultural fire, fire produced by humans, was first brought across the Bering Strait from Asia. When European settlers arrived quite some time later, they found Native Americans clearing forests for firewood and practicing the slash-and-burn agriculture necessary for the cultivation of maize. Europeans invited fire inside their homes. Domestic fires necessary to sustain human life inevitably led to accidents, and increasing population density among European settlers in the seventeenth century magnified the destructive potential of those incidents in which fire raged out of human control.[20]

Today every large city is served by a professional, paid fire department that takes sole responsibility for controlling and extinguishing serious fires in the municipality. The layperson who attempts to fight a serious fire (one that has produced extensive smoke or has spread throughout a room) without the aid of the fire department is generally condemned for his or her efforts by both the fire department and the public. Luckily, this course of action is rarely followed by the discoverer of a fire. Sociological studies have shown that the more serious a fire appears to be, the less likely it is that an individual will attempt to put it out without the aid of the fire department. Most people never consider fighting an extensive fire, just as they never attempt to capture a bankrobber. In some ways, the contrast between citizen and professional is more clearly delineated in the case of firefighting than in crime prevention, the other uniformed municipal service. After all, the category of "citizen's arrest" is unknown in firefighting.[21]

The existence of the "citizen's arrest" underscores the fact that policing, unlike firefighting, has never relied exclusively on volunteer efforts. Some policing, like firefighting, was considered the duty of the citizenry in early America. It was originally the obligation of the citizens to man the night watch in most towns, but the work was so unpleasant that most citizens paid substitutes to take their place. When city governments took over the responsibility of paying the night watch directly, in the early eighteenth century, they institutionalized the practice. By the time volunteer fire companies were first forming, very few "volunteer" policemen were left in America's cities. Firefighting was different, and the contours of that difference also demarcated the changing status of the volunteer fire department in the evolving city.[22]

During the seventeenth century, even sizable American cities had no firefighting force. Fire was the responsibility of all citizens. Fire codes in the urban centers of colonial America specified that each homeowner be in possession of two buckets, ready at all times for the transport of water to the scene of a fire. All adult male citizens were likewise expected to respond at the alarm of fire. In this way, early firefighting efforts paralleled early militia requirements. In both cases, the material investment in protection was at the level of the individual citizen. The origins of more organized methods to combat fire started in New Amsterdam, under the governorship of Peter Stuyvesant. The Dutch colony taxed its citizens to pay chimney inspectors in 1648 after several small fires resulted from careless chimney cleaning. The city also ordered tanned leather water buckets from Holland and introduced an official fire watch.[23]

Technological innovations and increasing urban density spurred on more organized and effective firefighting forces in other colonial cities. In 1718, Boston citizens organized the first volunteer fire company in America, complete with a small hand-operated fire engine and uniforms for its members. In 1736 Benjamin Franklin established and actively participated in a fire company in Philadelphia. His example, and increased municipal initiatives in urban safety, helped to introduce organized volunteer fire companies and fire engines in most of the cities of colonial America.[24]

By the early nineteenth century, every American city was protected by several fire companies voluntarily manned by the citizenry. The eighteenth-century fire companies were organized around small hand-pump fire engines, but later fire companies operated increasingly larger and more powerful engines.[25] The group of men willing at any time to abandon other activities in the name of fighting fires also grew over time. More men became volunteer firemen, and those groups, like their machines, became increasingly powerful. As cities grew in size and population, so did the number of fire companies. When one company could no longer combat fires effectively in a portion of the city, or potential firemen chose to interpret matters as such, members would leave to form another company. In 1790, Baltimore was served by three volunteer companies. By 1800, that number had doubled. By 1810, the number of Baltimore fire companies had doubled again. In 1843, there were seventeen fire companies in Baltimore, and by the time the department was replaced by paid men the number had grown to twenty-two engine, hose, and hook and ladder companies, with over one thousand active members. As I will detail in future chapters, volunteer firemen practiced both white- and blue-collar occupations, but they drew their identity first, and foremost, from their unpaid work as firemen.[26]

Although the first permanent fire companies in San Francisco were barely organized by late 1849, by 1852 they were correctly identified in the *Annals of San Francisco* as "a numerous and influential association."[27] Between 1853 and 1866, there were fourteen fire companies and three hook and ladder companies within the department, with a total membership averaging between 840 and 1,000 members over the years.[28]

They were also a successful association. The number of fires and damage to San Francisco decreased perceptibly in the 1850s. From 1852 to 1855, five major fires in the city caused only a little more than one million dollars' worth of damage. The two and a half years before that, 1849 to 1851, were marked by over nine major fires, costing the city twenty-eight million dollars in total.[29]

The growth of these fire departments was finally checked by external forces. Beginning in 1853, municipal and state governments began to replace volunteer fire departments with paid departments that were rigidly controlled, small in size, and designed to limit the excesses of their volunteer predecessors. By the steadfast effort of editor and reformer alike, these new organizations were propagated from city to city, until city dwellers relied on volunteer forces for only so long as a paid department was outside the scope of the city budget. By the 1870s, it was the institution of a city service like an efficient paid fire department that gave a settlement the right to identify itself as a proper city.[30]

Despite the strength of Jefferson's vision of a nation of cultivators of political independence, moral integrity, and foodstuffs, the cities of the early nineteenth century were prideful places. Residents measured their city's success not only in comparison to urban centers in Europe, but also to other American cities. Among the growing cities of early nineteenth-century America, competition for investments and resources was fierce. Cities relied on booster literature to assert their advantages over similar settlements, and increasingly it was not only the geographic and natural advantages of a city that attracted the attention and respect of competitors, but its urban services as well.[31] Thus the status of a city's fire department had significance beyond the fires it extinguished. A successful fire department could signal a bright future, while a disorderly department might forebode decline. By the 1850s in eastern cities, a paid fire department was considered progressive, and, more importantly, it promised a future of progress. A volunteer fire department had become a sign of the opposite. As editors drew a cumulative image of the rowdy, disorderly, and corrupt volunteer fire departments, the departments fell like dominoes.[32]

Synopsis: Fire-Man, Urban Citizen

This book charts the social, political, and cultural development of the antebellum city through the lens of the urban volunteer fire department. The volunteer fire department was an institution of profound significance to the life of the antebellum city. Not only did fire departments prevent a city from burning down, but they offered significant material benefits to their cities as well. Indeed, as the *Missouri Republican* pointed out, "There are many traits in the character of the fireman that render him the peculiar object of regard."[33] Public appreciation of firemen was certainly merited by the secondary services volunteer fire departments provided. Some gave money: the more solvent of fire companies were active in charitable causes in their cities. The Baltimore Mechanical Fire Company was, according to its historian, "conspicuous for one especial phase. This was its charitable disposition. Outside of serving without pay, its members never failed to contribute its share to all contributions to any worthy cause."[34]

"Firemen are proverbially generous, even to a fault, and as brave as they are liberal," praised a San Francisco paper on the occasion of the St. Francis Hook and Ladder's contribution to the Patriotic Sanitary Fund.[35] San Francisco's Sansome Company donated one thousand dollars to the Washington Monument Fund in 1853, "the largest donation ever made by any one association to the Monument," reported the *Alta California* proudly. "The company has always made itself prominent in acts of charity."[36]

Some fire companies offered a chance at self-improvement. Many of the first urban libraries were created by fire companies, some for use of the public as well as the firefighters. In St. Louis, both the Phoenix and Franklin companies, in the words of one historian, "tried to do something for their neighborhood[s] besides fighting fire" and spent thousands of dollars on libraries open to public and fireman alike.[37] In Baltimore, more than fifteen different library associations were created within the fire companies, several of which contained more than one thousand volumes. Although most Baltimore fire company library associations were intended for the self-improvement of the firemen, some were open to the public. The Baltimore *Clipper* reported that the Mechanical Fire Company library, whose rooms were "the handsomest in the city," contained more than four thousand volumes and was visited by an "astonishing number" of people, from "every section of the country." The Liberty Library Association, an adjunct to the company of the same name, allowed women access to their collection in 1850 and also set up an apprentices' library.[38] The Howard and Sansome companies in San Francisco also kept large libraries, the Sansome's numbering upwards of fifteen hundred volumes, many of which were donated to the city in 1860.[39]

Fire companies organized some of the first fire insurance in many cities. Baltimore's firemen created two insurance companies serving the city, and members of the Baltimore Fire Department elected the directors of the companies.[40] Volunteer firemen in San Francisco, Baltimore, and St. Louis, as in most cities, set up mutual benefit insurance companies for firemen and their families by mid-century. Any fireman who became a member of the association, by paying a small annual fee, was insured against injury while on duty. These associations also paid for firemen's burials and offered payments to firemen's widows and orphans. In St. Louis, even firemen who failed to pay their one-dollar dues were sometimes awarded compensation after fire-related injuries, as the Firemen's Fund Association tried to provide for all worthy firemen.[41]

Firemen opened up their firehouses for the use of the public, creating early civic centers within their own buildings. Baltimore firehouses were used as schools, and firehouses in cities across the country were often utilized by community groups. In 1856, the Women's Guild of the Fell's Point Mission held a week-long festival in the engine house of the Colombian Company, and the upstairs room in the Independent Fire Company was actually rented out to a "Female Sunday School" at one point. As the Baltimore *Sun* reported in 1843, the new building of the Watchman Fire Company in Baltimore, located in Federal Hill, contained "a public hall for that section of the city, the want of which has long been felt, and is now about to be supplied by this enterprising company." The enterprising Watchmen also placed an iron balcony in front of a second-story window, so that the space in front of the engine house could be used for political or other meetings.[42]

The Watchman firehouse increasingly became the site as well as object of urban celebrations. Their 1848 addition featured rooms specifically designed for "the use of public assemblies, parties, balls, and for various other purposes required by the prosperous and increasing population residing in the southern section of the city." In the period before the evolution of the service city, fire companies offered more than the extinguishing of fire. They not only protected cities from the threat of fire, but helped create community on the neighborhood level. In increasingly anonymous urban environments, the firehouse was a center for community and neighborhood cohesion. An investment in fire companies was thus an investment in both the social life of the city and in firefighting.[43]

The volunteer status and very form of the volunteer fire department also worked to endear it to journalistic observers. As the *Missouri Republican* reported, the fireman battled "from motives the most disinterested, with feelings of the most expansive benevolence, and without any hope of reward other than that which arises from the approbation of his own conscience and of his fellow men."[44] A voluntary association designed for the purpose of protecting property was a particularly attractive one to Jacksonian Americans. A British fireman noted in 1866 that "the arrangements for controlling and extinguishing fires, and saving life when jeopardized thereby, have become a popular and national institution in America, to a far greater extent than in any other country in the world; and it may almost be said, than in all of them put together. The system of volunteering seems to have been more developed, and to have taken a firmer hold there than elsewhere."[45]

As other foreign visitors were fond of commenting, Americans were enamored by "associations" in general. Alexis de Tocqueville reported that "in the United States, associations are established to promote the public safety, commerce, industry, morality and religion. There is no end which the human will despairs of attaining through the combined power of individuals united in a society."[46]

In an "era of associations" it was the perhaps the most noble association, free from obvious partisan or economic interest and dedicated to the protection of all, regardless of occupation, ethnicity or religion.[47] The volunteer fire department presented "a scene eminently and exclusively American," commented the Baltimore *Sun* on the occasion of the firemen's anniversary parade.

"It leads the world as an exponent of practical energy and genuine ability. . . . The material of the men and the means—their fitness one to the other, and to the purpose they profess—whether regarded as a grand demonstration of physical power and the efficiency of its application to public service—or as an exhibition of voluntary zeal for the common welfare—whether in the mass—in companies, or in the individual—it commends itself to universal admiration and respect."[48] As the Baltimore *Sun* outlined for its readers, the volunteer fire department was a mediating figure between sometimes contradictory forces at work in nineteenth-century America. It reconciled the physical virtues with moral powers, and it offered a vision of the mass as a harmonious concert of individuals. In firefighting, the singular purpose of the company, or mass, is governed only through the autonomous decisions of each individual firefighter. The volunteer fire department was not only the most crucial early city service from a practical standpoint, but also occupied a fertile and revealing space in the public imagination.

This fascination with firefighting on the part of Americans does not seem to have been a local phenomenon. This book focuses on volunteer fire departments that existed for different lengths of time, at different times, and in different regions of the country. This fascination can be traced in Baltimore, where the first volunteer fire company was started in the 1780s; in St. Louis, which organized its first fire companies in the early nineteenth century; and in the overnight metropolis of San Francisco, which organized fire companies just after the Gold Rush. Although these departments were organized in different periods, all were once praised as the most American of institutions, and also experienced almost identical developmental trajectories. All fell in public esteem in the 1850s, all were accused of certain transgressions, and all were dismantled and replaced with paid fire departments between 1857 and 1866. Despite regional and local variations in the political, social, and cultural contexts of municipalization—despite radically distinctive immigration patterns, patterns of class and political development and industrialization—the charges made against these departments were eerily similar. Common transitions in the perception of volunteer firemen by newspaper editors, politicians, and other city dwellers, between the first decades of the nineteenth century and the Civil War period, were intimately connected to the fall of republican ideals of citizenship and the rise of the businessman, the family, and reform politics in the mid-nineteenth century. The volunteer fire department was one casualty in the rise of a new city and new ideal of citizenship in this period.

This book charts this transformation. Chapter 1, "Paying Tribute," presents the firemen at the height of their glory in the early nineteenth century. Newspaper editors, property owners, politicians, and other city dwellers adored their fire departments. During the first few decades of the nineteenth century, and through the 1850s in San Francisco, the volunteer fire department was publicly lauded on a regular basis for its successful philanthropic activities and its successful firefighting. Volunteer firemen, the city's only reliable guards of life and property, visibly reduced the damaging effects of fire in the city.

The firemen did not go unrewarded for these efforts. They received a payment for their services, not in dollars, but in a tribute that served also to assuage the fears of all of those invested in the continued growth of the city. The volunteer fire department represented the hope that the city might not burn down, again. It provided citizens with nothing less than the faith to build and rebuild, despite overwhelming evidence of their own destructibility. The urban volunteer fire department offered its participants the fulfillment of a republican vision of citizenship. In return for risking their lives and competing for honor among equals in the name of the city, they received the regular acknowledgment of their civic virtue. Unfortunately, this relationship would not last.

Chapters 2 through 4 chart the decline and fall of the volunteer fireman. Each chapter centers on a key locus in the shifting relationship among volunteer fireman, antebellum city, and urban citizenship. Over time, the altruism of the volunteer fireman was recast as atavistic. These chapters explain how this happened, and why. The firemen's tribute in newspapers, poems, and on the stage declined. Volunteer firemen were increasingly identified by press and reformers as corrupters of youth, leading boys down the road to degeneration, rendering them unfit for decent employment or society. Press and reformers identified the brotherhood of firemen as potential corrupters of the entire urban political structure. Increasingly, "good" citizens from Baltimore to San Francisco began to ask each other, "Why are these men responding to fires, or more likely false alarms, rather than working? Why are they hanging around their firehouse, rather than home with their families? Can these men be trusted to protect our property?"

Chapter 2, "Manly Boys and Chaste Fire Engines: The Culture of the Volunteer Fire Department," focuses on the social functions of the fire company in the city. It deconstructs arguments that fire companies were working-class or ethnic clubs and reconsiders the role that gender played in constructing fire department culture. It also charts a transformation of the firehouse from site of civic pride, to locus for widespread disaffection about the morality of volunteer firemen. Press and politicians increasingly cast the all-male culture of the firehouse, a culture that embraced men of all occupations but held little room for the claims of the wife or mother, as a threat to the citizenry and to the public order.

Chapter 3, "Fights/Fires: A Glance at Violent Firemen," details a similar shift in the view of firemen's behavior outside the firehouse. As opposition to the firehouse mounted, so too did a nationwide perception of firemen as dangerously violent. Strangely enough, at exactly this same time, Mose the Fighting Fireman became a national hero of the stage. This chapter considers the extent and meaning of fireman violence and attempts to understand why departments with widely varying standards of behavior were subject to identical criticism in the 1850s.

Questions like these turned into points of contention between fireman and reformer in the 1840s and 1850s and revealed the growing distance between what the volunteer fire department had to offer the city (and the volunteer fireman had to offer as a citizen), and what the city expected from its fire department, as well as from its citizens.

Chapter 4, "Smoke-Filled Rooms: Volunteer Firemen and Political Culture," attempts to understand why firemen became involved in politics, and why reformers saw their political activities as so threatening to the civic body. In the 1830s and 1840s, reformers recast the fireman from model citizen to threat to the political order, and firemen in St. Louis, San Francisco, and Baltimore were publicly vilified for their forays into the political realm. This chapter follows the mounting hysteria about the political power of the fire department and assesses the accuracy of the accusations of political mobilization and corruption leveled against the fire departments.

Chapter 5, "Insuring Protection" chronicles the replacement of volunteer forces by paid departments. Although the decline in the reputation of firemen in both the political and social realms set the stage for their replacement, the costly transition to paid firefighting was not accomplished without a fight. Changes in firefighting aims and techniques, the rise of fire insurance, and new technology all helped undermine the authority of the volunteer fire department and legitimate the new order. Chapter 6, "Deluged and Disgraced," turns to the volunteers themselves and examines their reactions to paid firefighting. The firemen perform their own eulogy in this final act of the volunteer firefighting drama.

Although this study starts and concludes with the death of volunteer firefighting in urban America, the firemen get to live a long and dramatic life within its pages—full of conflict, camaraderie, heroism, and bluster. Ultimately, however, this is not a story about the firefighters, but about the relationship between the individual and society in the nineteenth century. The transitions that displaced the urban volunteer fireman were not localized in that organization but reconfigured the entire urban structure. On this note we leave their wake behind, and turn to their beginnings.

Chapter One

PAYING TRIBUTE

MAY 3, 1851—SAN FRANCISCO LAID IN ASHES . . .

More than three fourths of the city were nothing but smoldering ruins. Iron and zinc curled up like scorched leaves, and sent forth their brilliant flames of green, blue and yellow tints, mingling with the great red tongues of fire which flashed upwards from a thousand burning buildings. The hills were lighted up as if the sun was above the eastern mountain-tops, and trees, shrubs, herbage, and houses were as distinguishable in the bright light as at noon-day. Darkness hung over a large portion of the shipping where the broad and heavy smoke lay. People became paralyzed. Every few minutes the earth and air trembled, as great buildings were torn into fragments by explosions of gunpowder; and the air was filled with shattered timber, bricks and mortar. The multitude hung, as it were, upon the borders of this vast sea of flames. Few comparatively knew, or could know, what were the dangers and exertions of those who were within the range of the stifling and scorching flames. In less than nine hours from the beginning, more than twenty squares existed only in memory and the ascending volumes of smoke and flames which covered the site of the city. But the saddest sight of all was the destruction of brave but bewildered men, who, finding themselves suddenly surrounded by fire, rushed staggering and uncertain from flame to flame, in hopeless efforts to escape, until, strangled and scorched, they writhed and fell in view of hundreds who were completely powerless to save them. What a sad spectacle it was to look upon, the blackened remains of poor humanity, as they lay where they were burned by the fire which had destroyed the city.[1]

CURRIER AND IVES, the leading producers of popular artistic prints in antebellum America, produced ten separate prints honoring the urban volunteer fireman in two separate series, the "Life of a Fireman," and the "American Fireman." The former, which illustrated the activities of the New York Volunteer Fire Department, was among the most popular of all their prints.[2]

According to a twentieth-century art historian, "If Currier and Ives had issued only the six large folio lithographs which comprise 'The Life of a Fireman' Series, their reputation would have been fully established. These prints . . . depict with great accuracy all the excitement and color of the New York volunteer fire department in its boisterous heyday."[3]

Nathaniel Currier was himself a volunteer fireman in New York City in the 1850s, which partially explains his frequent choice of firemen as subjects for the firm's prints. Currier was also a staunch Abolitionist, however, and steadfastly refused to produce a "Life of the Abolitionist" series, despite the encouragement of his fellow activists. Had he thought that Abolitionism would sell prints, he most likely would have made such a series. The firm, self-proclaimed "Publishers of Cheap and Popular Pictures," was primarily concerned with the pecuniary aspects of the production of their art. The remarkable success of Currier and Ives prints, including those honoring firemen, was as much attributable to Currier's insight into the taste of the mid-nineteenth-century public as it was to the new printmaking and marketing techniques that enabled him to exploit that taste.

These are model firemen, respectable firemen. They are well built, neatly dressed, efficient, and openly admired by spectators in the background of the action. If a group of firemen is featured, it forms a highly coordinated unit. These firemen never rest, observers never heckle them, they never quarrel with firemen from other companies. They devote a great deal of time to saving people's lives rather than simply protecting property. In one print, *The American Fireman: Prompt to the Rescue*, a fireman carries an unconscious young woman, clad only in a light, delicate gown, away from the scene of a fire. In another print much acclaimed by the San Francisco *Fireman's Journal* in 1855 as "natural to life," "a fireman is seen emerging from one of the windows with an infant in his arms."[4]

There is little that is "natural" about these representations. Yet the success of the prints has been widely attributed to their realism. "The hypnotic fascination of a fire is present in all the Currier and Ives Fire Prints, but fortunately for the historian they went beyond this obvious appeal to leave a true document of firefighting methods and the actual scenes with a veracity often lacking in other areas of their pictorial coverage."[5] Artistic representation is a complex system of discourses, and, as John Tagg describes in *The Burden of Representation*, every representation belongs "to a distinct moment" owing its qualities to "particular conditions of production and its meaning to conventions and institutions." What discourses can we see operating in this "realistic" account of volunteer firefighting? If indeed the public loved the prints of Currier and Ives because their artwork offered a view of America that Americans found comfortably and happily familiar, then, fortunately for the historian, an examination of a print from "The American Fireman" series should reveal much about the vision of firemen held by Americans at the moment of that print's production.[6]

Figure 1.1. *The American Fireman, Facing the Enemy*. Louis Maurier for Currier and Ives, 1858. The fireman as saint and protector. (Courtesy of the American Insurance Association.)

The American Fireman, Facing the Enemy (fig. 1.1) was a print lithographed by Louis Maurier, one of Currier and Ives's principal artists, in 1858. In this typically idealized print, The Fireman is handsome, manly, and, despite his exertions, clean. His clothes are only slightly rumpled, and shirt and jacket are neatly buttoned. His expression is somewhat subdued and contented. A burned shell of a building in the background suggests that The Enemy, or fire, was extensive. It has been recently controlled, apparently by the exertions of this single man, the only figure in the print. The fire is reduced to a small flame, contained in the lower right-hand corner of the print, which the fireman physically dominates in his position atop a building.

This gentleman is clearly more than a particularly effective and fastidious public servant. In our "true document of firefighting methods," Maurier rendered the fireman in distinctly religious terms. His pose is similar to that of

Napoleon, Lafayette, or Washington in heroic representation of the period, all of which borrow formal idioms of earlier religious icons.[7] His aspect is similar to that of a standing St. George or other sainted warriors. The upright posture demanded by his heroic stance, complete with stiff back leg, is entirely unsuited to the activities of the working fireman. Although this fireman is encumbered by heavy hose, he bears his burden well. Like the iconographic saint, he also labors under the weight of specific formal elements that correspond to his ideal image.[8]

Antebellum Americans wrote romantic histories, they flocked to melodramas, and they generally celebrated heroic individuals, but there is something particular about Maurier's heroic fireman.[9] First of all, he is not an individual. Unnamed, he remains a representative fireman. Furthermore, the religious references in this representation go far beyond normal heroic conventions. Our fireman is slaying his dragon. He wears a bright *shield* on his helmet, rather larger in proportion to his hat than was the norm, and also sports another notable feature. Although the fire is contained *in front* of him, and is nearly totally extinguished, this fireman is surrounded by an aura, or halo of light, as if lit from behind. Perhaps instead he is lit from within. It would be difficult to interpret this glow as anything except a sort of inner fire, emanating from the fireman himself, traditional artistic representation of the status of the elect. This fireman has a halo.[10]

Why would an unnamed, representative volunteer fireman deserve a halo? Perhaps because his foe is so serious, so deadly, so terribly frightening that it could only be compared to the devil. As a clergyman speaking to a group of firemen explained, "The efforts of the Fireman and the clergyman are closely allied; one fights the fire-fiend in this world, while the other looks after the spiked-tailed gentleman who attends to the heating arrangements in the next."[11]

Only to a perception informed by the conventions of the fireman's tribute, or fireman's hagiography, could this be considered a realistic portrayal of firefighting activities. Here we see the volunteer fireman as religious icon. And here we see our first indication that the volunteer fireman was no mere volunteer.

The urban volunteer fire department was an institution invested with meaning. To businessmen and boosters, it augured a future either brilliant with possibility, or fated to decline. Other urban residents invested it with even greater significance. Contemporary descriptions of the departments reveal a relationship between community and volunteer fire department radically different from the respectful if generally negligent distance of twentieth-century city dwellers from their city services, or of the antebellum populace to other city services such as the police. Currier and Ives produced no print series in honor of urban policemen that Americans could hang in their drawing rooms. The relationship between city and volunteer fireman, as revealed in newspaper articles, political tracts, popular literature, and contemporary histories, was never neutral. Baltimore's volunteer firemen received lavish tribute through the 1830s. In the 1840s this began to change, and their popularity as expressed in newspaper coverage began a steady decline, culminating in the mid-1850s, when efforts to replace them with paid firefighters began in earnest. The relationship between firemen in St. Louis and their public followed a similar chronological trajectory. In San Francisco, the volunteer firemen and their firefighting were the subject of adulation through the mid-1850s, when reformers began to publicly condemn their organization. In all three of these departments, the firemen fell from favor within a surprisingly short period of time.

Clear, if not always rational, concerns dictated the disgrace and fall of the volunteer departments. A common acceleration, a fevered pitch, and frequent overreactions by both politicians and papers unified debates that otherwise differed in each city. The tone of the often one-sided debates over fire department politics and violence, discussed in chapters 3 and 4, appear at first glance hysterical. But when framed by the earlier reception of the volunteer departments, in the years in which the volunteers were in favor, a pattern emerges from these debates, and it becomes clear that the relationship between the antebellum city and volunteer fireman was never a rational one.

> In Europe, over the Fire King, we have seen highly disciplined bodies of men achieve great triumphs: we have watched them at their work—cool, systematic, aye, and daring too—in short, in the steady calmness of doing their duty. But here, where the fireman's work is a labor of love how different! The dash and spirit, the enthusiasm displayed—each fireman's soul in arms, one common cause, one universal chivalric spirit that sees or will see no danger, animating all, worthy of being ranked with the highest displays of bravery, and ennobled far above all instances of courage displayed in human carnage furnished us in the annals of battles.[12]

Journalism in the nineteenth century was wildly hyperbolic, but even by its own standards the acclamation tendered to volunteer firemen was remarkable in both its quantity and its terms.[13] The tribute to the firemen of San Francisco, quoted above, was not occasioned by any particular display of universal chivalric spirit. It was not offered after a valiant effort at a fire. Newspapers across the country praised firemen on every possible occasion, or, as in this case, on no special occasion at all. They praised firemen in editorial, letter, and poem. A poem was composed for the Union Fire Company after a fire appeared on the front page of the Baltimore *Sun*. A short sample of the abominable if enthusiastic lyrics of this typical tribute to the urban firefighting force will suffice:

To the Union Fire Company

Hail gallant sons of fire!
Hail salamanders brave!
Who dare the destroying angel's ire.
Nor dread the grave.
If ye can save,
The helpless from a doom so dire.[14]

While the mythological salamander could withstand fire, the volunteer fireman, sadly, could not. The bravery of the fireman was regularly noted, and praised in the fireman's tribute. The fireman was like a soldier, fearless in battle. "As the soldier loves the ensanguined field and the havoc of the fight, so the fireman loves the battle of the raging flame, and the fierce conflict of the red fire king," an orator declared to the firemen of San Francisco. But although a military motif was a favored one in the discourse of the fireman, the fireman was inevitably judged the superior. As the *Alta California* professed, firemen were "ennobled far above all instances of courage displayed in human carnage."[15] A poem in the San Francisco firemen's own newspaper noted that

Their fame is not of battle field—
of deadly, mortal strife—
But higher, nobler for than this—
'tis hope, 'tis human life![16]

The San Francisco *Evening Bulletin* agreed: "There is no instance in history of unrewarded, self-sacrificing effort—whether it be noted in military or civic chroniclers than that to which the journals of the day tender their faint ephemeral praise in mentioning the deeds of the Fire Department. . . . No soldier's triumph, even in defense of country, equals theirs, for theirs is not a victory stained with blood."

Because firemen were not tainted by the blood of human opponents, newspapers proclaimed their victory more noble than that of the soldier. This was a popular conclusion for both prose and poem.

A war more glorious than the strife
that ends in taking human life,
And fills the warrior's grave;
No! rather 'twine the chaplet now,
Around the gallant Fireman's brow,
Who risks his life to save.[17]

But if any soldier were to equal the achievements of the volunteer fireman, certainly it would be the classical warrior. Firemen were frequently compared to classical warriors both directly and indirectly by writers who revered the warrior for his contribution to the life of the ancient polis. As Hannah Arendt wrote about the ancient predecessor to the nineteenth-century city, "to belong to the few 'equals' (*homoioi*) meant to be permitted to live among one's peers; but the public realm itself, the *polis*, was permeated by a fiercely agonal spirit, where everybody had constantly to distinguish himself from all others, to show through unique deeds or achievements that he was the best of all (*aien aristeuein*)."[18]

The fireman, like the classical warrior, was engaged in an agonal struggle. Yet the volunteer fireman also practiced what Alexis de Tocqueville identified in the 1830s as the "best suited of all philosophical theories to the wants of men of our time," the principle of "self-interest Rightly Understood." "Americans," he wrote, "show with complacency how an enlightened regard for themselves constantly prompts them to assist one another and inclines them willingly to sacrifice a portion of their time and property to the welfare of the state."[19]

To volunteer to fight fires was not only to distinguish oneself with unique deeds, but also to pledge allegiance to the growth of the city, and to express in the purest form possible one's community spirit and enlightened self-interest. While contemporary observers generally chose classical imagery to praise their volunteer firemen, they also acknowledged the particularly American aspects of their endeavor. As the Baltimore *Sun* commented on the occasion of one of the many firemen's parades in that city, the volunteer firemen offered "a scene eminently and exclusively American . . . it leads the world as an exponent of practical energy and genuine ability."[20]

In other words, the urban volunteer fire department offered men the fulfillment of a particular ideal of citizenship: the opportunity to volunteer their very lives in the service of the city, and the regular acknowledgment of their civic virtue. The comparison drawn by writers between firemen and classical heroes in this tribute literature was not simply a poetic convention but held real political significance to American city dwellers. As historians including Drew McCoy, Gordon Wood, and Philip Ethington have shown, Americans in the Jeffersonian and Jacksonian period were schooled in romantic republicanism.[21] They turned to ancient Athens and Rome for a model on which to construct society. Firemen, like classical warriors, both distinguished themselves in the public realm and enabled the contemporary polis to practice its republican liberalism, in Ethington's definition, "a political language which traced the welfare of civil society to the ethical conduct of those who governed," and maintained that there was a single universal good that would both transcend and enable personal gain. According to Ethington, this republican liberalism, modeled in part on the ancient polis, defined political culture in American cities in the antebellum period.[22] "In our eyes," grateful Baltimoreans confessed to their fire department, "at each victory over the fiery vesta your chief becomes the Miltiades of another Marathon."[23] Or as the elegant lines of another tribute to the firemen mused:

Now mann'd are the brakes, and the elements fighting,
Like Trojans and Grecians for Helen of Troy,
Or Spartans defending the pass of Thermopylae,
Or Bonaparte's stand at the bridge of Lodi!
. . .
Hail! Noble, chivalrous, bold, daring fireman,
Who struggles to save, though enshrouded in flame,
Who offers up life on philanthropy's altar!
Your name is inscribed on the portals of fame.[24]

The fame of the volunteer fireman was to be eternal, and not simply because fame rhymes so well with flame. In Arendt's vision of the classical polis, the citizen could achieve immortality through noble deeds performed in the public realm, deeds like those of the fireman.[25] In the antebellum public sphere, the gendered discourse of republicanism offered political and social authority to the heroic and charismatic man. The man who could achieve great deeds in the public sphere could ensure both his worth as a citizen and his status as a man. Within the ruling republican-liberalist political culture of the antebellum era, then, a man's worth was determined not by socioeconomic status, but by his heroic individualism, and noble citizenship.[26]

The language used by journalists indicates that the volunteer fireman was exactly that heroic individual celebrated over all other men within republican liberalist culture. In the words of our poet he was noble, chivalrous, bold, and daring. He offered up life on philanthropy's altar. The glory of the fireman would live on, the tribute promised, in legend and in physical memory. The *Alta California* proclaimed it "well worthy also . . . to have his likeness preserved in our council chambers as was the hero's we have named amongst the stoic philosophers."[27]

For a period of time in a volunteer fire department's development, almost any notice of a fire, no matter how brief, was generally followed by a positive assessment of the firemen's performance. Typical reports of fires in Baltimore in the 1830s and 1840s included the following praise: "The firemen, as they always are, were prompt in attendance, and worked with their accustomed energy to subdue the flames." "It was only by the almost superhuman efforts of the firemen that the flames were confined to the square in which it originated." "The firemen were on the spot with their accustomed promptness, and succeeded in saving the surrounding property, though some of it is of a very combustible character."[28]

The *Missouri Democrat* rarely failed to praise its firemen when reporting a fire in St. Louis. In September 1856 they reported that "our firemen deserve all credit for the bravery and perseverance manifested by them in their successful efforts." The following month they proclaimed that "it was only by the active and energetic efforts of the various fire companies that the destruction did not extend over to the block on the east side of third street." While in November they reported that "the [theaters] were saved by the intrepid energy of the firemen who upon the threatened peril hastened to the spot . . . though in a situation fraught with danger."[29]

California journalists shared the enthusiasm of their colleagues in the East and Midwest. In Sacramento, "all unite in awarding the Department unlimited praise for the skill displayed and endurance exhibited in checking the fire and saving property adjacent."[30] In San Francisco, comments like "well may California boast of her firemen" and "great credit is due to the fire companies for their arduous labors at this fire" were ubiquitous. How, in this culture of excellence, was a reporter to find the words to describe the performance of the San Francisco fireman? One perceptive account simply declared, "Our firemen all and always do so well that it would seem invidious to particularize any."[31]

Newspapers honored the firemen in other ways as well. In Baltimore, St. Louis, and San Francisco, the volunteer fire department was always news. Descriptions of the details of the social life of firemen were considered legitimate stories and featured prominently in the columns of city papers. No detail about the elections of individual companies, visiting firemen, or other department business appears to have been too small for note. When fire companies from Philadelphia arrived in Baltimore in 1851, readers of the Baltimore *Sun* learned the intimate details of the visit in lengthy articles spread out over three days. Readers heard what train the firemen arrived on, where the firemen planned to stay, and what the Baltimore firemen wore when they met the visiting firemen. "The Deptford [Company members] were out in a new and beautiful uniform, the hats of New York pattern, and ornaments in front with a polished brass plate, bearing the name of the company, white wool shirts, with scarlet rolling collars." Gifts given to the Baltimore firemen were described in similar detail, as were the food and toasts given at the firemen's banquet.[32]

Any return home of the Baltimore firemen was also news. In 1844, the *Sun* reported on the Liberty Fire Company: "This excellent company returned on Saturday evening from their visit to Philadelphia. They were escorted to their quarters by the Mechanical and New Market [fire companies]. They appear to be highly pleased with their visit and the attention bestowed upon them."[33] Baltimore's press and its readers celebrated the return of the Liberty Company as surely as did the Mechanical and New Market companies.

San Franciscans who were not themselves members of the Broderick Engine Company were able to share in the pleasure of that company's gift to New York firemen thanks to the conscientious reporting of their press:

> *Presentation.*—A meeting of Broderick Engine Company, No. 1, was held last evening, at their house, on Bryan Street, for the reception of a splendid life-size portrait of John Decker, Esq., ex-Chief Engineer of the New York Volunteer Fire

> Department. . . . We understand it is the intention of the Company to place it on exhibition at one of our prominent picture stores.[34]

This life-size portrait of the ex-chief engineer of the New York Volunteer Fire Department was displayed, and not necessarily because of the quality of the artistic reproduction. Indeed, the reader never learns the name of the artist who produced the work. This fireman's portrait was deemed worthy of display because it was a representation of a fireman. As tribute, the object itself was worthy of public notice. When a special firehat was given to a member of the Monumental Engine Company, San Franciscans not only learned the details of the manufacture of the hat and its presentation, but were also told where it was on public display for their closer examination. As graven image, the New York fireman's portrait was doubly worthy of note.[35]

Early nineteenth-century fires were reported in a manner which, by modern standards, appears disingenuous. Not only were firemen excessively praised in most reports, but they appear to have been excessively praised even when their performance was severely flawed. In a fire in Baltimore, although the firemen made an "almost superhuman effort. . . . There was a rumor that a child was burnt in one of the houses." The reporter dismissed this rumor, apparently unwilling to entertain the possibility that the firemen would allow a child to die. "We could not learn that it was a fact, and are disposed to doubt it."[36] This description may simply have reflected good will on the part of the journalist toward the firemen, but so careful were journalists to praise firefighting that it is sometimes difficult for the modern reader, and likely the contemporary reader as well, to determine what actually occurred at fires in this period. These firemen are closer to Currier and Ives's firemen than fallible beings. "The Herculean exertions of our incomparable Fire Department, at this conflagration, cannot be overrated. The buildings burned, together with their contents, were of the most combustible materials. The steam machine of the Pennsylvanians did splendidly, but even without its aid, the fire could not have extended beyond one block in which it originated."[37]

Did the firemen perform well at this fire? If buildings burned down, but the firemen were Herculean in their exertions, by what criterion was their performance being evaluated? Did they show up promptly? Were they intoxicated at the time? In the case of some of the massively destructive fires of this period, in which only the valor of the firemen was reported, the clarity of the bias of the reporting is striking. Reports of fires in the newspapers of early nineteenth-century cities are close in detail and sympathy to those contained in the existing fire company ledgers in Baltimore and St. Louis, written for posterity by firemen. Both are full of superlatives and are rarely critical. In San Francisco, the differences between the reports of fire in the *Alta California*, or *Evening Bulletin*, and in the firemen's own paper, the *Fireman's Journal*, are even more revealing than their similarities.

On the evening of June 14, 1855, a very destructive fire occurred which was reported in both the *Alta California* and the *Fireman's Journal*. Both papers commended the firemen on their performance. The *Fireman's Journal*, in typical form, reported that "the firemen . . . by their united efforts, untiring work and the discipline of their men, succeeded in getting the fire under control." But the firemen's own paper also reported an accident that "appears to have given considerable dissatisfaction to a large portion of the Department, for the reason that they think 'It [the fire] was allowed to grow too large.'" In the *Alta California* the accident was described in one sentence, at the end of the article, under "Incidents of the Fire": "The left wheel of Engine No. 12 was smashed by coming in contact with the Engine of Monumental No. 6." The *Journal* provided more detail:

> The fire would not have gained so great a headway had it not been for the untoward accident which happened to two of the most powerful engines in the Department. Monumental 6, and Pennsylvania 12, the former, in consequence of the brakeman being tripped up by a loose plank in the street, while going down Dupont street hill, and all control being lost, ran into No. 12, which was taking suction at the cistern. . . . Those companies were delayed some five minutes in their work, and the fire spread.

According to a fireman, the scene of the fire was disordered as a result of clumsiness or bumbling by the volunteer fire department. Yet no suggestion that the firemen were in any way responsible for the damage of the fire was reported in the *Alta*. This paper was content to report that "the utmost efforts of the Fire Department were unable to stay the flames." The *Fireman's Journal* seemed to have been premature in consoling the firemen that "although the citizens look upon the members of the Department as being invincible, yet they are not infallible, and are just as likely to be thwarted for a while, as any other organization."[38] The public never learned from the *Alta California* that the firemen were other than infallible. Why would the press fail to report the obvious, that the accident had impeded the firemen? That firemen would cast their exertions in the best possible light is wholly understandable, but what investment could the newspapers of these cities have in such a representation of the fire department?

Invested in Firefighting

Journalists flattered their firemen by reporting their activities favorably and asserting their superiority not only over soldiers and others on the "ensanguined field," but over other firemen. "For many years past the Fire Department of San Francisco has had no superior, if equal, in the Union," reported a typically proud newspaper item.[39] Another, which listed the fires occurring that year, was titled, "The San Francisco Fire Department is the Most Efficient in the World."[40] After observing firefighting in "the eastern cities" a reporter from the *Missouri Republican* showed "no hesitation in expressing the belief, that the Fire Department in St. Louis is *more* efficient than any we have witnessed in any of those places." But citizens in eastern cities would hardly have agreed with him.[41]

Journalists had good reason for flattering their firemen. In the industrializing city, self-interest, wrongly understood, may have appeared to residents to have run rampant. Firefighting, dangerous work provided in the interest of the city, presented a reassuring contrast in a particularly American form. A volunteer fire department was

> No hireling of a city's purse,
> no clique to be obeyed,
> Their motto published to the world
> is "Voluntary Aid."[42]

The San Francisco volunteer fireman was here honored because he was above partisanship, he obeyed no clique. Tocqueville's ideal citizen, his self-interest, rightly understood, led him to firefighting.

While firemen were sometimes praised because they were volunteers, they were more often praised for precisely the opposite reason. Volunteer firemen were not really *volunteers*. The Baltimore *Sun* described the anniversary of their fire department as "a day of public tribute on one side—the tribute of admiration from one class of citizens to another; and from bright eyes and smiling faces, to gallant hearts, manly forms and a daring and honorable vocation."[43] But this "tribute" is not what it at first appears, generous praise of a gracious public. This was tribute in the older sense of the word—tribute as payment made for protection. This was the tribute that Currier and Ives' fireman as knight might demand from the countryside. This homage—in newspaper, poetry, picture, and story—was one aspect of what was essentially a relationship founded on protection. This was the necessary tribute of a public otherwise defenseless in the face of the Fire King and his invading hoards.

Investing in Protection

> A flame creeps through, and out at the windows—and the door of a mansion, in whose chambers sleep the innocent and the young. The destroyer seems to lull the sleepers to deeper forgetfulness, and as death hurries toward them, the alarm bell strikes, and ere its first tones send their voices far, the fireman leaps from his couch and rushes to the tenement. The cry is passed that they must perish; "Not so," he answers, and careless for the ties that bind him to home and life, he mounts to the blazing rooms, and pushing through the suffocating smoke, snatches from its cradle, and from death, the loved child and bears it safely to its mother's arms, or wakens those who profoundly slumber on the fiery brink. . . .

> Shall not such be praised? Shall not such be blest by everyone who loves humanity who loves the fearless and the good?[44]

Beneath the layer of melodrama coloring passages such as these lay a profound fear of urban conflagration, a fear that makes the firemen's tribute intelligible. In the cities of the early nineteenth century, and through the 1850s in San Francisco, "those who profoundly slumber on the fiery brink" included everyone. Many of the readers of these lines had experienced "the destroyer" at first hand, and had personal associations with the profound spectacle of the conflagration. For these urban residents, the question was not, "Shall not such be praised?" but "Is praise alone enough?"

The vulnerability of the early-nineteenth-century city to the ravages of fire was wholly apparent to city dwellers. Every American city suffered extensive fires in the early nineteenth century, and fire was a leading danger to both life and capital. Over a twenty-one-year period in the first half of the century, St. Louis sustained over ten million dollars of damage from large fires. Baltimore was more fortunate and lost only two million dollars of property and goods to large fires between 1832 and 1855, but still experienced a large fire almost every year. Between 1849 and 1855, San Francisco suffered through seven major fires causing over thirty-one million dollars of damage, including a fire in May 1851 that destroyed three-fourths of the city, and which left San Francisco in ashes.[45]

The language that early chroniclers used to describe their assailable status also conveys the terror urban residents held of fire. *The Annals of San Francisco*, written in 1855, is only one of many sources to label San Francisco from 1849 to 1852 a "doomed city." Near-constant conflagrations in this period "filled the superstitious and timid with dismay and irrepressible terror," its authors wrote.[46] "Those days of dire conflagration made the blood run cold," remembered a reporter.[47] Another San Francisco resident asked: "Who can forget the sensations of fear and dread which struck the hearts of our citizens at the sound of the alarm bell. With its stroke noon or midnight, appalled men and affrighted women rushed frantic at the sound; our streets became alive with an excited multitude. Fire was regarded as a fearful adversary, dreaded and unconquerable."[48] The "terrible blow" of the St. Louis fire of 1849 "paralyzed the city for some time."[49] Of this same conflagration in St. Louis, another historian wrote: "The sufferings among the poorer class was heart-rending, their families scattered in every direction throughout the city, without shelter, many obliged to sleep upon the ground, without a morsel of food, and only the clothing they had upon their backs. Nothing like it could be imagined, and the whole population were struck with terror at the dismal scene."[50]

Nothing like it could be imagined, because great fires are, literally, unimaginable. But they also consume the imagination. According to Carl Smith, while accounts of the great Chicago fire invariable claimed that the experience of that fire was beyond verbal representation, the fire also provided the vocabulary with which residents of that city understood the unrest of the late nineteenth century.[51]

While there is no constant correlation between city size and frequency of urban conflagration, there is a correlation between great fires and periods of turbulent growth in cities.[52] The early nineteenth century was just such a period for many American cities, and fire was their premier threat. Buildings were constructed quickly, with little regard to fire safety, and both open hearths and dangerous early manufacturing techniques contributed to the flammability of the early city. Starting in the 1820s, St. Louis was increasingly at risk as multiple-story, common wall, and wooden frame buildings began to appear, and warehouses storing flammable materials such as oils, tobacco, and grain were built in already crowded areas. San Francisco, "until after June 1851 . . . a perfect tinderbox," suffered from similar stresses. Shipping further threatened both of these cities as well as Baltimore. In all three cities, wharves connected directly to planked streets and were often piled with dangerously combustible materials.[53] Each city sported its own particular causes for alarm as well:

> Failure of water supply and high wind with a fleet of "fireships" to spread the fire along the river front, were the conditions most favorable to actual conflagration in St. Louis, where they were greatly exaggerated by narrow streets and easily combustible buildings. In Baltimore, with buildings of the least combustible character, high wind alone was enough to make previous preparation almost ineffective, while in San Francisco a like result followed complete failure of water supply.[54]

Certainly an omnipresent threat of fire would "appall the stoutest heart" and debilitate the strongest community.[55] The volunteer fire departments, which were all either created, as in San Francisco, or expanded and stabilized, as in St. Louis and Baltimore, in the wake of particularly destructive fires were a first effort at combating this enemy.

Given the number and destructiveness of fires in these cities, the gesture of creating fire departments was not in itself sufficient to assuage the fear of city dwellers. For homeowners to rebuild their houses, or for business owners to rebuild their stores, they need to have some degree of faith and optimism that another conflagration is not immediately forthcoming. How could city dwellers not be paralyzed in the recognition that urban fires were inevitable, and deadly? What the fire department provided, then, was not only physical protection from fire, but symbolic reassurance. The fire department was a firefighting institution, and a firefighting charm.

Perhaps its second incantation was the more significant. As a charm, the urban fire department addressed a fear that extended beyond the rational. Fire signified, and continues to signify, a great deal. In Western belief systems, fire holds a sacred place. Visions of Hell and Purgatory are constructed around fire, and fire has long been used in Europe as well as America to punish heretics, witches, and other threats to society. Witnesses to historic fires commonly described the spectacle in terms of the Apocalypse. Peoples from the Aztecs to the Greeks have held that the cycles of history would end in fire. In English, the words "fire" and "purify" even have the same etymological root.[56] Fire can signify evil, or it can cleanse, but it always destroys. Fire was no neutral threat to the city. Its associations undoubtedly amplified the response to urban conflagrations. The terror caused by fire was not easily overcome in a flammable environment, and in these extenuating circumstances required sustained and diligent exertions to combat.

Stephen J. Pyne has helped to explain the human obsession with fire by arguing that "perceived fire is not a reflection but an active alter ego, a pyric double." When one looks into a fire, the division between Other and Self begins to break down.[57] But Gaston Bachelard, in *The Psychoanalysis of Fire*, has gone the farthest in his attempts to unveil the different elements of people's ambivalent and obsessive relationship with fire. According to Bachelard, the imagination elevates fire and attributes values to it. (Perhaps it is for this reason that these city fires are so often described by contemporary observers as *raging* with *great fury*.) "They call upon all their own passions to explain a shaft of flame. They put their whole heart into 'communicating' with a spectacle which fills them with wonderment and which therefore deceives them."[58] Fire is at once life itself (since to be living is to be hot), and much greater than life, capable of subsuming life and of feeding itself. "In comparison with the intensity of fire, how slack, inert, static and aimless seem the other intensities that we perceive. They are not embodiments of growth. They do not fulfill their promise. They do not become active in a flame and a light which symbolize transcendence."[59]

Antebellum accounts of fire describe exactly such a transcendent entity: "Fearful glare illuminated the sky, the devouring flames, appearing instinct with life, shooting and stretching themselves on every side as though striving to seize in their fiery annihilating embrace the tenements adjoining their devoted victim."[60] Urban dwellers anthropomorphized fire into "a fearful adversary, dreaded and unconquerable." The *Missouri Democrat* reported that St. Louis borders were understandably "terror struck" when their building caught on fire in 1855. "Some were conveyed down into the street while lying in their beds, paralyzed with fear." Who but the transcendent could even attempt to do battle with this most intense and powerful of fiends? The answer, of course, was the firemen.[61] "Beneath these fierce flaming banners on the roofs of the threatened buildings, and here and there within a few inches of the blazing timbers, might be seen the firemen—San Francisco firemen—fighting as they only can understand who have seen them engaged in one of their fiery battles."[62]

The firemen were thus elevated to their particular nineteenth-century status by forces unconscious as well as historical. In the flammable environment of the growing city, protection was of supreme importance. Thus, the mere announcement that there was a group of men organized to fight fire was not sufficient to protect or to reassure. The volunteer fire department had to be physically created. But it also needed to be envisioned as something great, as more than the sum of some brave men and their equipment. In fact, the volunteer fire department had to be re-created as a transcendent force that could and would battle a transcendent foe. It was only in the second creation, of a mythical firefighting force, that the faith of the citizens rested.

And that faith was what enabled them to rest. "Our citizens sleep calmly in their beds, our property owners rest content in the security of their possessions, by reason of their increased confidence in the fire department." San Franciscans rested calmly, and trusted that "the reign of the fire-king has passed, and this red-handed terror of the former day has succumbed to a nobler and more powerful foe."[63] This second creation, of a "nobler and more powerful foe," and of a force potent enough to protect against fire, was exactly what the editorials and popular representations of the firemen attempted. They were investing in protection:

> He reviewed the enterprises of the day—telegraphs and railroads, which were to connect the Atlantic and Pacific, and closed with an eloquent and thrilling peroration to the Monumentals, in which he painted the dangers, bravery and self denial of the firemen. . . . The burning house, the crackling flames, the agonizing call of the mother to save her child and the gallant rescue by a fireman, amid the benedictions of thousands of spectators, were graphically delineated. "Such," he said, "Is the intrepid fireman—and such, I am sure, are you all. Humane, noble employment—It must ever have the blessings of man—and be the care of Heaven."[64]

There was often nothing realistic about the accounts of firemen's exertions, because the purpose of these reports had much more to contend with than representing the truth. The community needed to know that the firefighters had met the challenge, in a form worthy of their continued faith:

> FIGHT OF THE FIRE: The Grand battle between the gallant firemen and the devastating element was made at the corner of East and Commercial streets. The boys did not hope to save the building, but they were determined that the flames should neither cross that thoroughfare nor endanger the shipping at the docks opposite. The building, a two-story frame, old as San Francisco, and as combustible as a powder mill, was seized by the fire, and seemed devoted to imminent destruction. But the fire found a master.[65]

The praise of the volunteer firemen in these newspapers is so common, and so repetitive, because any report on fire had the duel responsibility to convey news, and also to reassure the reading public that the Devouring Element was at bay. "We did not intend, when we took our pen to write this paragraph, to pronounce an encomium upon the character of the fireman," the *Missouri*

Republican explained on one occasion. But after considering the "sufferings and toils endured by the members . . . we felt the full force of the obligation under which we, as a member of this community, have been placed; and feeling it, we could not forego the pleasure of acknowledging it."[66] The reporters and editors of the *Missouri Republican* pronounced an encomium, even when they did not intend to, by the "full force" of their "obligation" to the firemen.

The repetitive praise of these volunteer firemen in antebellum newspapers helped the public sleep safely. These newspapers helped assuage their readers, and helped maintain the cult of the fireman. As Tocqueville observed in *Democracy in America:* "If there were no newspapers there would be no common activity. . . . A newspaper then takes up the notion or the feeling that had occurred simultaneously, but singly, to each of them. All are then immediately guided towards this beacon; and these wandering minds, which had long sought each other in darkness, at length meet and unite. The newspaper brought them together, and the newspaper is still necessary to keep them united."[67] The daily paper presented a perfect forum for the repetition of the firemen's tribute on a public scale, and the heroization of the fireman in the public sphere. As E. L. Godkin wrote in 1865, "The modern newspaper is the equivalent of the Greek agora, the only means possessed by the citizens of interchanging thought and concerting action." To the extent that there was a sphere of communication in the nineteenth-century city, the newspapers created it in the symbolic assembly place of their newsprint. Because of the power of newspapers in antebellum America, while the newspapers were united in their tribute of the firemen, the public was as well.[68]

This public tribute of the firemen did more, however, than reassure readers that they might sleep safely. It also rewarded, and paid, the firemen. While volunteer firefighting appears to defy self-interest, tribute, in this case, was as actively sought as it was given. While the newspapers united in praising the selflessness of the volunteer firemen, the firemen were actually looking after their own self-interest (rightly understood). Tribute was honor, and honor, in the republican-liberalist political culture of the antebellum city, was the primary payment volunteer firemen took for their duties. Like capital, honor was cumulative in this political culture, and firemen recognized that the greater the honor, the higher the yield they would receive in respect and authority.

Firemen took the tribute given them by newspapers as payment for their heroic efforts. This, was not, however, the only payment volunteer firemen gained from their duties. They received tangible benefits for their efforts as well. Firemen in most cities were exempted from jury duty and militia service, and fire companies were among the few widely supported public institutions in a period when the public good was defined in terms of the interests of a very small proportion of urban citizens. Robin Einhorn, Sam Bass Warner, and Michael Frisch have all concluded that in the "private city" of the antebellum period, services were intended for and provided to those who paid for them through taxes on property. City governments reviled expenditures, especially those that could lead to the redistribution of wealth, either in the interests of the poor or the rich. "Nineteenth-century American city governments were designed to minimize the redistributive effects of general funding by removing as many of their services as possible from the general funding process—keeping property taxes low and general budgets small," writes Einhorn.[69]

Yet governments levied taxes in order to present these "volunteers" with contributions for their maintenance from the first years of their existence. Fire department allocations prove an anomaly amid urban privatization in cities across the country. From 1829 to 1849, the city government of St. Louis paid $52,000 of the $116,205 of expenses incurred by the St. Louis Volunteer Fire Department. The San Francisco and Baltimore departments were similarly funded. Governments allocated money for the fire department hose and paid large salaries to chief engineers if a department had one. In all three of these cities, firemen petitioned their city councils for extra funds, claiming that they were unable to do their job without more appropriations. Volunteer companies were actually paid by the public through bonds, hearth taxes, and chimney fines levied by city governments.[70]

City councils underwrote the cost of new engines and houses, each of which could easily run to many thousands of dollars. Baltimore's Deptford Company house was built in 1843 for six thousand dollars, four thousand of which was provided by the city.[71] These firehouses resembled city halls or churches more closely than the modest twentieth-century firehouse. They were houses which in some cases could be mistaken for castles, befitting the status of these knights. Journalists enjoyed comparing their firemen to classical figures, but firemen more often chose medieval or renaissance themes to represent themselves. The Independent Fire Company attempted to reproduce a famous Florentine marble tower built around 1300—in the middle of Baltimore in 1853.[72]

Ambitious firemen in St. Louis and San Francisco erected other monuments in their honor. The Vigilant Fire Company of San Francisco built themselves a Gothic castle in 1856, complete with a forty-foot tower, wainscoting, gothic arches, and an ornamental shield inscribed with the company motto, "*We come to save.*"[73] Huge towers originally served a practical purpose, for they provided a place to dry leather hose. But their symbolic function long outlasted any practical ones. As the architectural historian Rebecca Zurier has written, "Like towers on Medieval palaces they offered another way to fly an architectural flag and call attention to the building from far away."[74] As city landmarks, these buildings signified to all residents the proper home and status of the urban knights.

Firemen were not always subtle in their demands for tribute, even of the specie sort. After fires, firemen traveled from door to door, asking for contributions and exacting tribute from their (sometimes) grateful and (always) defenseless public. The San Francisco *Fireman's Journal* in 1855 reported with dismay that "the habit has lately sprung up in the Department of making demands upon the businessmen and residents near the locality of fire, for contributions for this or that company." Those approached for "contributions" were understandably hesitant to refuse.[75]

This fireman's tribute was not simply a journalistic convention, but is apparent in letters and offerings from individuals and groups to the firemen. Thousands of Americans hung Currier and Ives firefighter prints in their homes, and numerous public and private groups offered gifts to their firemen. These gifts were often symbolic or fashioned out of precious metals. Within a week, two San Francisco fire companies were presented with "costly and beautiful" American flags made by a local woman.[76] The *Alta California* regularly reported gift presentations, including one from a group of ministers' wives, to the "gallant and efficient arm of our Fire Department." The Howard Engine Company was given "presents costly and beautiful." The godly women presented the Howards with, among other things, "a superb Bible, bound in the costliest style, with leaves splendidly ornamented with gold, and lids fastened with a massive gold clasp. On the cover, in gilt letters, the words 'Howard Engine Company.'" The accompanying presentational letter made a clear statement about the nature of the transaction and the relative position of the two parties:

> We, the Undersigned ladies of this city would respectfully present to you the accompanying volume, as a slight testimonial of regard for the untiring energy and philanthropy which has ever marked your conduct, when called upon to do battle with the devouring element with which you are at war. . . . Be assured, our prayers shall ascend to the Throne of Grace that you may be prospered and encouraged in your arduous duties, while on earth, and when called to render your account at the bar of God, you may here the plaudits, "Well done good and faithful servants, inasmuch as ye have done it unto one of the least of these, ye have done it unto me."[77]

Here the protected pay tribute to the warriors, to the servants of both society and God. The ministers' wives commend the firemen for their philanthropy, but more so for their "arduous duties" in the ongoing battle with the Great Foe—the Devouring Element. They even promise that God himself will be forthcoming with further tribute.

Although this Bible was offered by gift givers more enamored of religious terminology than other tribute-making groups, the form of the tribute and the respect shown by these women to the firefighters was not unusual. A female admirer of the Liberty Fire Company of Baltimore offered her favorite company "a wreath formed of hair, containing a lock of each of the members."[78] The Vigilant Fire Company of San Francisco even received homage from the women of Marysville during a visit to that town. "After the dinner the different companies marched into town . . . and also to the ladies of the town, many of whom were standing on the balconies showering bouquets on the firemen. . . . Nobody would take any money from the No. 9 boys."[79]

While firemen certainly appreciated financial rewards, they exacted the bulk of their payment through symbolic and verbal tribute. This was right and proper, claimed some within the departments. The San Francisco *Fireman's Journal* criticized the practice of collecting money after fires. If "those benefited by their services see fit to remunerate them in a manner compatible with the character of these gentlemen, we have nothing to interpose," but the firemen would better glory in their status.

> If the costly edifices erected for the Department—the elegance and magnificence with which its members are surrounded—The care and attention bestowed upon the organization since its inception—The kind words with which its members are greeted on every side, and the interest evinced in time of duty, in time of pleasure and of mourning are not a sufficient return from the citizens of San Francisco for the services performed as firemen, then let the cloak of duplicity, which has covered the members of the Department be cast aside, and let them abandon the proud eminencies of honor and position, they have so long occupied.[80]

Indeed, the volunteer firemen were paid well in the early years of their existence in the form of community adulation and status enhancement. While firemen practiced a wide variety of paid occupations, as described in chapter 2, honor and respect provided firemen with a way to raise themselves above the common man, regardless of their class or income. Proof of their status filled the early nineteenth-century city. Currier and Ives's "Life of a Fireman" series could be found in middle-class homes. Theaters held benefits in their honor which were advertised throughout the city. They could read of their stature in the newspapers, and they could see their likenesses elevated in poems and stories. Firemen were heroes of melodramas on stages across the country.[81]

Firemen could also hear their praises sung in the many musical pieces written in their honor. Bands composed music for firemen events of every sort, and every city boasted a fireman's quadrille or polka. Among the most famous was "The Fireman's March," written in San Francisco by Charles Schultz, a noted composer and volunteer fireman. This rousing tune found great popularity among firemen and public alike and was seemingly played at every fire-department-related event in the early 1860s. Serious compositions, like Francis Johnson's "Philadelphia Firemen's Anniversary Parade March," also honored the firemen. In the "Fireman's Quadrille," the most dramatic example of this genre, a New York concert audience in 1853 was treated to a symphony featuring real fire bells and the synchronized efforts of three fire companies responding in realistic form to flames projected out of the ceiling of the theater. [82]

Figure 1.2 The Hook and Ladder Quick Step, composed and respectfully dedicated by Albert Holland to Baltimore's Pioneer Hook and Ladder Company. The Pioneers were just one of the many fire companies to receive musical tribute from an adoring fan. (Courtesy of the American Insurance Association.)

Like Currier and Ives's firefighting prints, the "Fireman's Quadrille" appealed to antebellum audiences for a number of reasons. They honored the firemen, providing them payment for their voluntary services to the health of the city. They offered audiences the thrill of the rescue as entertainment. While fires were terrifying, firefighting was also entertainment in Jacksonian America, and large crowds of spectators gathered at fires. By unnerving and entertaining the audience simultaneously, the "Fireman's Quadrille" made explicit the relationship between pleasure and protection that drove the public adulation of the firemen to such a large degree. And perhaps, not least of all, these representations were so popular because they reassured their viewers that they were protected, that the fire was subdued by their urban saints.

A Fragile Relationship

In the years after the formation of the volunteer fire department, a symbiotic relationship between protector and protected developed in urban America. Tribute rendered by the defenseless enabled Americans to build and rebuild cities that not only could be destroyed by fire, but, as their own experience so painfully illustrated, unquestionably would. This tribute created and maintained a faith in the impossible, in the existence of a power equal to that of fire. While it lasted, this tribute also provided firemen with adulation and status, with cultural capital in a political culture that elevated the heroic individual above the mass of urban residents. As long as they received their tribute, fawning reports in urban newspapers, musical compositions, popular prints that equated them with saints, and wreaths made of locks of hair, these firemen were less selfless volunteers than Tocqueville's ideal Americans, looking after their self-interest (rightly understood). This tribute was at least as significant a payment as were the more tangible benefits offered to volunteer firemen, including their elegant firehouses and exemption from jury duty.

But unfortunately for the volunteer firemen, this reciprocal arrangement was impermanent. Increasingly in the mid-nineteenth century, as urban Americans began to question the propriety of their firemen's behavior, they also began to chafe against the tribute demanded by them. As is discussed in chapter 5, the rise of alternative mythical protectors also undermined the position of the firemen in this arrangement. Technology, insurance, and professionalization offered the same security from fire that the firemen offered, without the demands of tribute.

The decline of tribute, and decline of the firemen, became mutually reinforcing. A Louisville fireman, writing to his San Francisco brethren, warned them of the necessity of maintaining their tribute. He hoped that they would "succeed in kindling a feeling of sympathy and approbation in the minds of your community, whose genial warmth and glow may never be extinguished." In Louisville, they had not been so successful, and the results were sobering. "The fire department here is but a shadow of its former self, caused, in part, by a want of the proper feeling on the part of some of those of our citizens," he wrote in 1855. "For it is but natural that men, who have no personal interest in staying the progress of the fiery element, other than the good of their fellow men—I say it is no more than we have a right to expect, that a lukewarmness should take hold of our firemen, when they find that their labors, night and day, through the cold of winter and the heat of summer, are unappreciated and go unrewarded by those who are the recipients of all the benefits arising from their exertions."[83] Citizens would be unlikely to provide tribute to "lukewarm" firemen battling "a flame and a light which symbolize transcendence."[84]

As firemen fell in the estimation of the public, some firemen blamed the collapse of this tribute relationship. In 1855, the same year that the Louisville department noted the ramifications of their loss of status, David Dana, a fireman and historian of firefighting, offered his solution to similar ailments among firemen which appeared to be sweeping the country. Rowdyism, disorder, and violence among firemen all had their source in the declining respect of the public, he argued, just as "the loss of a due self-respect in the parent is sure to be followed by disrespect from the child." His remedy was that "the public should raise the fire department in their estimation,—should respect them."[85]

But how does one demand respect? Unfortunately for the firemen, the political culture of republican liberalism, the culture that celebrated the volunteer fireman for his agonal struggle against fire, for his manly deeds, and for his self-interest rightly understood, came into crisis in the 1850s. In its place rose a different political culture, one which identified interest in terms of class and ethnicity, and one which elevated the businessman over the manly fireman as the ideal citizen.[86] As voters and press reexamined the behavior of their firemen, they found that the volunteers were no longer so worthy of praise and adoration. It suddenly "became evident that privileges had to be accorded to those who gave their time and services freely, which always might and in some frequent cases did, degenerate into uncontrollable license."[87] Journalists and voters across the country asserted that their volunteer firemen had been accorded privileges that had degenerated into uncontrollable license, into offensive and uncivilized behavior, into regular displays of violence, and into political power. As reformers began seriously to question the social norms of their firemen, the firemen were forced to acknowledge the limits of their tribute. By the 1840s in St. Louis and Baltimore, and by the late 1850s in San Francisco, close observers were likely to note that while Currier and Ives's heroic fireman might still grace the parlor, another fireman altogether was haunting the engine house.

Chapter Two

MANLY BOYS AND CHASTE FIRE ENGINES: THE CULTURE OF THE VOLUNTEER FIRE DEPARTMENT

THE BEST-SELLING magazine of the 1850s was *Godey's Lady's Book*, edited by Sarah Hale for a female audience. *Godey's* featured saccharine romantic stories, didactic cautionary tales, interior-decorating tips, and illustrated reports of new fashions for the well-dressed lady. *Godey's* had a circulation of 70,000 in 1850, 100,000 in 1856, and 150,000 by the Civil War. Hale has been called Domesticity's greatest advocate, and indeed *Godey's* magazine seems to have been designed to advance the interests of the newly emerging American middle class. An explicitly gendered publication, it graced the equally gendered parlors of middle-class women across America.[1]

Marcus Boruck, volunteer fireman and editor of the San Francisco *Spirit of the Times and Fireman's Journal*, probably never considered himself a competitor of Hale's, but like her, he edited an explicitly gendered publication appealing to one segment of the population. Both of these editors avoided controversial topics and hoped primarily to entertain their audiences. The *Fireman's Journal* also graced some elegant parlors, although it seems unlikely that those two publications ever shared space on a table.

Boruck directed his paper toward a male, and manly, audience. This entertaining and informative weekly journal offered the firemen of the 1850s and 1860s the latest in fire department and sporting news as well as a dose of "light reading," much of which pertained directly to gender. On one particular Saturday in 1859, a fireman could choose between four compelling articles on the front page of the paper, all of which intended to advise his sex on the subject of that other sex. The most prominent item, "A Bachelor's Opinion of Woman," celebrated the unmarried state shared by most volunteer firemen in San Francisco and other cities. "Better be hung, drawn and quartered than invest any portion of your life in a matrimonial speculation," argued the narrating bachelor of the title. He proceeded to support his case with a frightening tale of a man who had once been a volunteer fireman.

> My married friend sneaks in and out of his house like a hall thief; he glances timidly behind him as if fearful of a sudden onslaught of tongue or broomstick; he never gets what he wants in the victualling line, or any other domestic refreshments to suit him—and his life is like his shirt, a thing of patches and shreds—with nothing but a memory of the fleeting joys of his honeymoon and of the days

> of his unmarried freedom, to enliven for the moment his grief-oppressed mind. His children bawling in the dining-room, his wife bawling in the kitchen, his dog yelping in the yard, his cat mewing and spitting in the cellar, a parrot in the hall squalling, a hurdy-gurdy playing "Shouldn't buy tripe on a Friday," and the general alarm of fire all over the city and an engine house and bell over the way—these are the morning and evening home experiences of my married friend.

Of all the indignities of his married life, the most intolerable one suffered by this piteous archetypal married man is that he has been severed by matrimony from his engine house, even as a general alarm of fire rings. He is not physically restrained from running with the engine—we know that he sneaks in and out of his house at will. But in truth his engine house is no longer his home. His life of unmarried freedom has been replaced by one that is a mere prison, so inferior in every way to that of the bachelor volunteer fireman that even his shredded shirt compares unfavorably to the fancy uniforms worn by the volunteers.

Another small item on the page, "Freak of a Jealous Husband," relates the story of a man who locked his wife in a "large iron cage . . . so low that she cannot stand straight in it." In this story it is the wife who is imprisoned, but the message is the same. "Truly, it is better for a jealous-pated [*sic*] man to remain single all his life."

But the choice to remain single is not without its painful side, as the final two gender articles on this page of the *Spirit of the Times and Fireman's Journal* admit. In the poem "Nobody Seen It," a woman describes a kiss stolen on a staircase, which only the blushing roses and singing birds of a garden bear witness to. The sentimental tone of this article is reinforced by "The Mission of Woman," which asked the firemen, "What gentleman is not more or less a Prometheus?" After the nineteenth-century man of fire had identified with his forebear, he was asked, "Who has not his rock, his chain, and his liver in a deuce of a condition? But the sea-nymphs come—the gentle, the sympathizing, they moisten our parched lips with their tears; they do their blessed best to console us Titans: they don't turn their backs on us after our overthrow."[2]

Although, strictly speaking, a fireman did not need to be married to enjoy the comfort of a sea-nymph, or to steal a secret kiss from a lovely woman, both of these are activities that could easily lead to marriage. So the volunteer fireman had a choice—between the firehouse and jealousy, between a damaged liver and a gentle sea nymph, between desertion after his overthrow and a fate compared unfavorably to a medieval execution technique.

One wonders why an institution devoted to fighting fire would expend so much debate on questions of marriage. This is especially curious considering that the choice to marry was not readily available to all volunteer firemen. In

San Francisco in 1860 there were still almost two men to every woman, and 39 percent of firemen that year were married. In St. Louis in 1850, only half of the adults in the city were married, and less than 25 percent of unskilled workers and 19 percent of clerks had wives. Adult men outnumbered adult women in St. Louis by a 3:2 margin or greater throughout the antebellum period. Although there were slightly more women than men in Baltimore in 1830, immigration in the later decades brought three new men for every two new women into the city. In the 1840s and 1850s, men exceeded women in their twenties and thirties by a large margin.[3] All three of these cities were characterized by a gender imbalance, and even those men who desired wives were often disappointed. Why then was there so much ambivalence toward marriage among these antebellum volunteer firefighters?

As this issue of the firemen's paper makes evident, gender norms, and specifically masculine norms, were absolutely central to the nineteenth-century volunteer fire department. The activities of the firemen while fighting fires, in their highly structured social engagements and in their firehouses, were all bound up in the expression of a masculine ideal, an ideal shared by firemen regardless of occupation. They constructed the firehouse as an alternative home, supposedly free for the most part from the influence of women, but really defined by women. The gendered nature of so much of the firemen's discourse indicates how central notions of masculinity were to this all-male-institution. By attempting to banish women and the specter of marriage from the firehouse, where copies of the *Fireman's Journal* circulated freely, they allowed women entry in imaginary and print form where they were physically forbidden.[4]

Another female figure loomed large in the firehouses as well—the fire engine, which was fetishized and adored. The fire engine was the female figure at the center of the masculine culture of the volunteer fire department. This culture shared elements and activities with an emerging working-class culture, and was often confused with this culture by contemporary observers. But the volunteer fireman's primary cultural alliance was never to a class. Volunteer firefighting mitigated class differences by upholding an extremely appealing vision of masculinity, which was itself not tied to socioeconomic status, a masculine image suited to the prevailing republican political culture. As discussed in chapter 1, within republican-liberalist political culture, men identified their virtue, and the virtue of others, not by socioeconomic factors but by individual charisma, bravery, and service to the city. Volunteer firemen proved their virtue by their agonal struggle, and newspapers assured them of their virtue as citizens, regardless of their paid occupation.

The fraternity of firemen encompassed manual laborers and great merchants, members of all ethnic groups, and even married men, who were drawn together not only by the tribute offered volunteer firemen, but also by the appeal of fire department culture. This culture offered masculinity freed from the constraints of class, and the home freed from the constraints of the middle-class domestic sphere. What the fire department offered men was an opportunity to race, parade, wear a uniform, and match strength with other like-minded men, regardless of occupation.

While republican liberalism prevailed in antebellum cities, this classless masculine culture was publicly validated. But during the middle years of the nineteenth century, the gender norms of the volunteer fire department caused increasing trouble for the firemen of St. Louis, Baltimore, and San Francisco. Changing conceptions of gender, child-rearing, and the importance of the home all worked against the values of the fire department, and the masculine culture celebrated by volunteer fire departments came under attack by an increasingly powerful middle-class family order. The businessman increasingly argued that his value as a citizen and a man lay not in his public service, but in his success at work, while women took control of the home as their separate sphere. With the rise of the new order, the alternative families created within the firehouse were hung, drawn, and quartered by their nemesis, the middle-class family.

Choosing a Fire Company

It is impossible to understand the gendered culture of the volunteer fire department without knowing what kind of man was likely to become a volunteer fireman, and what factors led him to choose one fire company over another. The limited number of surviving membership lists for St. Louis fire companies makes it difficult to draw firm conclusions about firemen in that city. In St. Louis, ethnic and class factors appear to have been important in determining the choice of one's company. Certain companies in this department were clearly identified as consisting primarily of Germans, or Irish. Indeed, St. Louis's Phoenix Fire Company published their by-laws in both German and English.[5]

Although ethnicity was a significant factor in St. Louis, fire companies in this city were not the ethnic clubs Bruce Laurie has claimed they were in Philadelphia. Almost all companies with surviving membership lists in St. Louis show a variety of names—German, Irish, Jewish, Dutch, and British. In San Francisco and Baltimore, the heterogeneous ethnicity of the fire department is even more pronounced.[6]

Based on data from the 1860 census, it is possible to make some preliminary observations about nativity in the fire departments of both San Francisco and Baltimore. The fire companies of San Francisco did not have strong ethnic characters, with the exception of the Lafayette Fire Company, which was composed almost entirely of Frenchmen and conducted meetings and published their constitution and rule book in French. One-third of the department in 1860 was foreign born, in a city where one half of all residents were immigrants.[7]

In the 1850s and 1860s, San Francisco fire company members were more often publicly identified with East Coast cities than with any other factor. According to a member, the character and "pedigrees," the "records and traditions" of the companies arose from these associations. "The Empires and Manhattans and Knickerbockers were New Yorkers. The Howards were Bostonians—The Monumentals were Baltimoreans." The Pennsylvania Company was, naturally, supposed to be composed of men from Philadelphia.[8]

Very few firemen were actually born in the cities that gave "character" to their companies. Only the Monumental Company showed any pattern of nativity in keeping with its reputation. Of the twenty-seven members of the company identifiable in the 1860 census, over a quarter were born in Baltimore. Only two of the thirty-two identifiable members of the Knickerbocker Company were born in New York, as were three of twenty-two members of the Manhattan Engine Company. Only four of twenty-three members of the Howard Company were born in Boston. Of the very few members of the Pennsylvania Company who appeared in the 1860 census, only two listed Pennsylvania as their place of birth.[9] One of these men, a thirty-five-year-old married paperhanger named E. F. Batteurs, was the only non-white member of the San Francisco Fire Department. His race was listed as mulatto, while that of his wife was listed as white.[10]

Nor did all San Francisco firemen gravitate toward the company associated with their place of birth. All French-born firemen belonged to the Lafayette Company, but all firemen born in Boston did not belong to the Howard Company, nor did all firemen born in Baltimore belong to the Monumental Company. Even taking the high rates of nineteenth-century mobility into account, the "characters" of the San Francisco fire companies do not seem to have been based on actual patterns of nativity. Even the Lafayette Company at one time had a president who was born in England.[11]

Only one company, the Pennsylvania, had no listed members who were foreign born. The majority of other companies were between 20 and 43 percent foreign born, with a department-wide average of 33 percent. Members born in Germany, Ireland, and England were fairly evenly distributed among the companies, and even the Knickerbocker Company, which limited its membership to American citizens, was 31 percent foreign born, with members coming from all three of the previously listed countries. Almost all companies contained at least one or two members with Jewish last names. In sum, ethnicity does not seem to have been a significant factor in choice of fire company for those members of the department who were foreign born, with the exception of Frenchmen. The foreign born were almost evenly distributed throughout the city in 1860 and were represented in every fire company. Nor did a majority of members born in Baltimore, Boston, Pennsylvania, or New York belong to any one company. Although members of these companies may have lived in certain cities before moving to San Francisco, there appears to have been little correlation between the character of the companies in 1860 and their members' places of birth.[12]

Because there is no surviving complete membership list for Baltimore's fire department, it is difficult to draw firm conclusions about ethnicity in that department. But fragmentary evidence drawn from select company membership lists and the 1860 census indicates that most or all of Baltimore's fire companies contained some foreign-born firemen, and that foreign-born firemen were also more likely to join some companies than others. Irish and German firemen were more likely to join both the New Market and Deptford companies than the Pioneer Hook and Ladder or Mechanical companies, although both the New Market and Deptford companies contained a majority of Maryland-born firemen in the late 1850s. Fire company membership lists from earlier years support the conclusion that Baltimore's fire companies were not ethnically exclusive clubs; all include some German and Irish names.[13]

Nor does it appear that firemen in San Francisco and Baltimore chose their fire companies because of proximity to place of residence. Once again, evidence from Baltimore is not conclusive, but an examination of firemen's residences from the 1860 census indicates that members who were still in Baltimore a year after the department was disbanded were no more likely to live in the wards of their firehouses than they were to live in wards where other firehouses were located.[14]

There was also a large degree of spatial diversity among San Francisco firemen and their houses (see maps 2.1, 2.2, and 2.3). Only a minority of firemen in this city seem to have belonged to the fire company closest to their place of residence. In part, this is due to the fact that almost all firehouses were clustered downtown, within a fourteen-block area. By 1860, any fireman who lived downtown had thirteen firehouses within walking distance from which to choose

When the residences of volunteer firemen are mapped in relation to the firehouses of San Francisco, it becomes clear that most downtown companies contained members who lived all over the city. In other words, in most downtown fire companies, members did belong to their neighborhood fire company. The Sansome Hook and Ladder Company, as illustrated in map 2.1, provides a good example of a typical downtown fire company from the perspective of the wide spatial distribution of its membership. Based on available data, the Crescent Engine Company appears to be alone among downtown fire companies in its neighborhood-based pattern of fire company membership. The statement that volunteer firemen "endeavored to live as close as

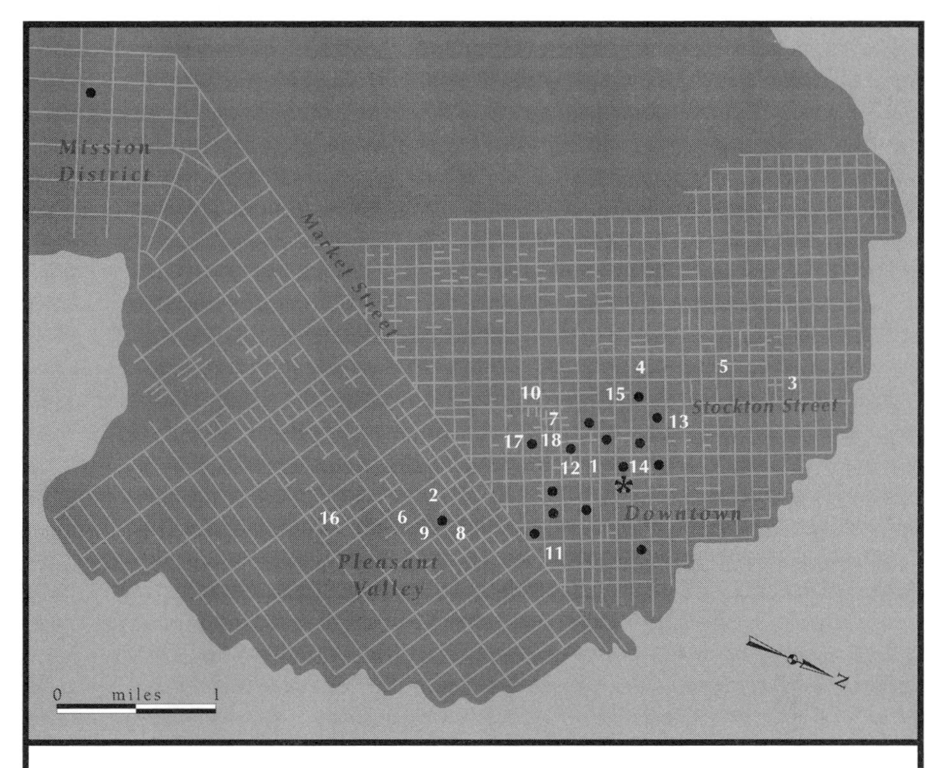

Sansome Hook & Ladder Company #3

23 Members residences in 1860 drawn from the San Francisco City Directory
Total membership in 1860 = 46

1 A. F. C. **Engert**,* salesman (29, unmarried, born in Prussia)
2 G. A. **Van Bokkellen**,* wholesale stationery (28, married)
3 F. A. **Bartlett**,* clerk (35, married)
4 C. E. **Gibbs**,* broker and merchant (28, married)
5 W. S. **Snook**,* insurance (33, married)
6 C. H. **Vail**, broker (30, married)
7 A. A. **Snyder**,* builder (34, married)
7 J. A. **Sperry**, importer
8 G. **Hudson**,* attorney (36, married)
8 W. G. **Badger**,* importer
9 W. B. **Edwards**,* merchant
10 C. **Ferguson**,* deputy city tax collector
11 T. J. **Haynes**,* merchant
12 W. T. **Hoffman**,* occupation unknown
13 J. B. **Larcomb**,* carpenter
14 A. **Maltbie**,* bookkeeper
14 H. B. **Coit**, physician
15 R. A. **Van Brunt**,* bookkeeper
16 J. **Blackwood**, storekeeper
17 D. **Hubbard**, occupation unknown
18 J. H. **Embury**, insurance
* B. C. **Horn**, importer (lives in Oakland)
* W. T. **Coleman**, importer (lives in New York)

* Member of SFFD since 1855

Map 2.1 The Sansome Hook and Ladder Company

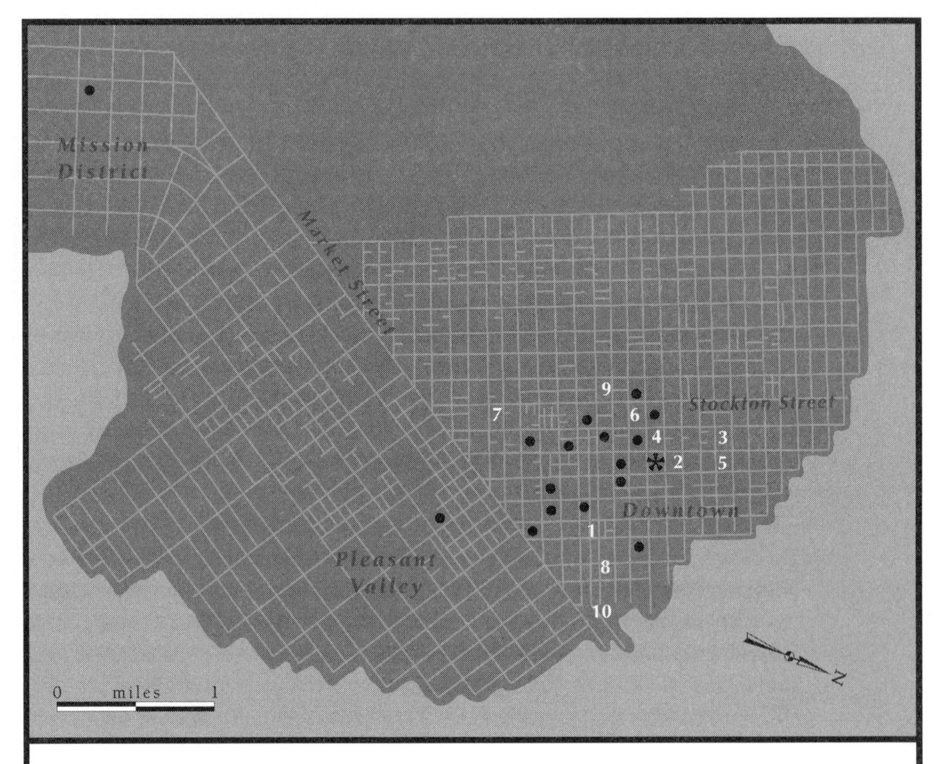

Crescent Engine Company #10

26 Members residences in 1860 drawn from the San Francisco City Directory
Total membership in 1860 = 56

Residents of Crescent Engine House

- **S. McNickoll**, tanner (26, unmarried, born in Australia)
- **F. Atkinson**, laborer (24, unmarried)
- **B. Ballou**, bellringer (42, unmarried)
- **F. Bussardett**, jeweler (23, unmarried)
- **N. Cromer**, butcher (27, unmarried)
- **P. Dolan**, clerk (23, unmarried)
- **F. Evans**, blacksmith (24, unmarried)
- **L. Morse**, butcher (25, unmarried)
- **Wm. Mount**, stevedore (30, unmarried)
- **John O'Brien**, baker (27, unmarried)
- **J. O'Brien**, hatter (27, unmarried)
- **John Past**, engineer (24, unmarried)
- **Chas. McCann**, driver

1 **D. Roach**, waiter (20, unmarried, born in Ireland)
2 **C. S. Biden**,* SFFD President and printer (18)
2 **B. Shirley**, bootfitter
3 **D. Gates**,* shoemaker (35, married)
3 **E. A. Rigg**, occupation unknown
4 **Wm. Farley**,* saloon owner
4 **Jos. Yeager**,* SFFD constable
5 **J. Foster**,* hotel owner
6 **Chas. Russell**, barkeeper
7 **L. Hess**, occupation unknown
8 **J. Joice**, occupation unknown
9 **H. Klein**, occupation unknown
10 **F. Osmer**, occupation unknown

* Member of SFFD since 1855

Map 2.2 The Crescent Engine Company

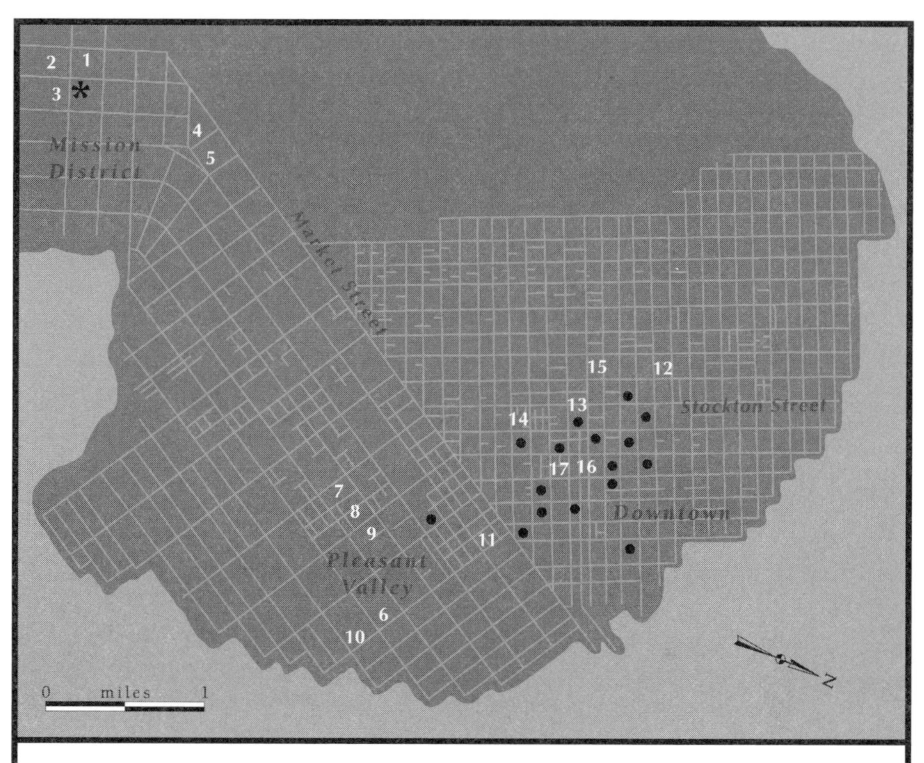

Young America Engine Co. #13

22 Members residences in 1860 drawn from the San Francisco City Directory
(Total membership in 1860 = 65)

1 **I. V. Denniston**,* farmer (29, unmarried)
1 **J. G. Denniston**,* farmer (35, unmarried)
1 **E. Valencia**,* farmer
1 **J. B. Moulton**, hotel proprietor
1 **Michael Lynch**,* SFFD Secretary and purveyor of groceries
2 **T. Dorland**,* judge (50, unmarried, born in Canada)
2 **Arthur Quinn**,* music hall proprietor
3 **Wm. Corbett**,* physician (51, married, born in Ireland)
4 **L. O'Rourke**, gardener (28, unmarried, born in Ireland)
5 **C. P. Marshall**,* purveyor of oysters
6 **John Dunne**, boatmaker (31, married, born in Ireland)
7 **J. C. Corbett**, barkeeper (29, unmarried)
8 **E. T. Pease**, merchant (married)
9 **J. J. Denny**, contractor (46, married)
10 **M. Fennell**,* contractor (40, married, born in Ireland)
11 **L Wintringer**, driver
12 **Wm. Langerman**, merchant (36, married, born in Bavaria)
13 **J. C. Wadsworth**, pantry man (28)
14 **James Grant**,* merchant
15 **J. W. Bell**, New York dept. of Wells Fargo
16 **G. N. Ferguson**, stable keeper
17 **E. H. Parker**, importer and insurance agent

* Member of SFFD since 1855

Map 2.3 The Young America Engine Company

possible to the engine house" perhaps applied only to the Crescent Company (see map 2.2).[15]

The Crescent Engine Company was the fire company that contained the smallest percentage of white-collar members and that, next to the Manhattan Engine Company, contained the greatest proportion of members who worked at unskilled occupations (see table 2.2 for the occupational composition of fire companies in San Francisco). All of its locatable members lived in the downtown area, including H. Klein, who lived on fashionable and expensive Stockton Street. The area west of Stockton Street was occupied mainly by white-collar residents in 1860, while the area east of this street was the main business district and had a more mixed residential pattern.[16]

The fire company with the greatest spatial distribution was also the one located farthest from the downtown area, the Young American Engine Company (see map 2.3). This company was situated far from the developed residential or business areas, in the neighborhood of the San Francisco Mission. The Young America Company, which also contained the largest percentage of foreign-born members (62 percent), had a largely white-collar membership. The high occupational profile of this company provides a strange contrast to the neighborhood in which it was located. The Mission District was a largely blue-collar district of industry and cheap housing. Yet 78 percent of Young America Company members worked at white-collar jobs, while only 3 percent worked in semiskilled positions and 3 percent in unskilled positions. Based on this evidence, it seems safe to conclude that merchants and businessmen in this company were probably drawn to it by investments in nearby industry and warehouses.[17]

For members of this company who lived in the surrounding residential neighborhood, this was the logical choice of fire company from a logistical perspective. Men like Michael Lynch, the secretary of the fire department and purveyor of groceries; E. Valencia, a farmer; and Judge T. Dorland, a fifty-year-old unmarried man born in Canada, lived in the immediate neighborhood of the firehouse. All three had belonged to this fire company for at least five years, which indicates their permanent status in San Francisco and a pattern of relatively high persistence.[18]

Other members of this company, including E. H. Parker, an importer and insurance agent, and J. C. Wadsworth, a twenty-eight-year-old pantry man, lived in the downtown area, directly across the street from other firehouses, and had to travel over two miles to reach their own company house. Although contemporary observers and historians have noted that some suburbanization of San Francisco had taken place by 1860, and that families, especially, tended to move outside the downtown area, there is little evidence of residential segregation by married firemen. Both married men and single men lived in the immediate vicinity of their firehouses as well as some distance away. This material shows no clear linkage between spatial distribution and marriage rates.[19]

This evidence makes it difficult to explain fire company membership in Baltimore or San Francisco in terms of nativity or even as neighborhood allegiances. In San Francisco, there is no clear pattern of age, occupation, or place of birth among firemen that correlates with their distance from the firehouse. Although the company with the lowest occupational profile, the Crescent, had the smallest spatial distribution, and the company with the highest occupational profile, the Young America, had the largest, in many companies the white-collar members lived closer to their houses than did some laborers. William Corbett, a fifty-one-year-old physician, lived across the street from the Young America house, while another member of his company, L. Wintringer, a driver, lived far across town.

In the high-profile Sansome Hook and Ladder Company, two importers listed as members lived outside the city (see map 2.1). One of these men, W. T. Coleman, president of the 1856 Vigilance Committee, probably had some trouble responding to the fire alarm from his home in New York City.[20] Six members of this company—three merchants, one attorney, one store keeper, and one broker—lived in the Pleasant Valley neighborhood, in the immediate vicinity of the Tiger Engine Company house, choosing to reside in an exclusive neighborhood and commute to the firehouse. It seems unlikely that these members regularly attended meetings and fires. None of these men were older than the members of the Tiger Company who lived nearby, but they did have a higher occupational profile. This indicates that occupational and class factors played a larger role in determining choice of firehouse in San Francisco than did factors such as ethnicity and neighborhood.

Yet even this generalization is difficult to sustain. In the Knickerbocker Company, located just two blocks from the Sansome house, the members living farthest from the engine house had a lower occupational profile than those living near the house. In the Howard Company, also located downtown, merchant members appear to have been evenly distributed in relation to the location of their firehouse.

Nor is there evidence of spatial distribution of firemen in Baltimore by occupation or age. Men of all ages belonged to fire companies in Baltimore. While a third of the firemen locatable in the 1860 census were still in their twenties, a year after the department was disbanded another third was in their thirties, 24 percent were in their forties, and nine percent were in their fifties or sixties. These firemen were fairly evenly distributed among the four fire companies for which there are extant membership lists for the late 1850s.[21]

It appears that in San Francisco and Baltimore, firemen of all ages, occupations, and places of birth chose fire companies with little concern for either logistics or ethnicity. A man did not become a fireman or choose a firehouse because of occupational or ethnic allegiances, or because he lived in a certain area. Evidence from two very different cities proves that fire companies were neither ethnic nor workingmen's clubs, in most cities. But if firemen were not joining fire companies to express their working-class republicanism or to support their ethnic allegiances, why were they joining them?

The Brotherhood of Firemen

Within the republican-liberalist political culture of the antebellum city, membership in a volunteer fire company provided a means of gaining respect and adulation for the volunteer. It supplied the volunteer with tangible benefits like insurance, abstention from jury and militia duty, and prestige. It offered a means to status in a highly democratic period, and offered men a way to tend to their self-interest, rightly understood, while proving their value as citizens.

Volunteer firefighting also provided a man with a community. Social historians have shown that men newly arrived in cities in the nineteenth century were likely to join associations as an antidote to the anomie produced by a disorienting environment. Associations, including volunteer fire departments, provided cohesive social networks for individuals which could replace the bonds of family left behind. They were one response to what Mary Ryan characterizes in *Cradle of the Middle Class* as "the social and psychic discomfort of an increasingly mobile, segmented, and impersonal social order."[22]

In these cities, the volunteer fire department functioned much like an extended family. Companies were highly competitive with one another, and the structure of volunteer departments allowed companies a great deal of autonomy. Firemen generally tried to avoid making intradepartmental conflicts public, however, in order to preserve the reputation of the department as a whole.[23]

Indeed, firemen believed they were a part of a brotherhood. As a Sacramento fireman wrote, "For my part, I care not to what Department a man belongs, whether it be San Francisco, Stockton, Placerville or Yreka; if he is a fireman enrolled for the same purpose, fighting under the same banner, I am ready to extend the hand of fellowship."[24] Firemen from New Orleans, Baltimore, New York, Charleston, South Carolina, and many other cities wrote to the *Fireman's Journal* with news of their organizations. The firemen of one city often sent ornamental fire hats, portraits, or banners to a company in another city with the same name. And when firemen left one city, like New York, Boston, or Baltimore, for another city, like St. Louis or San Francisco, they often remained in touch with the old companies through correspondence and gift exchange.[25] A Baltimore fireman who moved to New York in 1856 kept up contact with his old fire company by publishing a monthly humorous paper for them. The *Pickwickian* provided news about life in New York often in the form of humorous drawings, gossip about the Baltimore firemen, and *The Fireman: or the Ambitious Boot Jack, in any quantity of volumes*, a farcical novel.[26]

Figure 2.1. The Brotherhood of Firemen. In this poster from the 1850s, the men of the Protector Engine Company display their solidarity under the watchful eye of the company fire engine. No rowdy firemen here! (Courtesy of the American Insurance Association.)

The volunteer companies coordinated department-wide parades and balls, and also joined together to host companies for elaborate visits to their city. In 1848, the Relief Fire Company of Cincinnati visited their "brothers" in St. Louis. In 1850, the Union Fire Company in St. Louis made a reciprocal visit, although a fierce cholera epidemic was raging in Cincinnati. The Cincinnati firemen made up for the miasma by spending four-thousand dollars on entertaining the St. Louis firemen over the course of their visit. "Our four days sojourn in the city of Pork was one continuous round of excursions, picnics, banquets, balls and parades, and all were loud in their praises of the appearance and behavior of the visitors," remembered a St. Louis fireman. When they returned to St. Louis "loaded with banners, pictures, old relics and silver horns," they were met and escorted to their firehouse by "scores of friends, representing every company in the city."[27]

An excursion of San Francisco's Howard Engine Company to Stockton in 1855, extensively covered by both the *Fireman's Journal* and the major papers in San Francisco, was a similarly giddy and extravagant affair. The Howards were on three different occasions "loaded down with bouquets of flowers," and were treated to, on one occasion, "one of the most *recherche* dinners ever gotten up in the state." The next day they dined on "fruits of all kinds . . .

game, meats and lighter viands were inexhaustible. Costly wines and liquors were also brought into requisition." The firemen of Stockton took their San Francisco brethren to the circus, to a night-long ball (where women were preumably present, although not explicitly mentioned), to the gardens of Stockton and on a tour of the Stockton Insane Asylum. There, "an hour was spent in viewing the building and speaking with its unfortunate occupants on the subject which their thoughts appear to dwell on most." They were then serenaded by a band in the courtyard of the asylum.[28]

At the end of this glorious visit, where "friendships were made . . . which will never be severed until the grave closes over those who enjoy them," the firemen were not content to exchange silver horns and banners. In front of "almost the whole male population" of Stockton, were "two or three hundred men exchanging hats, coats, shirts and belts of all colors, sizes and descriptions, embracing and bidding adieus. The very collar of 'Boxer', the Monumentals's dog, which accompanied the 'Howards' on their excursion, was changed, and that of the 'Eureka's' dog substituted in its stead."[29]

What the dog-collar exchange may have meant to Boxer remains obscure in the historical record, but these celebrations were extremely meaningful to their human participants. The elaborate social life of the volunteer fire company served a crucial function for its participants. Nineteenth-century cities, which contained large numbers of young dislocated men, suffered from a lack of traditional family structure. In Baltimore during the period 1840–1870, people over the age of fifty were rare.[30] The average age of all St. Louis residents in 1850 was twenty-one, and nearly one-third of all residents were between twenty and thirty years of age.[31] In San Francisco in 1852 the mean age of adult males (twenty-one or older) was thirty-one. Both St. Louis and San Francisco had rates of geographic mobility in the 1850s far higher than the 56 percent average rate Stephan Thernstrom has estimated for nineteenth-century American cities. Between 1852 and 1860 there was a 95 percent turnover of population in San Francisco, and within four years, between 1850 and 1854, two-thirds of St. Louis residents had left.[32]

Young and mobile, the populations of these cities were likely to choose living arrangements that emphasized their lack of familial bonds. In St. Louis in 1850, one-third of all residents lived in boardinghouses, and 29 percent of the population lived in units containing more than ten people.[33] The fire company became an alternative family in these cities, with the firehouse substituting for a home. Unlike boardinghouses, they contained the luxuries of real homes. "Many of these houses are really magnificent," commented the *True Californian* about San Francisco's engine houses.

> Their apparatus is kept burnished and brilliant; their meeting-rooms are neat and comfortable and their parlors most luxuriously and splendidly carpeted, furnished, and decorated. In many are found magnificent pianos; hanging on the

walls are valuable paintings, and upon the shelves of their book-cases are expensive libraries of standing books. Many people have been disposed to grumble at this exhibition of extravagance, thinking that the city had purchased these things; but this is not the case, as we have shown. The "fancy fixens" and embellishments have been added by the liberality and zeal of the firemen themselves or their friends. . . . In different parts of the city are located some dozen magnificently furnished, well warmed, and finely lighted rooms, to which the young men belonging to the Fire Department have free access. Here they meet their friends, and talk over the events of the day.[34]

Baltimore's firehouses were renowned for their fine libraries. In the Mechanical Fire Company library, "The walls of the spacious saloon unoccupied by the shelving, are handsomely adorned with a large number of scenes of fires, &c, which give the interior a fine appearance."[35]

The middle nineteenth century was a period when changes in marketing, production, and consumption patterns led to increasingly decorous and decorated homes among those who could afford them. Homes, and the furnishings within them, could demonstrate not only the taste but the character of their occupants. As the renowned landscape architect Andrew Jackson Downing wrote in 1850, "much of the character of every man may be read in his house." Clearly these firehouses, complete with books, prints, pianos, and other signs of consumption, could compete in appearance with homes where *Godey's Lady's Book*, rather than the *Fireman's Journal*, was the featured reading.[36]

But was the firehouse a true home? Could it also serve as a sanctuary from the competitive world of the workplace, as proponents of the domestic sphere envisioned the sacrilized home?[37] There is ample evidence that it did just that. The draw of the firehouse was clearly stronger than the sum of its decorations and reading materials. Like any other homes, the engine houses of St. Louis were "warming places," as a volunteer firefighter in St. Louis in the mid-nineteenth century remembered:

Just as soon as supper was over, it was away to the engine house. There you would be sure to meet from twenty to thirty members, some playing checkers or dominos—with everything orderly and if it was winter, with the stove red-hot, the engine being placed as near it as could be without blistering the paint. . . . The fire was kept up during the night by some of the members of the night-watch. The engine house was a warming place for them. When the time came for some of the members to go home, they would be told: "Don't go yet; there will be a fire to-night certain."[38]

There is evidence that many firemen never did go "home." A romanticized memoir of the San Francisco Fire Department claimed that "at night nearly all the members of the various companies slept in the engine houses without beds, covered by their firecoats."[39] Forty-four members of the department listed a firehouse as their primary residence in either the 1860 census or city directory of that year. Based on evidence from those two sources, the firehouse's permanent residents were substantially younger than members of the department overall, less likely to work at white-collar jobs, and, without exception, unmarried. They were also more likely to be native born than other San Francisco firemen (see table 2.1).

While the firehouse might, in appearance, resemble the sacrilized family home, and while it might also, like the family home, serve as a sanctuary from the competitive world outside, it failed to fulfill the larger promise of the family home. The firehouse did not appear to awaken higher thoughts in its residents. As Lori Merish, among others, has concluded, by the 1830s a new ideal of "pious consumption" legitimated the belief that "refined domestic artifacts would civilize and socialize persons and awaken higher sentiments."[40] The refined home would work to save society, by elevating the base nature of men.

Clearly the firehouse failed in this crucial respect. However refined it might appear, the firehouse supported behavior that would never have been acceptable in a sacrilized home. While we do not know much about the behavior of the San Francisco firehouse's permanent residents, we do know that the late-night behavior in firehouses in St. Louis was less than decorous. In 1853, neighbors of St. Louis's Laclede Fire Company petitioned the company about "the noise and confusion which occur almost every night in front of the Engine House. . . . It is a source of annoyance to the families adjacent."[41] Married members of the largely German Phoenix Fire Company in St. Louis pleaded that they could not be responsible for the late-night revelry in their house. "Nearly all the members are engaged in some regular Business requiring their constant attention during the day and at night they are glad to seek quiet and repose with their families. They have enough to do besides spending their time at the engine house unless their duty as firemen calls them there and it is owing to this cause which prevents the officers and members from being at the house in order to enforce proper conduct about the house."[42]

The members of the Phoenix Fire Company were clearly divided over the proper use of the firehouse—and divided over the social dimension of volunteer firefighting as well. Some members, most likely including permanent residents of the firehouse, chose to spend both their days and nights at the firehouse. If San Francisco's model is at all applicable, these were probably men who, like San Francisco's permanent residents, were single, held lower-status jobs, and were younger than other members. For these men, the firehouse was clearly their home, and it was a home that would not be ruled by the same standards of order and decorum followed in sacrilized family homes. The members of the department who submitted the complaint, by contrast, were

TABLE 2.1
Profile of San Francisco Volunteer Fire Department, Firehouse Permanent Residents

	High White Collar	*Low White Collar*	*Skilled Laborer*	*Semi-skilled*	*Unskilled Laborer*	*Total*[a]
Firehouse residents	5%	20.5%	43%	20.5%	11%	100% (N=44)
Department overall	18%	41.5%	27%	8.5%	5%	100% (N=427)

Age Distribution[b]

	20–25	*26–29*	*30–35*	*36–39*	*40–49*	*50s*	*Total*
Firehouse residents	55%	27%	9%	0%	9%	0%	100% (N=22)
Department overall	23%	20%	35%	9%	10%	2%	99% (N=251)

Firehouse residents, mean age: 27 Median age: 25
Department overall, mean age: 31 Median age: 30

Other Comparative Information[c]

Percentage of firehouse residents married: 0%
Percentage of department overall married: 39%
Percentage of firehouse residents foreign born: 18%
Percentage of department overall foreign born: 33%

[a] Class composition of 44 fire department members listed in either the 1860 census or 1860 San Francisco city directory as permanent residents of a firehouse.
[b] Ages of 22 firehouse permanent residents listed in 1860 census.
[c] Department members located in 1860 census.

those who did not, or could not, revel in the firehouse all night. They did not do so because they had biological families and worked as well at "some regular Business requiring their constant attention."

Both gender and class concerns guided the internal debate over the uses of the firehouse. In St. Louis, married men of regular business debated the use of the firehouse with largely unmarried men of unclear business. This internal critique of the proper use of the firehouse centered on preventing violence and maintaining the public respectability of the firehouse in the neighborhood. But the rights of the family found little open support within the firehouses. Although some firemen were married, a fireman was generally considered to be lost upon his marriage. A short article entitled "Another Gone" could only mean one thing in the firemen's paper. Marcus Boruck wrote upon the "loss" of one friend, "We wish our friends would not send us 'wedding tokens' as they make us sad." A Sacramento fireman described the reaction of a Sacramento company at "the loss of their favorite 'bald head.'" They "evinced their disapproval by a serenade on very uncouth looking instruments, and dis-cursed most inellegant [*sic*] music, until their once brave chief, consented to pass the 'Flagon' for the last time on earth, never more to 'pull' from its inviting 'snoot' while life lasts."[43]

Many firemen, like the director of a Baltimore fire company, resigned from all firefighting duties upon their marriage. The sorrowful secretary of his company wrote that the director "took it into his head to run away and leave us, but he did not go single-handedly, he took with him a lady whom he now claims as his Wife, alas! Poor Mac [the Mechanical Company]. Your men are shipping off one by one until the number has dwindled down to a few poor old bachelors, such as the writer of this."[44]

In his study of nineteenth-century masculinity, Anthony Rotundo concluded that while many young men had as intense and intimate same-sex relationships in the antebellum period as women had, the men's relationships were far more transitory than were women's. While women might remain intimate friends for life, close male relationships generally did not survive after marriage. The loss of intimacy between men is one of the things these firemen bemoan when they bemoan a fireman's marriage. A married fireman could still fight fires, but his love of the company would be second to that of his wife.[45]

In San Francisco, at least, a majority of firemen were single. In 1860, only 10 to 20 percent of firemen in their twenties were married, and 39 percent of the total department overall. Marriage rates among San Francisco firemen also indicate that there were confirmed bachelors in the department. While between 57 percent of firemen in their early thirties and 70 percent of firemen in their late thirties were married, only 53 percent of firemen in their early forties were married.[46] In Baltimore, a majority of firemen appear to have been married; only 21 percent of Baltimore firemen locatable in the 1860 census were single.[47] But for either married or single firemen, the brotherhood of firefighting allowed for the experience of an intense single-sex culture in marked contrast to that of the nuclear family.

In another sense, as well, a fireman *was* "gone" at marriage. "Since the assession of so many families to our population," the *Fireman's Journal* complained in 1855, "the Firemen have become scattered throughout the city." The result of which being that they "never hear the Hall Bell in the night." Evidence from San Francisco does *not* indicate that married men who remained firemen lived farther from their firehouses than unmarried members did in 1860, but this was the perception of a worried observer. Geographical distance from the main alarm of fire in San Francisco was probably not responsible for the sorry response of these married men, but competing claims may have been. A fireman away from his firehouse at night was less likely to note an alarm, but a fireman with his family was also less likely to respond to an alarm. A warm bed might be a strong incentive for temporary hearing loss.[48]

The presence of married men in a fire company does not indicate that staid behavior was the firehouse norm. Pleas for order, and for less raucous behavior, are repeated over and over in the surviving minutes of both the St. Louis and Baltimore volunteer fire companies, indicating that they were given little serious consideration. Despite or perhaps because of the firemen's sentimental celebration of women in stories like "The Mission of Woman," firemen proudly rejected many of the values associated with the family.

John Kasson, Karen Halttunen, and others have argued that the development of etiquette in the nineteenth century was a middle-class response to the excesses of democracy found in the new industrial economy of urban society.[49] Formality and restraint, which grew increasingly important as markers of status among urban Americans of the emerging middle class, were anathema to firemen. Indeed, restraint was incompatible to both the duties and spirit of firefighting. As one fireman put it, "Formality is but another name for restraint of body and mind, and that is a fireman's pet horror."[50]

Temperance, perhaps the most significant antebellum reform movement led by evangelical Christians, also failed to catch on among firemen. Minutes of the Baltimore Fire Company meetings document the copious consumption of wines and liquors after fires and at department picnics, as well as a short-lived attempt at forming a temperance league in one of the companies.[51] The Dashaway Association, a very successful temperance group started by F.E.R. Whitney, ex-chief engineer of the San Francisco Volunteer Fire Department, succeeded in drying out the Howard Company, one of the most prestigious companies in San Francisco, but failed to find much success among members from the department at large.[52]

The editor of the *Pickwickian* regularly mocked both propriety and the manner in which Baltimore firemen flaunted standards of propriety in his humorous monthly sheet. Under a drawing of an intoxicated, unshaven individual, wearing what could be a fireman's hat, the editor composed a "letter" from the "Young Men's Un-Christian Association" to the Pioneer Hook and Ladder Company. The YM(un)CA explained to the firemen that they were hoping to expand their organization. "In casting about for a field in which to operate, its attention has been directed to that of the *Asso*[ciation] of *Firemen* as one peculiarly appropriate, composed as it is for the most part of '*Bummers*' like ourselves. We may proudly hail them as *Brethren* and co-labourers in endeavoring to get drinks when we have no '*Rocks*.' "

The YM(un)CA proposed to the firemen that they join together to start a "*sinking fund*, so that when we should want a drink we could go and get it respectably without begging from *Foreigners* as we have been doing." They also proposed to deliver lectures on Sunday on when to drink and where to drink.

In a final insult to propriety, the Young Men's Un-Christian Association proposed to "do away with . . . loafing around churches, meeting houses and Sunday schools. These meetings are to be held in the Engine Houses or in your *Bunk Room*." The letter was signed with the non-pen-names of the *Pickwickian's* three editors. The YMCA, an organization set up by middle-class men to help promote self-control and to prevent vice among urban youth, is mocked in the *Pickwickian* for those very reasons. It would be difficult to imagine a more scathing indictment of the culture and values of the emerging middle class.[53]

Classless Masculinity

The apparent critique of middle-class values in this *Pickwickian* article should not mislead the reader about the membership of Baltimore's Pioneer Hook and Ladder Company. Although the language sounds similar to the working-class republicanism documented by Sean Wilentz among antebellum New York working men, this was no bunch of laboring rowdies. The company's president at this time was the very proper Charles T. Holloway, who later became the chief engineer of Baltimore's paid department and fought for increased propriety and morality among the paid forces. This company kept a library, and a majority of members practiced white-collar occupations. In 1859, the year the department was disbanded, 55 percent of Pioneer Hook and Ladder members were listed in either the 1860 census, or 1858 city directory, as being engaged in white-collar occupations.[54]

The contradiction between this language and its audience raises the question of class in the fire department. Thus far, I have avoided using class terms to describe these volunteer firemen, because I do not believe that it is either useful or accurate to identify firemen who belonged to the same companies, but may have practiced different occupations, as being members of different classes. Culture determines class, and firemen, whatever their paid employment, were culturally *firemen*. While some of their behavior may have resembled that of the emerging middle and working classes of the period, that does not mean that the behavior itself, or its practitioners, was necessarily classed. Indeed, the brotherhood of volunteer firemen invites us to reconsider what meaning class really had to individuals in the middle of the nineteenth century.

In his study of the political culture of San Francisco, Philip Ethington concluded that for white males, "social consciousness . . . was largely a product of . . . political life" during the antebellum period. Within the governing republican liberalist culture of the antebellum era, "group identities of class and ethnicity mattered as yet very little."[55] Volunteer firemen were celebrated within that political culture for their heroic deeds and agonal struggle, regardless of their other, paid, occupations. Within the volunteer firemen's own culture, class did not define behavior, and masculinity was not predetermined by a man's class. "Un-Christian" behavior was celebrated by firemen in all three of these cities, despite the presence of white-collar men in the firehouse. The terminology used in the *Pickwickian* is itself revealing: these firemen do not mock middle-class behavior, but Christian behavior. Indeed, as Stuart Blumin

TABLE 2.2
San Francisco Volunteer Fire Department, Occupational Composition in 1860
(in percentages)

	High White Collar	*Low White Collar*	*Skilled Laborer*	*Semi-Skilled*	*Unskilled Laborer*	*Total (100%)*
Department overall	18	41.5	27	8.5	5%	N=427
Broderick #1	14	41	38	0	7	N=29
Manhattan #2	15	19	31	12	23	N=26
Howard #3	31	41	25	3	0	N=32
California #4	16	32	37	5	10	N=19
Knickerbocker #5	14	37	21	28	0	N=43
Monumental #6	16	45	34	2.5	2.5	N=38
Volunteer #7	21	33	21	17	8	N=24
Pacific #8	13	47	20	13	7	N=15
Vigilant #9	18	47	29	0	6	N=17
Crescent #10	3	33	37	10	17	N=30
Columbian #11	0	52	33	14	0	N=21
Pennsylvania #12	12	56	32	0	0	N=25
Young America #13	26	52	16	3	3	N=31
Tiger #14	5	47	32	16	0	N=19
St. Francis H&L #1	13	52	26	9	0	N=23
Lafayette H&L #2	42	33	17	8	0	N=12
Sansome H&L #3	52	39	9	0	0	N=23

Note: Total membership = 859; identified in the 1860 census or San Francisco city directory.

himself admits, the term "middle class" was not widely used until the postbellum period, nor was the middle class fully formed in the antebellum period. What these firemen identify themselves against is not a *class*, but evangelical Christianity and the decorum of its converts. This decorum was odious to firemen, not because they were themselves not religious, but because the culture that emerged out of the Second Great Awakening was a feminized culture, a culture of self-restraint.[56]

Firemen might have parlors, but they would not participate in the restrained parlor society mocked by Herman Melville in *Pierre*: "The true charm of agreeable parlour society is, that there you lose your own sharp individuality and become delightfully merged in that soft social Pantheism, as it were, that rosy melting of all into one, ever prevailing in those drawing-rooms."[57] This was true even when, as in San Francisco, firemen were more likely to be merchants than true *bummers*. In 1852, according to Peter Decker, half of all of San Francisco's volunteer firemen were merchants. By 1860, almost 60 percent of them practiced white-collar professions, and every fire company except one contained some high-white-collar members (see table 2.2). Even among the firehouses' permanent residents, 5 percent held white-collar jobs.[58]

Nor was the San Francisco department alone in its diverse membership. In Baltimore, "the most prominent citizens affiliated with the Fire Companies, and it was in the engine houses that most of the town talk was heard."[59] When three surviving company lists from 1814 are cross-referenced with the city directory of that year, the results indicate that Baltimore volunteer firemen in this decade were evenly split between white- and blue-collar members, but that almost 30 percent of firemen engaged in high-white-collar occupations.[60]

The percentage of both high-white-collar and low-white-collar members declined over time in Baltimore, but not to the degree that one might expect. An analysis of four surviving membership lists from 1858, the year before the department was disbanded, indicates a surprisingly large number of white-collar members, given the department's bad press and reputation for disorder in that decade. Of 219 active members locatable in either the 1858 city directory or the 1860 census, 40 percent practiced white-collar occupations and 9 percent practiced high-white-collar occupations. These figures do not include honorary members of the companies—those who supported the department financially but were not required to fight fires themselves. Nor do these figures include veteran members—those who had served seven years of active duty and now held emeritus status. Honorary and veteran members of Baltimore's department in many cases identified themselves with volunteer firefighting as vigorously as any young volunteer fireman, and were even more likely to practice white-collar occupations than the active members.

But even the blue-collar members of Baltimore's department vary from the working-class model of firemen in Philadelphia and New York. A large fraction of skilled laborers in the department were listed in the census as owning real property. Of the forty-seven skilled laborers locatable in the census, ten of them, or 21 percent, owned five-hundred dollars or more of real property. Six skilled laborers had over one-thousand dollars of real property. While John S. Hogg, a thirty-five-year-old carpenter and active member of the Mechanical Company, practiced a blue-collar occupation, owning eleven-thousand dollars of real property, he was also a substantial member of his community. Clearly, Baltimore's department was not a working-class department, even in the year that it was disbanded.[61]

There is no reason to believe that other fire departments were working-class institutions either. A Cincinnati fireman remembered that "it was no uncommon thing to see the old solid citizens in their broadcloth and gold-rimmed spectacles" actively fighting fires with their employees.[62] A fireman in St. Louis remembered a similar scene: "Merchant princes and clerks, professional men and loafers . . . threw aside whatever they were doing as soon as the alarm bell sounded."[63]

All departments were celebrated by their members for their heterogeneous composition, and white-collar men often held positions of authority in the house. But the behavioral standards of the emerging middle class, described by Stuart Blumin, Anthony Rotundo, Mary Ryan, Mark Carnes, and others, did not dictate the behavior of the firemen.[64] These were neither middle-class nor workingmen's voluntary associations. Nor were they associations, like the Odd Fellows, that succeeded in mitigating class distinctions, in Blumin's words, "through the recruitment of members from all classes and the pursuit of a specifically interclass fellowship." To the extent that volunteer firefighting mitigated class differences, it did so by offering an extremely appealing vision of masculinity, which was itself not tied to socioeconomic class.[65]

Volunteer fire companies were not middle-class associations, either. They failed to adopt temperance ideals in a period when temperance separated classes in all three of these cities. They did not stress self-improvement or moral discipline, and they certainly did not reinforce the family as a social institution, common characteristics found by Don Doyle in the middle-class associations of Jacksonville, Illinois.[66]

Within firehouses, some of which displayed signifiers of middle-class respectability, men of different occupations fraternized, and sometimes they practiced activities usually associated by historians with working-class culture. Men drank in the firehouse, and sometimes they fought. Occasionally the fights were of a formal nature. Robert Dunn was expelled from the Laclede Fire Company when he did "to the great scandal of the company and disturbance of the neighborhood bring hither into our engine room two men as Principals to fight a prize fight—they, the said Robert Dunn and Wm. Boyd, aiding and abetting them in the capacity of seconds." Generally, the fights were of a more banal sort. The Laclede records also report that "Peter Holden did while in an intoxicated state come into our engine room and then and there violently assaulted a member of the company," for which he was not expelled.[67]

Indoor fighting fell outside the realm of acceptable firehouse behavior and was condemned. But physicality was absolutely central to the masculinity of the fire department. Most firemen did not stage fights in their firehouses, but they did enjoy less violent displays of strength and physical competition. When the Lafayette Fire Company of San Francisco, a company composed primarily of Frenchmen, built a gymnasium in the rear of their house, they placed a notice in the San Francisco *Fireman's Journal* inviting "their fellow members of the Fire Department, for exercise and social recreation."[68]

The Lafayette Fire Company contained a membership in 1860 which was 42 percent high white collar, and 33 percent low white collar (see table 2.2). It would not have been unusual for middle-class men to visit a gymnasium; indeed "sport," with its promise of health and the release of work-related tension, grew in popularity among the emerging middle class in the antebellum period. But, according to historians, sports clubs were also overwhelmingly divided along class lines in this period. The gymnasium of the

Lafayette Company, and the fire department in general, was particular in that it brought men of different backgrounds together in their appreciation of physicality.[69]

Exercise, both in and out of the firehouse, was very important to these white-collar firemen as well as to their laboring peers. Firemen of all occupations exhibited an interest in both strength and appearance which defies class analysis. Uniforms were one part of the appearance of the companies which inspired special care. Every fire company had at least two uniforms, one of which was an elaborate parading uniform, of fine fabrics and bright color. The Liberty Fire Company of Baltimore chose to parade in 1851 in black pants and drab coats, white hats with gilt lettering, patent leather belts with brass plates, white comforts and gloves. Their motto on this occasion, "Where Liberty dwells there is my home," held a special meaning for firemen who considered the Liberty house their actual home.

The Howards, "arrayed in the new and tasty uniform lately adopted by that company," met an adoring San Francisco public in 1859 sporting blue flannel jackets and white patent leather belts, with the name of the company in sunken black patent leather on the front, and the company number also in black patent on the back. The Howards, known in San Francisco as a "white glove company" because of the high occupational status of its members, chose uniforms that differed only in color and detail from the Manhattan Engine Company, whose membership was almost a quarter unskilled laborers.[70]

Fire company minutes are full of debates over the choice of fire hats or uniform trim appropriate for upcoming parades. After several aborted attempts at deciding on a new uniform, the Phoenix Fire Company of St. Louis was driven to forming a "committee on hats" in 1845. A poem published in the *National Fireman's Journal*, "The New Company at Smithersville—A True Story," warned firemen of the danger in excessive sartorial concern. It ended with the stanzas,

> But too late—the work was done;
> The frame row it was gone—
> Burned while the boys were dressing.
> It was a lesson never forgot,
> For they said, right on the spot,
> "We'll do different.
> We'll not stop to don our clothes
> When we hear the fearful news
> That a fire is raging,
> But in every day attire,
> We'll hasten to the fire,
> And dress up after."[71]

As a historian of the Cincinnati Volunteer Fire Department is quick to point out, however, "notwithstanding a suggestion of Lord Fauntleroy in the costumes, there was no lack of masculinity in the wearers. These men were rough and rugged individuals."[72] Strength was essential to working the fire engine and to fighting fires and played a large role in constructing the classless masculinity of the volunteer fire department. Just as in recent years modern firemen have claimed, as an excuse for excluding women, that only men had sufficient physical strength to fight fires, nineteenth-century volunteer firemen found part of their personal identity in the strength they believed made them good firemen.[73] David Dana, a Boston volunteer fire chief and chronicler of volunteer fire departments, wrote in 1858 that "from necessity members of a fire company must be chosen from those who follow laborious pursuits, for with rare exceptions, men of sedentary employments, and pursuits entirely mental, have not the physical capacity for endurance to discharge the duties of fireman." But young clerks in the fire companies of San Francisco, Baltimore, and St. Louis would have disagreed with him.[74]

Firemen in every city staged frequent contests in which each company would try to pump water farther or higher than the other in front of crowds of spectators. These contests were known among firemen and reporters as tests of "muscle" as well as of machine. The final battle between the hand-pump—and the steam engines which replaced them—was generally viewed by fireman and onlooker alike as a battle between "muscle" and steam. For this reason, the use of horses to pull fire engines was seen as particularly shameful. A Sacramento fireman, with the nom de plume "Machine," wrote: "There has been strong talk among the members of Sacramento 3, about purchasing a horse to run with their engine to fires. They say, with some truth, that their engine is so heavy it is impossible for them to ever be first at a fire. In my humble opinion, if the same enthusiasm existed in that company that there did a year ago, horse power would be no *whar* [where]."

He then contrasted Sacramento No. 3 with "our new company, Young America 6. . . . The most of her company are composed of good solid, hard-fisted mechanics, ever ready for duty; who, when they put their muscle on a brake, are bound to make it tell."[75] The press also reveled in the masculinity of the volunteer fireman. They often focused on the physical attributes of the firemen in their descriptions of parades, social events, and even fires. Firemen were described as "stalwart fellows," "manly looking men," and "as fine specimens of the bone and sinew of the land as could be desired." Here is the fireman as Currier and Ives icon: brave and strong, dependable and manly. The antebellum press thus generally validated the firemen's own masculine self-image.[76]

Some historians have identified this celebration of muscle as a marker of class in the mid-nineteenth century. Sean Wilentz identifies similar celebration among New York's volunteer firemen as part of a working-class or mechanic republican ethos. Elliot Gorn has written convincingly that among working-class New Yorkers, muscle and grit were the sole sources of power in the streets, and that as their economic prospects became circumscribed in a changing economy, "a combative, physical way of life . . . offered the action, adventure, and autonomy denied in the workaday realm. . . . Volunteer fire companies offered a chance for real heroics, rough masculine camaraderie and colorful display."[77]

A working-class ethos is clearly evident in the comments of "Machine" in Sacramento and probably also played a role in producing the fights in the firehouses of St. Louis. But the limitations of a class analysis of this behavior become evident with the most cursory examination of the firemen of San Francisco. The manly posturing in San Francisco, in a department that was largely merchant class or white collar, can be accounted for neither by historians of working-class masculinity, nor by historians of middle-class masculinity. San Francisco firemen in companies with high occupational profiles refused to use horses to pull their engines. Both white-collar firemen and their laboring peers in San Francisco took part in ritualized displays of strength, physical competition, and elaborate costuming. And through most of the 1850s at least, they were celebrated by the public for doing so. If, as Wilentz argues, celebrations and symbols, like those of the firemen, emerged to "define the rifts of class between masters and journeymen," why would white-collar workers participate?[78]

Accounts of working-class fire companies in New York and Philadelphia fail to explain accurately the presence of white-collar men in organizations that supposedly expressed working-class norms. After a subtle description of patrician participation in New York's fire companies until 1845, Amy Bridges makes the mystifying claim that "the gang, the militia company, and even the fire company were largely organizations of the working classes."[79] Wilentz, Bruce Laurie, and others have argued that names of white-collar workers appear on firehouse rolls only transitionally. These historians agree that the fire companies of the eighteenth century were largely white collar, but that these members were gradually replaced by blue-collar workers by the 1830s, who set the new rowdy tone to the companies.

In both Baltimore and San Francisco, white-collar workers took part in all firefighting activities until the last years of their departments' existence. White-collar members were not transitional. Baltimore's Independent Fire Company offers a good example of the kind of occupational stability that characterized most fire companies. Membership lists from 1814, 1838, and 1856 indicate that there was an almost complete turnover in membership of this company every twenty years. Five members in 1814 were still around in 1838, and seven members in 1838 were still active in 1856. Only one member, William B. Parish, a cabinetmaker, remained an active member of this company over the entire forty-two-year period. About half of the members who remained in the company for eighteen or more years were merchants, but two clerks and a watchmaker were also long-standing members of the company. One member appears to have experienced upward mobility while he was a member of the Independent Fire Company. Joshua J. Turner, a carpenter in 1814, was listed in the 1838 city directory as a lumber merchant.

Although individual members may have changed, from an occupational standpoint, the company remained much the same in 1856 as it had in 1814. The Independents, as they called themselves, did not change into a working-class company over time. An 1814 membership list shows that the company at that time was 51 percent white collar and 30 percent high white collar. In 1838, the department was 42 percent white collar, and only 23 percent high white collar. By 1856, however, the white-collar members had made a comeback. Just three years before the department was disbanded, the Independent Fire Company was 52 percent white collar and 29 percent high white collar. At no time did this company have more than one or two semiskilled or unskilled members. In sum, the Independent Fire Company remained much as it had been—a heterogeneous company with virtually no semiskilled or unskilled members.[80]

Baltimore's New Market Company was somewhat different. The occupational status of this company, low from the outset declined over time. However, even this department retained a substantial number of white-collar members. In 1814, the New Market Company was 36 percent high white collar and 47 percent white collar. There were no locatable semiskilled or unskilled members of the department in 1814. By 1857, the company was composed mainly of skilled laborers. Thirty-two percent of members were still white collar, but there were virtually no high white collar members still active in the company: only four, or six percent of members locatable in the 1858 city directory or 1860 census. Also notable was the increase in semiskilled and unskilled laborers in the company by 1857. Together they made up 12 percent of the company in 1858. In both 1814 and 1857, the New Market Company had the lowest occupational profile of any company in Baltimore for which there is a surviving membership list. Widely considered "a bad lot" by other firemen, this company was active in rioting from the early part of the century, as I will discuss in the next chapter.

Yet note that even in the New Market Fire Company, nearly one-third of the members in 1857 practiced low-white-collar occupations. Although virtually no merchants were willing to fight fires in a New Market uniform, a sizable number of merchants were still willing to become "contributing" members of the company. Even the New Market Company, notorious throughout Baltimore, kept a mixed membership until the bitter end.[81]

The surviving membership lists from 1856 of the Franklin Fire Company in St. Louis also support the view that companies retained heterogeneous memberships. Of sixty-seven members with listed occupations, eight are what Stephan Thernstrom identifies as white collar, or lower white collar, primarily salesmen; the great majority of the rest were skilled laborers. According to company minutes, six of the eight white-collar members played an active role at fires and meetings.[82]

Nor was this an unusually sedate company. In 1856, the entire department in St. Louis was under intense condemnation by the public for fighting and rioting, in which the Franklin Company was not free from fault. This was an active cross-occupation company which expressed social norms that should not be categorized according to class. They were fire department norms, and they appear to have been shared by the departments of Baltimore, St. Louis, and San Francisco. The merchant firemen of Baltimore in the 1820s and of St. Louis in the 1830s are described as "manly," as are the rowdy firemen of the later decades in these cities. The Pioneer Hook and Ladder Company of Baltimore had a majority white-collar membership at the same time that its members satirized middle-class pretensions in the *Pickwickian*.

The vigorous masculine culture of the fire department undoubtedly attracted men to firefighting. The middle decades of the nineteenth century were a time of crisis for urban men. Working-class men increasingly were forced to acknowledge the limits of their economic opportunity, while men of the emerging middle class were forced to balance discordant home and work environments. Masculinity itself had reached a crisis point for both groups, and specific class-related social activities emerged to fill the needs of these men. Middle-class men joined literary clubs and temperance and other reform organizations. Or, as Mark Carnes has shown, they joined fraternal orders with rituals that promoted "emotional transition from an identification from feminine domesticity to the relentlessly aggressive and competitive demands of the masculine work place."[83]

Many urban workers, by contrast, repaired from their anonymous workplaces to saloons, where they found the camaraderie and respect missing from their jobs. They also found fistfights, dogfights, and rat-bating contests, organized by saloon keepers as entertainment. One primary way working-class men earned the respect of their peers was through their physical strength and ability to dominate others. Indeed, physical violence was central to urban working-class masculinity, which celebrated bare-knuckle boxing as well as less orchestrated exhibitions of virility. Personal acts of physical violence were common within saloon culture, and common also among working-class street-gang members.[84] By the 1830s, we have been told, both working- and middle-class men had developed masculine cultures that offered approval and respect distinct from any performance in the workplace. These two visions of masculinity were increasingly opposed to one another.

The volunteer fire department offered a third option. It offered some of the trappings of the middle class—fine houses, libraries, even an occasional piano—along with the physicality and excitement of working-class culture. It offered a home that was a "warming place" for the firemen. It offered a form of masculinity that was accessible and appealing to men of any social strata, without the constraints and hierarchies of middle-class forms, and with narrower perameters than working-class forms. Firemen held banquets, tea parties, and balls like middle-class men, but they had no elaborate rituals like those of middle-class fraternal organizations during this period. Firemen fought in their firehouses, on occasion, as working-class men might, but were always reprimanded for it. The ideal of decorum prevailed even when its practice failed. What the fire department offered men was an opportunity to work as a team, to put their masculinity on display, and to compete with their physical equals, regardless of occupation.

And there is evidence that many men were looking for just this option. Jeffrey Adler has illustrated the way in which antebellum travel literature attempted to lure East Coast residents to St. Louis. "Travel writers insisted that St. Louis was young, dynamic, and a bit untamed." They emphasized the vigor of the city and the challenging frontier conditions. "Romantic and exciting images of urban life in the rough-hewn West captured eastern notice."[85] Bored young clerks and mechanics alike flocked from Baltimore to St. Louis, and from both Baltimore and St. Louis to San Francisco, looking for adventure. Along the way, they joined fire companies.

If young urban men hoped to play out fantasies of robust masculinity, they found that the fire companies provided one excellent outlet for doing so. "When we look at the present race of men who daily crowd our thoroughfares . . . we are inclined to think that instead of advancing in physical beauty, we are sadly retrograding," bemoaned the *Fireman's Journal* in 1856.

> California at one time, was peopled by a class of men proverbial for their manly vigor and ruddy health, and that too at an era when nearly all who flocked to her shores were compelled to undergo the most extreme privations and hardships. . . . Living in "tents" and "roughing" it in the most approved manner of Pioneer Life seemed to have the effect of developing the system both physically and mentally. . . . It is a noticeable fact however, that the emigration of later years, has consisted almost totally of men . . . not inured to toil and hardship. As a body the physical formation of these men are not so muscular or so well developed as those who preceded them and rapidly settled the country.

The *Journal* concluded by suggesting exercise as an antidote. "Merely taking a walk is a poor substitute for the more active and manly exercises that develop the frame." Fighting fires is not specifically mentioned here but was obviously considered a manly exercise fitted to reinvigorating the men of San Francisco and renewing an era of manly men.[86]

The fact that fire company culture was the joint creation of men of different occupations does not mean that there were no divisions within departments along class lines. Letter writers to the *Fireman's Journal* and *Alta California* frequently condemned a department's "white kid glove members" and "aristocratic members" who consistently failed to appear at fires. They "would no more think of putting their delicately gloved hands to the brakes of an engine than they would of committing suicide," as one letter writer put it. Boruck also demanded that "inferior cigars" not be smoked in the Board of Delegates meetings, seemingly making a different sort of class critique.[87] Poems appeared in the *Fireman's Journal* upon occasion condemning the man who boasted of being a "gentleman." The "gentleman" in the poem had "a patrician air," of course, and a "well-cut coat," but lacked any real honor or virtue. He was precisely the sort of man who would never attempt to fight fires.[88]

But this rhetoric needs to be put in its proper context. As European observers to this country loved to note, Americans both embraced professed equality and scorned aristocratic pretensions.[89] By the 1850s, virtually all men considered themselves entitled to be called "gentleman." The real object of scorn among firemen was not the merchant or lawyer, but the man who would not remove his kid gloves at the demand of the fire. What these letters and poems expressed was not a working-class republicanism, but pride in the role and duties of the fireman and in a citizenship based on the fireman's very real contribution to the health of the polis.[90]

The brotherhood of firemen was a limited brotherhood, and class, ethnic, and especially turf divisions emerged in these departments, as I discuss in chapter 3. But these facts should serve to highlight the remarkable heterogeneity of the volunteer fire department, as well as the firemen's unified norm of manly behavior. At a time when masculinity was increasingly defined by class, the fire department transcended class through the creation of a shared masculine identity.

Gendered Fire Engines and Absent Women

If the volunteer fire department was a place where the constraints and divisions of class were subsumed into an expression of masculinity, where did women fit in? In this world of the bone and sinew man, the place of women was difficult to reconcile. Women helped raise money to buy fire equipment. Women helped to sew the elaborate uniforms the firemen wore when visiting their brother firemen in other towns or while parading. Gifts from "lady-friends," like the "wreath formed of hair, containing a lock of each of the members of the Liberty Fire Company" of Baltimore, graced most firehouses.[91]

A San Francisco firemen who once fought fires in New York claimed that he had "visited a very large number of Engine, Truck and Hose houses, and I have yet to see the first house that does not contain some handiwork of the fair sex." These creations were, "of course, conspicuously exhibited and highly prized," according to an outside commentator.[92] But except for one eccentric and very rich female in San Francisco, women themselves entered the male sanctum only in discursive or symbolic form, with two significant exceptions. Women might be allowed inside illicitly for dancing and other revelry. Such commingling would have been unusual, but at least one house steward in St. Louis was expressly ordered to prevent such behavior.[93] In addition, on special celebratory occasions women would be paraded through the halls of the firehouse and be offered light refreshments.

Of course, in the traditional home, women held near total authority during the nineteenth century. Within the domestic sphere, women controlled the appearance of the home, and they elevated the character of their husbands and sons through good example, moral suasion, and well-chosen decorations.[94] As we have seen, although firehouses might look like virtuous homes, firemen do not appear to have been morally elevated by their surroundings. Firemen, both men and keepers of homes, expressed some hostility toward this feminine authority and attempted to keep it out of the firehouse. When the new Monumental engine house was opened in San Francisco in 1855, one fireman wrote:

> Upwards of *seven hundred and eighty* ladies visited the building between the hours of 11 A.M. and 5 P.M., partaking of the hospitality of the "Sixes," and viewing the beauties of the entire establishment. The ladies expressed their astonishment at the beauty and taste shown in the selection of the interior arrangements of the house, with the avowal that they "could not have done better," in which there must be more truth than poetry, coming as it does from those who are somewhat tenacious of their rights.[95]

Not only was the physical presence of women in the firehouse strictly regulated, but they are also strangely absent in descriptions of fire department activities. The Missouri Fire Company of St. Louis spent fifty-two dollars on claret, brandy, champagne, and cigars at a picnic in 1858 in which "each member of the company was allowed to invite one male friend." In some cases, women fail to appear even when invited. In newspaper descriptions of fire department balls and dances, women are sometimes completely absent, while the "grace" of the firemen receives ample discussion.[96]

Although women were usually absent from the world of volunteer firefighting, one "lady" was the absolute focus of her company, occupying the place of honor in each house: the engine itself. "Among the many interesting episodes in the life of a true fireman, none partake of so much importance as the housing of his cherished and favorite apparatus. It savors more of the act of a careful husband, providing for the wants of a much loved wife, than anything else we can compare it to." Or rather, Marcus Boruck later elaborated, "To many of them she *is* their wife, and like all good husbands they wish to nourish and care for her."[97] A Sacramento fireman wrote of a new engine: "She looked like a bride decked for the bridegroom, and seemed to excite admiration in all beholders."[98] Such metaphors were not viewed as fanciful by the volunteers who uttered them. The often inaccurate historian Herbert Asbury correctly identified "the great affection, amounting almost to worship, in which [the volunteer fireman] held his engine."

> To a fireman an engine or a hose cart was always feminine; he invariably spoke of it as "the old gal" and often addressed it in endearing terms. It was not unusual to see a jubilant fire laddie publicly kiss his machine, and embrace as much of it as his arms would surround, after it had worsted a rival in fair contest. . . . As a lover proves his admiration for his lady by presenting her with baubles for the embellishment of her charming person, so did the fireman express his adoration for his engine in terms of paint; and the more he loved the machine the greater was his desire to ornament it with brightly colored pictures of his own selection.[99]

The fire engine was the firemen's "bride" in cities where women were scarce and matrimony, as we have seen, was treacherous. "She" was a subject for adoration and competition. A poem published in San Francisco expressed the firemen's pride in their engine:

> We want our engine painted,
> To look as good as new;
> We want her rubbed down well and polished,
> And nothing less will do,
> Want her levers filed up smoothly,
> To make 'em shine like steel;
> Want her tongue set up a little,
> And a new flange on her reel . . .
> We want her wheels well gilded,
> And keep this in yer head—
> Paint her just as you're a mind to,
> So you only paint her red.[100]

Unlike modern fire engines, hand-pump machines were not generally painted red, although most firemen were as particular about how they were painted as was the company in the poem. Existing fire department minute books in St. Louis chronicle endless debates over the manner and extent of decorations to be made on engines. Engines in Baltimore "exhibited a profusion of elaborately carved and gilded work." In San Francisco, an engine described to be "as handsome as a young bride" was covered in gold leaf and crowned with two "golden ladies," iron statues of idealized feminine figures, heavily gilt.[101]

Idealized female figures were also one of the most popular subjects for the painted panels that decked the sides of these fire engines. Newspapers and surviving illustrations of these engines show a striking variety of figures: Minervas, Liberties, Guardian Angels, Justice, Oceana and her nymphs, and female Indians. In *Women in Public: Between Banners and Ballots, 1825–1880*,

Mary Ryan describes a wide realm of uses to which such idealized female figures were put in antebellum America. "Women, beautiful in form and splendidly attired, evoked a being different from, apart from, and attractive to the male creators of civic culture, and as such she served as a canvas on which to paint abstract values in appealing but transcendent fashion."[102] For many firemen these female figures did serve as "transitive semiotic devices," passing meaning beyond women themselves to the civic culture, but to other firemen they were simply "pretty ladies," and like the gilt statues on the golden fire engine, not explicitly identified with any virtue or belief. That they were pleasant to look at, and a fitting decoration for the engine's greater beauty, virtually all firemen would agree.

As the firemen's rhetoric makes clear, the fire engine was believed to embody the values of the nineteenth-century woman. The members of the Pennsylvania Company of San Francisco described their engine as "chaste" when offering it for sale. At a banquet the statement, "Our engine—may she be like an old maid—always ready, but never wanted," was offered as a toast. An engine whose reservoir was "washed" at a fire or in a competition, either through a failure of the machinery or of the men at the brakes, was said to be "no longer virgin." Such a fallen machine was "thus discredited and subject to repudiation as soon as it could be replaced by a better one."[103]

The extent of the shame that could fall on a disgraced machine was indicated when the Missouri Fire Company's engine was "washed" at a contest with the Union and Central companies in St. Louis in 1845. "No one had seen in St. Louis 'such a woe-begone looking crowd' as the members of the Missouri Company after this disaster," commented one observer. Although the Missouri Company offered the members of the Union Company a deposit of one thousand dollars for a rematch, the Union Company declined "under the code, to a match with an engine which had been washed, and ceased to be 'virgin.' "[104]

The public also loved fire engines. Sam Brannan, a San Francisco businessman, spent ten-thousand dollars on a partially silver-plated engine for his city's Howard Company in 1853. A parade was held to show the engine off to the city, and Brannan was inundated by public demands to see the machine. The *Alta California* wrote paragraphs praising the engine, its mechanism, woodwork, engraving and painting of "three females at the bath, one of them dallying with a swan upon the stream."[105]

But the fireman's enthusiasm for the machine could easily develop into a mania, or fetish. There was a fascination and "romance" of "running wid de masheen," for which men would "ruin their clothes, undermine their health, lose their sleep, endanger their lives, and endure all kinds of hardships."[106] A heroic Boston fireman overtaken by this romance risked his life for that of his engine. "With a fireman's love of 'the machine' he grasped the rope and made his way through a raging sheet of flame, burning his hat, hair and clothes."[107]

Figure 2.2. No Mere Machine. In this poster of the Humane Hose Company of Philadelphia, an elegantly dressed fireman, trumpet in hand, gazes longingly at his "painted lady." The frontispiece of the hose truck shows women gathered in a domestic scene. (Courtesy of the American Insurance Association.)

An insult to a company's machine could also lead to a fight or riot, as occurred in both Baltimore and St. Louis.

The extent to which the machine could be fetishized is evidenced by stories of men who deserted their brides on their wedding nights at the sound of the fire alarm bell, stories that were understandably popular among firemen. In one such tale, "Necessity Knows No Law," published in California, a newly married man leaves for a fire. "The fact that he had assumed responsibilities of an extraordinary nature had not fully impressed itself upon him. . . . He cared not for new made wife, responsibilities or congratulations, but throwing aside the wedding habiliments, and assuming the garb of a fireman, rushed to the performance of this duty." At the moment before entering the nuptial bed, the fire engine intervenes. In another variation of this potent tale, a fireman's date resigns her own claims when the demands of the engine are made. "The lady immediately withdrew her arm from mine and said: 'Jump on your rope: don't you see they are passing your carriage?' " That a sexual choice was being made was highlighted by the woman's next comment, "Have no fears for me; no one will molest me."[108]

Descriptions of this fetish occur also in the testimonials of enemies of the fire department. The San Francisco *Evening Bulletin* ran one such testimonial "of a prominent merchant of New York and an old firemen . . . hoping that it may prove a warning to some of our young men, who are so infatuated with the 'machine' as almost to destroy their usefulness at any legitimate occupation." In this not wholly credible testimonial the "prominent merchant" maintains that after "joining the department quite young" and choosing the machine over his employment,

> for more than two years I was literally a loafer and a vagabond, notwithstanding the daily prayers and entreaties of my parents to forsake the companions who were leading me to destruction, both body and soul. The machine was my pride—my delight; what did I care for the fire, or how much it destroyed, if to arrest it would involve the ruin of my pet?—absolutely nothing. Those paintings and gaudy decorations were of far more importance, in my eyes, than all the buildings I made little or no effort to save. . . . I wonder even now at my infatuation, and look with horror upon the system which made me a very slave and perverted the better and nobler qualities of my nature. . . . Yet I had no lack of moral training . . . nor do I think that I was worse than hundreds now in the Department. I do not blame them, it is the accursed system that makes our youth such.[109]

Here is the most elaborate expression of the "infatuation of the machine," and also of the republican theory of gender, evident in the writings of Machiavelli and in the public ceremonies of antebellum America. According to Mary Ryan, "As objects of male sexual desire, women appealed to the passions that would inevitably corrupt civic virtue." Here the fire engine, the powerful female figure in the fire department home, has enslaved a citizen and perverted the nobler qualities of his nature. The emphasis on the painted and gaudy qualities of the engine also call to mind the fears and warnings of middle-class urban Americans of the "painted woman," the vicious and seductive female version of the confidence man, who, like the fire engine, gloried in debauching innocent young men.[110]

The republican-liberalist political culture of the antebellum city upheld the fireman as the model urban citizen for his heroic deeds. But a move away from that conception of citizenship is evident in this cautionary tale. The old republican language remains: the fire engine represented a means to a fireman's downfall by corrupting his virtue and making him "a very slave." But note also that the engine is demonized for destroying a young man's "usefulness at any legitimate occupation." This accusation, that firefighting could keep a man from a "legitimate occupation," is one that could, and would, be made of volunteer firefighting in general. It indicates that for the middle-class man, citizenship and masculinity were increasingly defined not by heroic acts, but by success at a paid occupation. A new model of citizenship was on the rise in antebellum America. The firefighters were in trouble when, as David Leverenz put it, "patrician enlightenment values were supplanted by a language of middle-class Christian capitalism."[111]

Families versus Firemen

The infatuation of the machine threatened the virtue of the citizen, and it threatened order in the work place. But the largest threat it posed was to the unity of the evangelical, Christian family. If the firehouse made a mockery of the pretenses of the sacrilized home by promoting immoral behavior within a supposedly didactic environment, the fire engine took the insult a step further. In the statement of the "prominent merchant" we see the battle between the Christian family and the fire department family over the very souls of their sons. Most companies had young followers who ran to fires with the engines and socialized at the firehouses. Legally they were allowed to do no more than tag along, as volunteer fire departments stipulated that no one under eighteen, or in some cases no one under twenty-one, could join a company.

These rules were not fully enforced, however. In 1854 a member of San Francisco's Columbia Engine Company was killed when a dog, tripping him, caused his head and body to be crushed under the engine. In their testimonial, the company mourned the loss of a youth, "scarce eighteen years of age," but the *Alta California* reported his actual age as sixteen. The 1856 membership list of St. Louis's Franklin Company list several eighteen-year-old members who had already belonged to the company for a year. One eighteen-year-old, Aug. Hefner, was listed as having joined the company at age sixteen.[112]

Corruption of youth was one of the most frequent and powerful accusations made against fire departments. In his annual report, the chief engineer of Cincinnati's new paid fire department compared the firehouse to a demonic nursery. "Under the present control, the engine-houses are no longer nurseries where the youth of the city are trained up in vice, vulgarity and debauchery."[113] A critic of the St. Louis department wrote that "youths not controlled by parental restraint, as soon as the shades of night closed in, sought the engine-houses, where hours were spent in the rehearsal of deeds of violence and crime."[114]

Fire companies tried to stem off this criticism by passing laws banning "boys" from the firehouses and attempting to keep them from running with the engines, but they appear to have been as ineffective as similar laws banning late-night revelry in firehouses. Many firemen had grown up around

Figure 2.3. Look Who's in the Firehouse. The firehouse might be a "demonic nursery," but Currier and Ives's "The Little Fireman" is rather angelic. *The Little Fireman*, 1859 lithograph. (Courtesy of the American Insurance Association.)

engine houses and agreed that such exposure was "the nucleus or training school for young men and boys under age, to eminently fit them at their majority, to be the best and most experienced of Firemen." One firemen, who "well remembers his apprenticeship when a boy as a member of 'Slowline' No. 2 attached the 'Union' Fire Company," claimed that organized groups of boys within the companies "were the flower of the organization to which they belonged, and no efforts were spared to make them all that practice could do as regarded speed, vigilance and efficiency."[115]

Most parents did not believe these were the best skills a boy could learn in his teen-aged years. Well-bred boys were supposed to express restraint in their everyday demeanor. They were expected to spend their time in church, in a proper school, or with their mother, who made sure that the home was a Christian and moral environment.[116] Who was making sure that the firehouse was a Christian environment? Reformers and families knew that the firehouse was not a safe or moral place to linger late into the night. The educational function of the firehouse was condemned by the larger society. Charles T. Holloday, the former Pioneer Hook and Ladder president and chief engineer of Baltimore's new paid department, celebrated in 1858 that, by ending the volunteer system, "we have destroyed one prolific source of rowdyism, and by abolishing one of their primary schools, have deprived our House of Refuge and our Jail of many an inmate and graduate."[117]

As parenting grew in importance among evangelical Christian, domestic families, the seeming threat posed by the fire department also increased. As men spent more time at work and away from the home, child-rearing patterns in America changed, becoming more gender-specific and subject to greater attention and concern for both husband and wife. Critics like Theodore Dwight bemoaned the new neglect of child-rearing duties among fathers. Catherine Beecher, in her guide book for new brides, *American Woman's Home*, offered overly busy fathers the example of "husbands and fathers who conscientiously subtract time from their business to spend at home, in reading with their wives and children, and in domestic amusements which at once refresh and improve."[118]

Domestic mothers more than made up for any loss of paternal attention their children may have experienced. Child rearing was approached by Christian women with a new fervor and intensity. Indeed, their foremost duty within the domestic sphere was to guide and shape the morals and character of their children. As Catherine Beecher wrote, "There is no more important duty devolving upon a mother than the cultivation of habits of modesty and propriety in young children." [119]

If in fact, the "first-duty" of proper parents was "to train up their own families to be useful members of society," as Beecher preached, a sure sign of failure would be the presence of a son, not by the fire*side* learning habits of propriety (or restraint, the "fireman's pet horror"), but in the fire*house* learning something else. Charges of corruption of the young stemmed not so much from the legitimacy of tales told by merchants about fire engine infatuation, but rather because the firehouse, in attempting to raise boys to become firemen, was usurping the privileges of the sacrilized home, and especially the privileges of the mother within the domestic sphere.

Clearly the firehouse did not provide the moral environment Christian parents desired for their sons. It was the very difficulty inherent in the project of raising virtuous sons in an immoral environment like the city which gave the charge of corruption such resonance with such parents. When sons occupied the liminal space of adolescence, a role which Joseph Kett has argued was never clearly defined in the nineteenth century, this problem was amplified.[120]

The culture of the volunteer fire department therefore posed a threat to several powerful emerging orders in the mid-nineteenth century. By offering men a comfortable place to spend all their free time within an alienating environment, a fire company was able to fashion its house into an extremely seductive, alternative home. Here was a home where a man need not worry about that "sudden onslaught of tongue or broomstick," or a shirt of patches and shreds. Instead, it offered the fulfillment of a vision of masculinity that celebrated strength, courage, speed, and appearance. This was a vision of masculinity which was not tied to class, in a period when class increasingly divided and defined cultures in America. And here was a culture that conceptualized masculinity and citizenship in terms of voluntary service to the city rather than dedication to some "legitimate employment." By embracing their alternative homes and their alternative vision of manhood, firemen, many of whom were white-collar in profession, made an enemy of the emerging cultural middle class.[121]

At the same time that the ethos of domesticity embued both the home and parenting with a new importance for the cultural middle-class, a similar and connected transformation in standards of public civility was also underway in America's cities. While the firehouse became a site of contention over gender norms in the middle decades of the nineteenth century, firefighter masculinity was constantly on display in the streets. It was in the streets that the real battle over volunteer firefighter culture was fought. In order to understand how this fight played out, it is necessary to consider some other battles fought by firemen.

Chapter Three

FIGHTS/FIRES: A GLANCE AT VIOLENT FIREMEN

HARRY: Come, Mose, let's be off.
MOSE: [Astonished] What! Widout a fight? No, sir-ree—I'm goin' to have a speech from the landlord—den for a knock-down and a drag-out—den I retires like a gentleman.

—*A Glance at New York*[1]

IN THE 1850S, Currier and Ives's volunteer firemen graced middle-class homes, Marcus Boruck's *Fireman's Journal* graced firehouse parlors, and a fireman named Mose graced the stage. The 1848 melodrama, *A Glance at New York*, launched the career of the second most famous volunteer fireman of the nineteenth century.[2] The character Mose Humphreys (fig. 3.1), commonly known as "Mose the Bowery B'hoy," but also as "Fighting Mose" and "Mose, Hero of a Hundred Muses," was a seegar-smoking, rowdy volunteer fire laddie who emerged from an otherwise ordinary production to magnetize the country in over one thousand performances in the 1850s.[3]

A Glance at New York, the only surviving Mose script of the nine that were written, provides ample reason for Mose's enormous popularity. As a scholar of the fireman has commented, "Almost from inception Mose had borne the hallmarks of legend in a vehicle whose features—brevity, violence, the unshaded contrast of villainy and virtue—bore the stamp of popular fable."[4] Mose is a democratic hero for the age of Jackson—always ready to fight or to woo, he proves himself the protector of both fools and babies. As his more elegant friend, Harry, says, "In spite of his *outre* manners, he has a noble heart."[5]

Mose was also, and primarily, a fireman. In his first appearance on the stage he professes, "I've made up my mind not to run wid der machine any more" because the chief engineer had hit him "over the goard wid a trumpet" for insubordination. Of course he cannot resist the lure of firefighting for long. "I did think yesterday I'd leave de machine, but I can't do it; I love that ingine better than my dinner."[6]

Mose was not the first fireman to grace the theater. Other firemen had featured as heroes in lesser melodramas, and real volunteer firemen and the

Figure 3.1. Mose, the Fighting Fireman. Mose loved to fight, but did real volunteer firemen find pleasure in it, too? Lithograph of actor F. S. Chanfrau in the character of Mose, 1848. (Courtesy of Peter's Collection, National Museum of American History, Smithsonian Institution, Photo 600446-B.)

theater had a long relationship in American cities. It was poetically suiting that a fireman should become one of the greatest heroes of the nineteenth-century American stage: theaters were, after all, among the most flammable of nineteenth-century buildings (see fig. 3.2). Theaters held benefits for volunteer firemen, and fire companies in San Francisco and elsewhere regularly patronized them and worshipfully supported particular actresses.[7]

Previous theatrical firemen were significantly less popular than Mose—and also less rowdy. Mose was the first fighting fireman to take to the stage. In *A Glance at New York*, he fights, or threatens to fight, in every scene in which he appears. He does not fight indiscriminately, however. He fights thieves and politicians, loafers and landlords, but is gentle with the naive country boy,

Figure 3.2. Highly organized companies of Baltimore firemen battle the "Burning of the Front Street Theater and Circus" in this 1838 lithograph with hand coloring by Geo. C. Warner. With their elaborate dress uniforms and manly heroics, volunteer firemen put their masculinity on display offstage as well as on. (Courtesy of the Peale Museum, Baltimore.)

George. "I wouldn't hurt him for the world," Mose promises. His fighting also never interferes with his duty as a fireman.[8]

Mose is at once the buffoon of the play and its most appealing character. He is respected by everyone he comes in contact with, from the most proper to the criminal.[9] He knows his way around New York, and insists on having fun whether fighting or working. He cradles a baby in one scene, and he treats ladies and deserving elders with respect. He is irrepressibly masculine, as suits a volunteer fireman. When his educated and refined friends decide to infiltrate a women's bowling league in drag and convince him to come along, Mose betrays them and his own masculinity by kissing a matron, who quickly forgives him his transgression.

And as Mose, his girl Lize, and fellow fireman Sykesy traveled across the country, they entered the popular culture of the day. His catch phrases, such as "get off dem hose or I'll hit yer wid a spanner," were quoted in papers and on the streets. Schoolchildren imitated his speech, and his likeness was reproduced in numerous lithographs and posters. He made guest appearances in circus and ballet performances, as well as in advertisements. He was a national phenomenon—and America's first urban folk hero.[10]

He became, for better or worse, the reigning symbol of the New York fireman and, to a lesser degree, the American volunteer fireman. The Mose character was based on an actual volunteer fireman, but there was no actual Mose. As a stock figure in a melodrama, his character was circumscribed by the conventions of the genre. The Mose figure is but one adaptation of a role played by servants or peasants in English plays, stylistically similar to and dramatically interchangeable with other mid-nineteenth-century cult characters like Sam Patch, or the stage Irishman. He was wildly successful as a caricature of a New York volunteer fireman and as a symbol of the fireman, not as an actual representation of one.[11]

There were misunderstandings and suspicions about Mose, however, for some of the same reasons that made him so popular. The notoriety of the fighting Mose parallels exactly the notoriety of real fighting firemen. Some audiences wondered if Mose, a fighting fireman, was an appropriate stage presence in cities troubled by actual firemen's battles. An 1856 Louisville playbill attempted to assuage any fears the audience might have about this rough but noble character. "No two characters have been more misunderstood than Mose and Lizey. This hero and heroine of humble life have been too often considered perfect rowdies and profligate outcasts, while the very reverse is the case. Mose it is true, is one of the fire b'hoys, full of fun, frolic and fighting, but without one vicious propensity in his nature."[12]

The suspicions of the Louisville audience were understandable, as the city was at the time plagued by "the riotings and shedding of blood which have been attendant upon fire alarms."[13] While the legendary Mose toured the country, real firemen were forced to face the stigma of "fun, frolic, and fighting." What is surprising is not that the theater director in Louisville had to reassure his audience, but that more audiences did not reject Mose altogether. The most adored stage character of the decade symbolized that which communities professed to abhor: the fighting fireman.

Mose's impact on the nonfictional world of the real urban volunteer firefighter was intense and lasting. As urban citizens first began to consider paying firemen to fight fires, rather than employing volunteers, the image of the rowdy, violent volunteer was put to use to justify the expense of municipal forces. That certain individuals infiltrated and "soon changed the aspect and personnel of the department from a band of friends and brothers to that of rioters, scalawags, and thieves" was reported in San Francisco, Baltimore, and St. Louis.[14] As the Mose character grew in popularity, so too did the belief that volunteer firemen were inveterate fighters. Indeed, a national increase in violence among urban firemen was noted, discussed, and condemned by more law-abiding reformers in the 1840s and 1850s. While Mose was celebrated for his fighting, across America real volunteer firefighters saw their institutions dismantled as a result of their own perceived violence.

At the end of the 1850s, as Mose's fame reached its peak, reformers came to the consensus that urban volunteer firefighters posed a serious threat to public order, and that firemen stood outside the law, answerable to no power greater than their own. While Mose could have a "knock-down and a drag-out" and then retire "like a gentleman," America's urban firemen found it impossible to fight and then retire with dignity and reputation intact, in part because of the fictional fireman.

This chapter will explore the context and extent of violence among volunteer firemen in nineteenth-century urban America by closely examining when and why firemen in Baltimore, St. Louis, and San Francisco chose to fight. Although firemen in all three of these cities were reputed to be "violent," firemen in different cities did not share in a uniformly violent culture, nor did they engage in identical modes of behavior. The paradigmatic form of fireman violence was the fire "riot," in David Grimsted's definition, an incident "where a number of people group together to enforce their will immediately, by threatening or perpetrating injury to people or property outside legal procedures but without intending to challenge the general structure of society."[15] Such a riot occurred at a fire or alarm of fire only once in San Francisco, twice in a short period in St. Louis, and countless times throughout the tainted history of Baltimore's volunteer fire department. Lesser violent activities, including melees, musses, fights, and rows, show even greater regional variation in cause and extent. This chapter will consider why firemen fought one another in the middle of the nineteenth century, and why the public reacted to fighting firemen as it did. Did firemen in different cities really exhibit similar behavioral patterns? Did urban volunteer firemen share a masculine culture in which regular acts of violence were sanctioned and necessary? If not, why did urban citizens in the late antebellum period believe this to be true?

The Firemen of Mob-Town

In the previous chapters, I have argued that volunteer fire companies were so appealing to men because they offered a comforting vision of the world during a period of economic and social transition. While industrialization forced working men to recognize the limits of their economic opportunity, and while many middle-class men were forced to balance discordant work and home environments, volunteer fire companies offered both honor and brotherhood to potential members. They offered the fulfillment of a republican ideal of citizenship, they offered status through the respect and tribute of other citizens, they offered fine houses, paid for by city governments and donations of neighbors in a period when only wealthy merchants could afford to relax in clubs with armchairs, and clerks often shared rooms, and sometimes beds, in boardinghouses. They offered men community, camaraderie, and a masculine culture that was not tied to class.

During a period when distinct masculinities appeared among working- and middle-class men, the volunteer fire department offered a third option—a vigorous masculine culture that combined aspects of working- and middle-class culture along with cultural forms singular to the fire department. While leisure activities were increasingly segregated by class, fire departments contained memberships that were heterogeneous with regard to class and ethnicity. Baltimore's volunteer fire department was primarily composed of men who practiced low white-collar occupations, clerks, shopkeepers, small businessmen, and those laborers who practiced skilled trades. In San Francisco, the volunteer fire department was substantially more elite in occupational profile but welcomed many skilled, and some unskilled, laborers. In both Baltimore and San Francisco, a higher proportion of volunteer firemen practiced white-collar professions than did the population at large. The volunteer firefighter was just as likely to be a clerk or merchant as he was to be a butcher, like Mose.

Volunteer fire companies offered a heterogeneous membership, some of the trappings of the middle class, as well as the physicality and excitement of working-class culture. The volunteer fire departments of urban America developed a vision of masculinity that was accessible and appealing to men of different social strata, and which offered men the opportunity to match strength with other like-minded men, regardless of occupation.

In Baltimore, this masculine subculture produced and supported extensive violence, but not because it became a working-class institution. Bruce Laurie and Sean Wilentz have attributed violence among firemen in Philadelphia and New York to transformations in the class and ethnic compositions of firefighting forces. In both cities, "perfectly respectable" departments were altered by the emergence of industrialism and population growth. The departments came under the control of working-class rowdies who engaged in increasingly violent expressions of their competitiveness until an exasperated public saw no choice but to replace them. In Philadelphia in the 1830s, "intercompany rivalries were still relatively benign." A decade later they had developed into "brutal clashes between warring white traditionalists." By the 1850s, arsonists were burning down rival firehouses, and firemen preferred to shoot at each other rather than fight with more primitive and traditional weapons like brickbats or fists.[16]

Although this narrative of decline may accurately represent the history of the volunteer fire departments of Philadelphia and New York, none of the fire departments considered here experienced this trajectory. Not only did the heterogeneous composition of these departments differ from that of Philadelphia, where, we are told, the white-collar workers fled in terror from their companies, but the actions of the volunteers differed as well. Baltimore's volunteer fire department certainly did not conform to the precedent of New York and Philadelphia. Baltimore's department was never working class. As late as 1869, the year in which the department was disbanded, 40 percent of firemen listed in the city directory or census practiced white-collar occupations. Nine percent of locatable firemen practiced high white-collar occupations, while 21 percent of the skilled laborers in the department owned five-hundred dollars or more of real property.[17]

Baltimore's department differed from the Philadelphia department in another way as well: it supported a culture of violence almost from the beginning. Unlike Philadelphia, Baltimore had no Benjamin Franklin to set the tone for its eighteenth-century department, and troubles in Baltimore started early. Between 1763, when the Mechanical Fire Company was formed, and 1782, when a group of firemen split off and formed the Union Company, there was peace in Baltimore. The motto of the second company, "In union there is strength," was quickly belied, however. According to an early source, "rivalry sprung up between the two companies," and the disaffected met in 1785 to form a third company, which, "with a view of reconciling all the then difficulty," took the name Friendship.[18]

The first surviving fire company records in Baltimore document early-nineteenth-century disputes. A meeting of the Mechanical Company in 1813 condemned the lack of orderliness at fires and a "great neglect of duty" by the company. One of the earliest entries in the Union Company's ledger is a resignation letter from a member who complained of being "badly insulted" by another member.[19] By the 1830s, Baltimore had gained the sobriquet "Mob-Town" because of its frequent riots, some of which originated within the fire department. Both newspapers and company ledgers document serious volunteer troubles, including a battle between two companies at the scene of a fire, and other scenes of disorder, including shootings and arson.[20]

Despite attempts in the early 1830s by both firemen and city to bring the firemen's behavior under control, the violence worsened. Although fights seemed always to center around the firehouse, or fire itself, firemen pointed to outsiders as the cause of the violence. In the first years of the 1830s, three firehouses were set on fire by unidentified arsonists. Riots were nearly weekly occurrences. Yet the press failed to identify firemen as the perpetrators. "When shall we be able to pass a Sabbath day without being called upon to record some act of disgraceful violation of the peace, some daring outrage amounting almost to bloodshed?" asked the Baltimore *Sun* after one of these riots. "Not, we fear, until the originators of these riots, the master spirits who excite the evil passions of gangs of thoughtless, unruly boys, and lead them on step by step from simple brawls to riot, arson, and murder, receive their just dues." The *Sun* did not suggest that the master spirits might be firemen.[21]

Firemen maintained that they were blameless in these doings, but fire companies began internal reforms. Company members signed pledges that they would discontinue the use of "ardent spirits at fires," and that they would "refrain from giving any cause of offense to the members of any other company." Rather, they would take care to remember "the honour of the company" of which they were members, and the "character of the Firemen of Baltimore."[22]

Much of the problem, however, lay in this question of "honor." It was unclear whether a volunteer fireman's code of honor would be better served by fighting, or not fighting. The ledger of the Mechanical Company in 1839 commends the Independent Fire Company for attacking the Patapsco Company (the Mechanical Company's particular enemy) because of the latter company's "continued disorderly conduct, and the low character of the man of fellows of which it is composed—a disgrace to the Fire Department of Baltimore."[23] In the eyes of the Mechanical Company, it was perfectly honorable for an honorable company to attack a company made dishonorable by its own fighting.

The Volunteer Fire Department Standing Committee also considered honor a legitimate reason to start a fight. "It will not be maintained," the committee declared, "that any company should remain quiet and permit itself to be taunted, insulted, or mistreated."[24] In fact, members of the committee were not above such concerns themselves. According to fire company notes, in 1840 a fracas was instigated by one of the members of the committee whose "taunts and vociferous noises" were sufficient to start a riot on a "most beautiful and moonlit night."[25]

This tacit recognition of an honor code that condoned violence under certain circumstances helps explain the great number of disputes brought before the Standing Committee. In the highly charged and competitive world of antebellum firefighting, insults lurked everywhere. The first years of the committee, between 1834 and 1840, saw an astounding array of cases, from relatively minor infractions involving racing, or of one company throwing water upon another, to serious threats, bludgeonings, theft, and "general outrages by firemen." The United Fire Company ran their hose carriage into the Washington Company's engine. Was it deliberate? Unclear. Was it reason for a fight? Yes. Was the threat "to split your head open" made by a member of the Columbian Company simply high spirits, or an insult to the member of the Deptford Company against whom it was made?[26]

Committee members clearly felt ambivalent about firefighter violence. They recognized that sometimes fighting was justified, and they were firemen themselves. They rarely reached any conclusions. Subcommittees were often appointed to look into disputes, but they do not seem to have reported back. Even when evidence was forthcoming, the committee was loath to lay blame within the department or pronounce any serious punishment, perhaps out of concern for the department's public image. After all, a volunteer fire company survived on the goodwill and financial contributions of its neighbors, and bad press was likely to decrease the firemen's tribute. It was not in the interest of the Standing Committee to make conflicts and violence more visible than they already were. The same parties reappear with similar complaints. The New Market Company, generally considered to be a "bad lot," was accused of "using implements and carrying clubs and weapons not required by their duties, and frequently applied to purposes subversive of the public peace." In one particular 1838 battle against the Union Fire Company, New Market members, or their "runners," killed two men. Yet no punishment occurred, and the firemen continued fighting. It is unclear whether the committee was astounded or resigned that two deaths did nothing to tame the disorder in the fire department. Indeed, the committee noted, "riots, turbulence, disgraceful conduct and personal violence have since repeatedly occurred. The name of the fireman has almost become a badge of obloquy, and an emblem of disorder."[27] Fire company records show that the deaths made little impact on the firemen, and that even firemen who condemned "disgraceful" companies could still take a lurid pleasure in the violence of others. "The Patapsco and Friendship came in collision and ended in a *glorious* fight," the secretary of the Mechanical Fire Company wrote in 1840.[28]

The Standing Committee must have done an excellent job keeping volunteer difficulties private. Far into the 1840s, the press refused to locate the source of rioting among the firemen. Perhaps this was due to the firemen's capable performances at a series of large fires, or the role the firemen played in controlling the enormous 1835 bank riot. On several occasions during the two-day confrontation, the firemen were attacked by the mob while trying to save the property of the mayor (also a director of the bank), among that of other citizens. Afterwards they volunteered their services to act as watchmen or temporary police officers. Their persona of dispellers of riots was a role naturally incompatible with their own riotousness.[29]

In any case, although firemen engaged in frequent and extensive episodes of violence, they were not publicly identified as violent in the 1830s. In 1838 the Baltimore *Sun* clearly attempted to exonerate the firemen of any charges of misbehavior. Although the paper acknowledged that, at one time, some people suspected that the firemen themselves were starting riots, "this opinion . . . is nearly exploded." The *Sun* offered an alternative explanation, elaborating and expanding upon the favorite excuse of the firemen. "We say the cause is this: Baltimore City, like all other large places, contains some five or six dozen flash fellows—fancy rattlers—men who are a sort of half and half—who dress with more ease than grace, and now and then with more grace than ease: a species of nondescript, being neither professional men, mechanics, or laborers—a something, nothing, a kind of wandering beings."

After elaborating upon the details of these "confidence men" who wander from eating house to tavern bar, flashing showy jewelry and drinking late into the evening, the article revealed their fiendish intentions. Intent upon fighting, "according to their own conception, a sort of civil drubbing, which some particular man, or set of men, has, in some way earned," their intention is conveyed "to the various engine houses, (at most of these in the evening are collected large gangs of half grown boys,) they hear of the coming battle with the greatest joy, and off they scamper to the battle ground." The article concluded that it was the responsibility of parents and masters to keep children and apprentices at home late at night, and that no one under the age of twenty should be allowed to collect in gangs or at engine houses.[30]

The confidence man is also the antagonist in the first Mose drama. Various confidence men, closely fitting the description offered by the Baltimore *Sun*, repeatedly trick and rob a country boy in *A Glance at New York*. Mose the fireman eventually saves the greenhorn from their clutches and then knocks them to the ground. In *A Glance at New York*, the fireman is the only protection against confidence men offered by New York to unwary visitors. In this article, Baltimore firemen were also clearly distinguished from troublemakers.

Outside agitators did help incite firemen's riots at this time, and in later decades as well. According to fire company minutes, rabble-rousers might shout inflammatory words at the firemen or throw bricks and stones at them during or after fires. Often these fights originated in political disputes between Whig and Democratic political clubs that associated at the privately owned firehouses or at taverns near the firehouses. In 1844, the secretary of the Mechanical Company reported that the engine of the Vigilant Company was "seized by a party of rowdies, who threw their hose in the Falls. The Columbia Carriage was likewise seized and partially destroyed. Beautiful Conduct!! Brick bats flew like hail, pistols were fired in every direction." This company believed that rowdies, and not firemen, were the source of their troubles. The secretary of this company was clearly concerned that "there is now no safety for those that are well disposed," and predicted that "something must be done or the department will be in the hands of these rowdies completely!"[31]

But firemen were not the innocent victims of rowdyism and political difference. The firemen also contributed to these scenes, and "disgraceful fights," in which "axes, torches, knives and pistols were freely used," were attributed by firemen to their brethren as well as to "rowdies" who might or might not be connected to the department.[32]

Yet in reports of riots at fires and false alarms in the 1830s and 1840s, firemen were rarely identified. On the rare occasions on which arrests were made, they were reported to be "youths not believed to be firemen" and unidentified belligerents.[33] Clearly, many of these individuals, arrested or not, were firemen. A particularly disgraceful fight occurred on Easter Sunday in

1844 after a false alarm. The secretary of the Mechanical Company recorded that the "Easter morning trial of apparatus turns into a fight in which members of all companies participated." The Baltimore *American* stated conservatively that they "observed a general melee going on, but as to who was at fault, or who were the belligerents, we could not ascertain." In 1838 legislation was passed making the intentional injury of a fireman a crime punishable by a month's imprisonment.[34]

A combination of internal reforms and a new municipal "minor law" banning minors from companies in 1844 worked to dispel both the boys and the riots for a time. The secretary of the Mechanical Fire Company commented with some amazement in April 1845 that the recent legislation "is found fully to effect the object for which it is designed—scarcely a boy is seen with any of the Reel Suctions. . . . A most admirable regulation and calculated to do away with the broils and riots which have disgraced the Fire Department for so long past."[35] But the minor law was soon ignored, and by the summer of 1847 rioting had again become, in the words of the secretary, "so bad that it is dangerous for peaceable persons to go to fires, for fear of being shot, or knocked down by a brick."[36]

After its two-year hiatus on disorder, the press returned far less sympathetic to the firemen. In an article titled "Firemen's Riots—What Can the Matter Be?" the Baltimore *Sun* scorned the excuses they had believed two years before. "We find bonfires built in some remote section of the city, merely to cause an alarm and draw the firemen together for the purpose of a fight, and have seen the apparatus of certain companies taken out when there was no alarm and run into a section of the city where a collision was most likely to take place." Although adult men, in the uniform of firemen, always appeared to be in charge, "when a collision occurs," the reporter sneered, "we have every assurance given that those who participated in them are half-grown boys, and not members of the companies."[37] Or, as another article stated skeptically, "It certainly seems strange that these rioters, if not members of the companies they run with, should be allowed to take out their apparatus."[38]

Apparently the public was losing interest as well. For the first time, the Mechanical Company Collecting Committee decided in December not to request funds from the neighborhood, due to "the impression which may have been made on the public, by the rioting of several Companies in the city." Instead, they decided that they "had better defer it until peace and harmony was restored."[39] That time never came. By late 1848 another person had died, and at least five observers had been injured by the flying bricks, missiles, and bullets that marked the firemen's battles.[40]

During the period of calm in the mid-1840s, "arrests of minors were made, all rioting among firemen ceased, and there were not near so many fires as now," as one fireman later put it. It appears that the Baltimore press took advantage of the peace and quiet following the passage of the minor law and reexamined its assumptions about rioting in Baltimore.[41] In the 1830s and early 1840s, at the height of fireman rioting, riots frequently took place that did not involve the firemen. Many of these riots were perpetuated by unhappy segments of the population to protest ills in society. During this period, riots occurred in Baltimore that were both expressive and recreational, to borrow Michael Feldberg's terms. The bank riot of 1835 was one of three riots in Baltimore in a two-year period clearly expressive of protesters' sense of economic or political injustice. An 1840 attack by "a large party of rowdies with the New Market and United companies . . . on a crowd of Whigs assembled at the Patriot office" offers another example of expressive rioting. "Several pistols were discharged by the Whigs but no one was killed . . . great political excitement between the Whigs and Democrats, threatening riot and bloodshed."[42]

Other riots, involving rowdies and firemen, appear to have been purely recreational in nature. These riots may have reinforced the solidarity of the group or upheld a group's honor code, but such riots did not express any larger dissatisfaction with the status quo.[43] The riots in which the firemen took part (according to their own records) were therefore easy for the public to blame on other troublemakers, and the confidence man–outsider figure served this purpose well. Firemen could not be expected to be in control in an environment where no one else was, either. If boys ran with their machines and knocked each other's heads in with bricks, well, they might have done as much elsewhere just as easily. The firemen blamed the police for not keeping order, and in fact had to act as police to protect public order during the bank riot. Furthermore, it was difficult for the public to decide whom to blame when the police consistently failed to arrest rioters.

But by 1846 there is evidence of a dramatic decline in expressive rioting as well as a decline in the number of riots *not* related to firefighting. Virtually no reports of riots without firemen can be found in the newspapers of the late 1840s.[44] The link between firemen and riots probably became clear in the 1845–1846 period of calm in the fire department. As a result, all later riots could be blamed on the firemen, who were clearly rioting for recreational purposes. Thus a solution to all riots was sought in relation to the fire department.

In fact, rioting among firemen had only marginally worsened. Individual riots of the late 1840s in Baltimore were particularly violent, and for a period in 1847 firemen battled one another weekly. There were also particularly violent battles in 1835 and 1840, as well as extended series of battles throughout the period. Rioting appeared worse in the late 1840s not simply because it *was* worse, but because there was no longer a background of lawlessness to soften its edges. "Mob-Town" may have been an appropriate description of Baltimore in the 1830s, but by the late 1840s the city's reformers were hoping for a more dignified title.

Firemen were perceived to be rioting more often because they were more likely to be identified in newspaper reports as rioters in the late 1840s, a fact possibly related to the rise of the fighting Mose in 1848.[45] Fights involving firemen were also more likely to be labeled "riots" than in earlier years. "A Riot and Brutal Murder," in 1849, is actually the story of a barroom brawl involving perhaps four people, all of whom unfortunately belonged to fire companies and one of whom was stabbed to death.[46] A postfire disturbance a week later was saved from becoming "a riot of considerable extent" by the "efficient and extraordinary efforts" of the police. An engine collision on Baltimore Street led to insults, followed by two injuries. A brick thrown by a member of the Watchman Company hit a member of the United Company on the head, and a United member retaliated by smacking a Watchman fireman with a pipe. The police, the reader is told, saved the day. "The very moment that manifestations of disorder appeared, [the police] were on the spot amidst the uproarious crowds that filled the street, and regardless of danger or injury promptly arrested the offending parties."[47] This event would hardly have merited a paragraph in the 1830s, but in the 1830s the police would also not have taken preemptive action. The melee would have taken its own course, either dissipating, as such events often did according to fire company records, or developing into a full-fledged riot.

What is clear from this passage is the new interest and demand for order in Baltimore, focused on preventing disorder, not simply controlling it. As in other cities, order was enforced in Baltimore by growing numbers of professional police. Police expenditures in Baltimore more than tripled between 1845 and 1855, and by 1856 an expanded and centralized Baltimore police was uniformed, reflecting and legitimating their growing semimilitary status in the city. In 1849 the mayor of Baltimore divided the city into fire wards to which the companies were then assigned and were allowed to leave only upon permission of the mayor.[48]

These two preemptive strikes against the firemen in 1849, one by the police at a disturbance and one by the mayor, could only produce the impression that a nonviolent fire department was nonviolent because it was externally controlled, not because of any internal restraints. In fact, the police were utterly unable to control a truly riotous crowd, as was made clear in Baltimore's election riots of 1856–1859, the most violent election riots in United States history. The perception that the police alone could provide control helped them to widen their own sphere of influence. Starting in the mid-nineteenth century, it also helped the police to legitimate ever-increasing force sizes and expenditures when they failed to provide that elusive control.[49]

There is no evidence of any firemen's riots or other major public disturbances by the firemen from 1850 to 1855, although there were a great number of false alarms and fires, averaging almost one of each per day in 1851. Two or three minor attacks by one company upon another are documented in the company ledgers, but these events do not seem to have resulted in major injuries, or to have been publicized.[50]

The decline in violence does not seem to have improved the public standing of the fire department. Perhaps this was because their behavior was now viewed within the paradigm of police control, their orderliness viewed as the result of effective policing. The press portrayed it as such, commenting, when a serious riot broke out in August 1855, that for some time "there has been every indication of a serious struggle between them [the New Market and Mount Vernon companies], though they have been kept in check by the police, who were always on the watch, in consequence of the anticipated rupture. Notwithstanding their vigilance, however, they have, at last, succeeded in their disgraceful designs." The results were indeed disgraceful: one fireman killed by a member of his own company (who was attempting to kill a policeman); one young bystander and a former fireman killed, the latter with a shot to the breast; three other men injured; and the crowd at large "armed, and for the most part, incessantly firing."[51]

Two further riots culminated the violent career of the Baltimore Volunteer Fire Department on election days in 1856 and 1858. The years 1855 to 1859, a period of Know-Nothing Party hegemony in Baltimore, saw a renewal of violence in the city in the form of election riots that neither political party was willing or able to stop. The reputation of the department had sunk so low by this time that a complete reversal of reporting is evident. While in the 1830s and early 1840s firemen were often above suspicion in melees in which they played a leading role, their final years are marked by riots in which their role was exaggerated. In the 1856 mayor's election riot, the New Market Company played a primarily defensive role in one battle of what was actually a series of simultaneous riots, all fought with firearms, across the city. Members of two Know-Nothing political clubs, the "Rip-Raps" and "Plug-Uglies," attacked the engine house of the Democratic New Market Fire Company for two or three hours, "unchecked and unheeded, by apparently any efficient show of police force," with "muskets, shotguns and blunderbuses." "It was a most surprising spectacle for a civilized community," scoffed the *Sun*. Two men died in this battle, and at least five others died in the riots that occurred in other parts of the city. The role of the New Market Fire Company was highlighted in the *Sun's* coverage of the riot.[52]

The less bloody but still shocking election riot of 1858 was particular in that firemen appear to have had nothing to do with it, despite the assertions of historians since. Perhaps it was fitting for the firemen to get credit for one last riot in their final year, after so many prior years of disorder.[53]

Given the strange trajectory of the Baltimore Volunteer Fire Department—a membership that clearly did not reflect the ruffian reputation it acquired in the 1850s, a long and involved history of recreational rioting that had no impact on the reputation of the department until the late 1840s, and increasing condemnation in the press of behavior that did not substantially worsen—it becomes difficult to accept traditional explanations for firefighter violence. Baltimore's volunteer fire department did not decline from a bastion of middle-class respectability to a mob of working-class and immigrant rowdies. Volunteer firemen in Baltimore rather found their traditional concepts of honor, and means of expressing that honor, increasingly under fire amid changing demands for order and respectability in the larger society. Behavioral norms in Baltimore had changed more than had the behavior of the firemen.

St. Louis Rowdyism

The violence of the St. Louis volunteers seems playful in comparison, more rowdy than riotous. Regional differences may have contributed to the less alarming tone of this fire department. Baltimore was a more characteristically Southern city in the antebellum period than St. Louis, which maintained strong economic and cultural ties to Boston, New York, and Philadelphia until the time of the Civil War. As historians including Edward Ayers and Bertram Wyatt-Brown have demonstrated, Southern men were quicker to resort to violence in the nineteenth century than were Northern men. In the South, maintaining individual honor required quick and unambiguous responses to even minor insults. Volunteer firemen in Baltimore might have resorted to violence with such regularity because of the sanction of a Southern honor code.[54]

For firemen in St. Louis, violence was never such an obvious choice. Firemen did not begin to fight in St. Louis until 1849 and employed primitive weapons in primarily minor skirmishes. Only one fatality can be directly attributed to the volunteer fire company's record of rowdyism, and up until their demise, firemen in St. Louis showed a willingness to reconcile with their sparring partners, highlighting the casual nature of most of this fighting. While they were never as violent as the firemen in Baltimore, firemen in St. Louis also shared in a culture that sanctioned some acts of violence. As in Baltimore, the record of firefighter violence does not fit a simple decline narrative.

The first five permanent fire companies in the frontier city of St. Louis were established between 1832 and 1835, with the first recorded fight occurring in 1849. This first fight was really a riot, although it was not referred to as such at the time. This may have been because the firemen did not attack one another but the Irish inhabitants of the appropriately named "Battle Roe." The fight resulted in worse press than injuries—although not as bad, of course, as if the firemen's victims had been "Americans." The Irish deckhands of this areas were known brawlers and engaged in frequent fights, often between two Irish gangs. Native-born residents of St. Louis were not sympathetic to these violent immigrants. One contemporary account of this thumping stated only that "a fight occurred between the firemen and a gang of Irish. The firemen came off the victors. Loss $130,000." In the report of a fireman, the Irish had "got what they deserves," after the firemen finished "run[ing] the Irish all over the upper part of town."[55]

Fire companies in St. Louis maintained their honor in the 1840s by racing to fires, raising false alarms, and stealing the engines out of other companies' houses. Engine racing was treated as a major problem by many of the companies, which passed legislation to expel any member who engaged in such an activity and warned of the "many evil consequences ensu[ing] from persisting in such practices such as unnecessarily injuring the apparatus and endangering the lives and limbs of members." The lives and limbs of nonmembers were also endangered by this practice. The Missouri Fire Company admitted to running over four people with their engine in two years, none of whom, amazingly, was seriously hurt.[56]

The 1843–1849 records of the Phoenix Fire Company, the "most turbulent" company in the department and the one containing "more of the Eastern rowdies than the rest combined," according to one historian of the department, reveal that the company in this decade had more interest in entertaining other companies, parading, and attractively dressing both its engine and members than in fighting (men or fires). The most disturbing event of the 1840s at the Phoenix firehouse was a threat made by a member to shoot the watchman if he rang the bell. This transgression occupies an entire month of debate in the journal. Fines were also instituted for members caught racing, or for ringing the bell in a false alarm of fire.[57]

Another St. Louis company expelled a member for "misbehavior and stating a gross falsehood to the company." St. Louis fire companies favored the threat of expulsion, and expulsion itself, as a means to control behavior; to accept a previously expelled fireman into your company was a mark of great dishonor.[58] Four offenses merited expulsion from the Laclede Company in 1850, "giving false alarm of a fire," "disobedience of the order of a Superior," "loud, vulgar, or obscene language either at the engine house or when on duty," and quarreling. These transgressions appear quaint in comparison to the offenses of arson, battery, fighting at a fire, and shooting another fireman that resulted in expulsions in Baltimore.[59] The Missouri Company threatened to expel any member who appeared drunk at a fire twice, or made any noise "deemed injurious to the character and reputation of the company."[60]

Even flagrant provocations of another company appear to have diffused themselves fairly well in the 1840s. The Missouri Fire Company stole the Union Company's engine out of their house "without authority" in 1846, in a clear violation of that company's honor, and felt no repercussions for four years. "Union Fire Co. awfull keen for a muss, they had better keep cool," the Missouri secretary remarked in 1848.[61] Only with the onset of the tumultuous 1850s could the fight they had "been expecting for some time" begin. The description of this fight reveals a joy in pure physical violence lacking in any of the surviving materials from Baltimore. The fight began as the Missouri Company returned home with their engine from a fire. As they passed the Liberty hose truck, the captain of the Liberty Company, known to the writer as "Big Six," ominously approached Mr. Dickey, assistant foreman of the Missouri Company.

> Big Six struck at Mr. Dickey but missed him. In turn, Dickey knocked him down, and so the fight began. Both companies fought like h—l. At last the Liberty Hose Co. run, and I thought the fight was ended, but not so, for just as we started home again, the Union and Liberty Companies came at us with stones, clubs, spanners, and wrenches. Our boys tried to stand their ground, but it was no use, they were too much for us. . . . There was as many as 20 of the Liberty and Union members at Mr. Dickey at once, and if ever a man fought hard, Dickey did, and I believe he would have undid them all, but one of the Liberty's members jumped on the fence and struck Dickey in the back of the head, which knocked him down.

The fight ended with Mr. Dickey's fall. Three Missouri members were injured, but only Dickey had to be carried home. The writer proudly announced that more Liberty than Missouri members were injured, but he closed with a sobering evaluation of the afternoon's activities: "All I wish is that there will never be such another fight again. . . . This scrape will be the means of breaking down the Missouri. P.S., we will have a slap at them again some day."[62]

Intradepartmental fighting began in St. Louis in 1850, but firemen continued to exhibit restraint. As the Missouri secretary indicated, firemen in St. Louis felt ambivalence about physical combat. They may have enjoyed the excitement of the battle and felt the desire to avenge previous wrongs with more fighting, but they could also hope that "there will never be such another fight again." This regret is entirely absent from the surviving records of the Baltimore fire companies.

The Union and Missouri companies seemed to drop their differences after this fight, although the Union Company went on to fight with the Liberty and Phoenix companies in 1852. The Missouri had the chance at another "slap" at the Liberty in 1854 when the latter company "accidentally" ran its engine into the path of the Missouri engine. The Missouri men practiced restraint, although the Missouri secretary did not mince words about the "dirty low blow hards" that made up the Liberty: "The D—n Rowdies are a perfect nuisance, and the company from its commencement was a querulous, low, rowdy company, and instead of getting better, they got worse. A bigger set of Cowards never pulled on a drag rope of an Engine." The secretary's comments upon this occasion reveal a firefighter code being broken by the Liberty Company and a real fear of the ramifications fighting would bring on the department: "It is this company of our once Respectable Department [that] from their first organization . . . would take in members expelled from other companies. . . . They now talk of breaking up, and the sooner the better for the city and department."

It was probably this fear for the reputation of the department, in the light of developments in Eastern departments, which kept fights from escalating into riots in St. Louis. A "muss" broke out in 1851 after the Washington Fire Company threw water on the St. Louis Fire Company, with "plenty of Brick Bats thrown by the St. Louis," but the Washington Company did not retaliate.[63]

Fire companies in St. Louis fought throughout the 1850s, but also repeatedly attempted to work out differences among themselves with apologies or meetings with other companies, indicating that the firemen hoped to limit the extent and ramifications of their rowdyism. In 1856, the Franklin and Missouri companies, which had fought on and off for several years, held a "friendly visit" as they both pledged to "stand by each other as friends, and to do all in our power to cement the bonds of friendship more closely than ever."[64] Problems between the Franklin and Liberty companies proved difficult to solve, however. Differences between the two originated when the Franklin was "attacked by members if the Liberty . . . on their way to take up some Hose" in 1851. After three years of occasional fights after fires and false alarms, the Franklin Company held a meeting with members of the Liberty Company to attempt finally to resolve their difficulties.[65] Fighting continued, and in 1855 the Liberty Company was suspended for six months for damaging the Franklin Company's engine, the same month that the Washington Company was suspended for breaking the windows of the Liberty.[66] The damage to the engine led to the only verified violence-related fatality in St. Louis. Before these two companies were finally reconciled, a Liberty Company member was shot and killed, the only documented case of a firemen in St. Louis using a pistol against another fireman.[67]

Within its own context, the fact that only one St. Louis fireman was shot is somewhat remarkable. Firefighters in St. Louis deserve credit for not resorting to firearms again. By the mid-1850s, nearly all firemen carried them for protection against mobs at fires, according to one volunteer who claimed he "would not have gone to that fire without his revolver under any consideration." Yet if guns were carried, they do not appear to have been drawn, or if drawn, they were certainly not fired at other firemen.[68]

On the eve of the Civil War, St. Louis was a town seething with sectional violence, where "Bibles and Sharp's rifles were associated as correlating agencies of civilization."[69] Advertisements for rifles appeared on the front pages of St. Louis's newspapers. Yet firemen in this city did not use firearms regularly. Fights in St. Louis emerged out of races to fires, competitions over fire hydrants, and turf disputes, as they did in Baltimore and other cities. Some St. Louis firemen enjoyed fighting. But the firemen of this city exhibited clear restraint considering the weapons on hand and the precedent set by departments on the East Coast. The volunteer firefighter culture in St. Louis sanctioned only limited forms of violence.

Although there may have been an internal control, and possibly even order, to the St. Louis fighting, by the mid-1850s the city's firemen had alienated the press and reformers as thoroughly as the Baltimore volunteers had done. In another ethnically based disturbance in 1854, the firemen attempted to impose their values outside their organization.

> While the fire was raging a number of the Washington Company boys entered a beer-house close by the place of the fire, owned and kept by Martin Graf, a German, and demanded some beer. Mr. G. set before them some mineral water, brandy and other drinks, stating that he could not give them beer as his beer pump was out of order. But the liquors were refused by the firemen. They then began to break the bottles in the house, and in other ways damaging the furniture in the room, when Graf drew a pistol and shot at a fireman called "Bogus Jim," slightly wounding him in the face. This cleared the house, but the crowd outside began to grow violent in denunciations and threats, when Mr. G. came to the door and again discharged his pistol at the crowd.[70]

Graf shot several people in the crowd and escaped, as a mob was only barely restrained from tearing down his house. Graf, the pistol-wielding German, took the brunt of the blame for this incident, although the row was "disgraceful in the extreme to our city," the *Missouri Democrat* reported. As in the earlier Irish-bating episode, the sympathy of the public was fully with the firemen. Perhaps if the St. Louis volunteers had limited their attentions and demands to immigrants and to one another, they could have continued in this manner for some time, harassing ethnic groups and throwing bricks at rival engines. But by the 1850s, the values of the firemen and the larger society were clearly diverging. The *Missouri Democrat* complemented the firemen on their "effective work in subduing the flames," at the fire near the beer house, but complaints about the firemen's behavior elsewhere began to increase.

As discussed in the previous chapter, the firehouse became a central cite of contention in St. Louis in the battle over behavioral norms. Firehouse neighbors complained of the constant noise and disorder emanating from almost all of the houses throughout the 1850s, a situation firemen were either unable, or unwilling, to rectify.[71] The mayor of St. Louis focused on the disorderly firehouse in his report to the City Council in 1855.

> It is a demoralizing system, for the members, particularly the more youthful, will and do congregate, as they feel free to do, in about their engine house, day and night, and on the Sabbath, in great numbers, and indulge in conversation and conduct, not only unbecoming, but highly indecorous and obscene. No one who has a decent regard for what is polite, refined or virtuous, has lived in the vicinity

> of, or passed near one of the houses in the evening or on Sunday, and not been disgusted with the exhibitions there witnessed.[72]

The polite, refined, and virtuous were more actively assaulted when missiles thrown in one 1856 battle between the Liberty and Franklin companies damaged several houses, not firehouses, in the neighborhood.[73]

Reformers in St. Louis may have felt particular concern over their firefighters' lack of decorum. Boosters and middle-class transplants from Boston and New York were actively working toward the gentility of East Coast cities in the 1840s and 1850s, and hoped to bring refinement to St. Louis at the exact time that the behavior of the firemen was degenerating. Refined men were not supposed to engage in the sort of personal physical violence that Mose specialized in. Etiquette books advised readers to follow Christian precedents instead. "When his enemy smites him on one cheek, meekness requires [the Christian] to turn the other, also, and for personal abuse to return acts of kindness." For reformers, the morality of the firemen became the object of outrage, as did the firemen's behavior in the streets.[74]

Given the larger transformations in the public use of the streets in America during the middle decades of the nineteenth century, it is not surprising that the street became a site of contention over firefighter behavior. As Richard Bushman has shown, the streets were an especially contested battleground in the struggle for refinement across America.[75] In the streets of America's cities, the refined were forced to interact with everyone else. As respectable women increasingly ventured out of doors for benevolence and shopping, activities consistent with their roles as virtuous consumers, businessmen and reformers created "an urban habitat designed especially for the ladies," in Mary Ryan's words. Public space was sanitized by the presence of women. Cities including San Francisco, New Orleans, and New York passed ordinances in the middle nineteenth century against insulting women in the streets, and shop owners worked to ensure that women felt comfortable traveling to their stores.[76] No decent woman would voluntarily submit herself to the "hordes of ruffians" who loitered around firehouses in New York in the 1850s, according to one account, "insulting and abusing women and strangers and making themselves as offensive and dangerous as possible." Men needed to protect virtuous women from the threat of such behavior. Firemen were not only actively visible in the streets, but in St. Louis, as in Baltimore, they were also actively crude in their behavior.[77]

It was appropriate that the final confrontation between the norms of the firemen and those of the polite, refined, and virtuous would transpire in the streets. Only two months after Mayor King's report on the indecorous firemen, he was interrupted on a walk by the Phoenix hose carriage, drawn by "a set of Wildmen and half-grown boys on the sidewalk . . . to the great detriment of the lives of Ladies and Gentlemen walking on that crowded thoroughfare.

I heard the yell as of so many savages . . . and ran to see what was the cause. Upon reaching 4th street I attempted to stop the parties who were engaged in the disgraceful act, but was not only disregarded, but insulted by a louder yell when they learned who I was."[78] The savages had squared off against the protector of ladies and gentlemen and won a Pyrrhic victory. In April 1857 the city of St. Louis passed an ordinance to provide for a paid steam fire department.[79] Legislated out of existence, the final year of the volunteer department was marked by arson and active resistance to the new, paid organization.[80] Nonetheless, as a department apologist pointed out correctly, "the record of dangerous injuries due to the spirit of 'sport' during its whole existence, is not comparable with that often resulting during a single season from the rivalry in sport among 'teams' of leading universities, between 1898 and 1905."[81]

St. Louis's fire department was never an unruly mob. Although members may not have shown sufficient respect for their elected officials, violence within the department was almost always internally controlled. But history has not been kind to the St. Louis volunteers; their record of violence continued to expand long after their institution was dismantled. The most famous nineteenth-century historian of St. Louis, John Thomas Scharf, spared no venom in his portrayal of the firemen as nearly Baltimorean in character (which, considering he had written *The Chronicles of Baltimore* nine years earlier, is perhaps not surprising). The volunteer system, he wrote, "had become a standing outrage" and was responsible for all manner of urban crimes. "The spirit of rowdyism which had grown up under it, not satisfied with an occasional demonstration at fires, turned to the highways and assailed the inoffensive citizen as he walked to his home."[82]

Perhaps not surprisingly, firemen also contributed to the mythologizing of fireman violence. Thomas Lynch, a veteran firefighter, apparently manufactured a dramatic riot in his 1880 history of the St. Louis Volunteer Fire Department. The supposed riot is undocumented in any previous work, including the leading newspapers of the period. The "Dog-Fight Riot" of 1853, according to Lynch, occurred when a firemen interfered in a fight between a large bulldog and its small victim in his "desire to see fair play." The owners of the bulldog resented the interference, and soon a riot between the firemen at large and the bulldog's supporters interrupted the peace of a St. Louis Sunday.[83]

Could Mose be responsible for these developments? Both Scharf and Lynch attribute the rise of rowdyism in the St. Louis Fire Department to the "acquisition of members . . . of a lot of refugees from justice and chronic roughs from the departments of the Eastern Cities."[84] Although the names of these rough characters are not given, both authors provide clues to their exact identities. According to Lynch, it was the "typical 'B'hoy,' or 'Syksey' " (another character in the fictional Mose drama). According to Scharf, "this class were those who styled the apparatus 'de masheen!' who said 'nah!' and 'yaas!' " Both of these authors indicate that Mose, in his most threatening and dangerous form, came to St. Louis at just the time when his character would have graced the stages of the city.[85]

Not only did Mose, in the form of East Coast rowdies, enter St. Louis, but Lynch reports that St. Louis began to produce its own "Moses" as well. "The character of 'Mose' brought out about this time at the theaters contributed largely to give 'éclat' to the sayings and doings of these parties, and especially in molding the future character of the younger members."[86]

The influence of Mose was far greater than either of these commentators realized, however. Mose was not only able to change the character of the department after his arrival, as they suggest, but to re-create its entire history in his image. Who but Mose would stand up for the rights of the literal "underdog" with his fists, as the firemen of the imaginary "Dog-Fight Riot" did? The victims of the real St. Louis firemen, the Irish in 1849 and the German tavern keeper in 1854, would have been beneath the notice of Mose, or at least they would not have featured large in his adventures. The persecutors of small dogs are precisely the sort that Mose would revel in fighting, and then telling of the fight. It appears that Mose not only enabled those outside the fire department to understand rowdyism within it, but also enabled members of this masculine subculture to construct their own behavior—and history.

The "Model Fire Department of the World"

Almost from the time of their organization in 1849, the firemen of San Francisco considered their department to be the "Model Fire Department of the World." In part this was due to the "strict observance of its laws, and . . . brotherly feeling which has always distinguished them."[87] In part it was because the San Francisco Volunteer Fire Department was among the most elite departments in the country. In 1860, after the Baltimore and St. Louis volunteers had been forcibly disbanded, San Francisco's department contained far more white-collar than laboring members. Nearly 60 percent of volunteer firemen in this city practiced white-collar occupations, and fully 18 percent were in high-white-collar jobs. The department was ethnically diverse, but less so than the Gold-Rush city it belonged to. In a city where only half of all residents were native born, one-third of all firemen were foreign born in 1860. San Francisco's department was a model of wealth, decorum, and middle-class trappings.[88]

Because they organized so much later than East Coast or Midwest departments, the firemen in this city understood the wages of violence. They correctly observed that "one blow struck in anger in the public street, while in the Fireman's garb, will be like a cancer, eating gradually into the vitals of the Department."[89] As a result, violence in San Francisco had a different character than it did in Baltimore or St. Louis. Each violent episode in San Francisco can be traced to a concrete source of "ill feeling" among the participants, and in each case the resulting violence was read by the participants as a legitimate, nontrivial reaction to perceived wrongs. The San Francisco firemen were not riotous like the Baltimore firemen, nor rowdy like their St. Louis brethren. They shared a code of honor, but it sanctioned very few expressions of violence. Like the other departments, however, the San Francisco volunteers alienated both press and politician with scenes of public disorder that were at odds with an increasingly orderly urban context.

Volunteer firefighting in San Francisco was not free from the rivalry and competition that marked other departments. Starting in 1849, when the department was organized, firemen raced each other to fires and allowed boys to run with their engines. The *Fireman's Journal* warned against another popular practice, "saving" hydrants at fires. This eroticized description gives some suggestion as to why the practice was so widespread. "No engine or hose company has any particular right to a hydrant; and a company has no right to send a member in advance to take possession of a hydrant, until they should arrive, to the exclusion of any other apparatus. The butt first at a hydrant ready to attach, in the event of a fire has the undisputed right to enjoy it, and a member of another company would not be justified in retaining that hydrant on the ground that his engine or hose carriage would soon be there."[90]

Yet those activities which provided the impetus for so many of the fights in other departments had little affect on the good feeling among firemen in San Francisco. As volunteer Robert S. Lammot wrote, "After it [a fire] is over, instead of stopping a while to have a fight—as they file past one another on their way home, you hear such cries as Hurrah for the 'Howard'! She's always the first in service—Three cheers for the 'California'—she is *some* at a fire—There comes the 'Monumental'! good for the Baltimoreans."[91]

Within the competitive culture of the volunteer fire department, antagonism and rivalry could and did appear. After a trial of apparatus in front of five thousand spectators, and a five hundred dollar wager, the Monumental and Vigilant companies nearly came to blows. They published insulting letters to each other in San Francisco's newspapers but were reconciled during the visit of a Stockton fire company to the city before a self-described "war of water" could become a "war of blood."[92]

Similar tensions arose for the same reasons between the Howard and Knickerbocker companies (which wagered six thousand dollars on a contest of machinery) and were heard to growl "instead of giving three cheers for each other as they ought to have done" when returning from a fire.[93] In the letters exchanged between these companies, also published, each company attempted to negotiate terms of the contest most favorable to them while accusing the other company of demanding unfair advantage. These correspondences finally degenerated into accusations of dishonesty on both sides, and the refusal of the Howard Company to compete at all, based on the assertion that, "judging from several previous transactions with [the Knickerbockers], there is no honor or probity among them as a company."[94] Although honor was at stake, no blows were exchanged between these companies.

San Francisco also suffered from many of the same external stresses that troubled other departments. Fights between boys running with engines occasionally began but were generally controlled by "the promptitude and decision of MEN in the department." Unruly crowds interfered with firemen in their discharge of duty. Firemen in San Francisco, like those in Baltimore and St. Louis, complained that there were often no police at the scenes of fires to aid firemen in crowd control.[95]

As in East Coast departments, youth gangs found San Francisco's firemen a tempting target. In 1855 rowdies attacked the firemen on at least three occasions, yet the firemen refrained from battling with rowdies. The most serious of the incidents occurred early one morning when the French membership of the peaceful Lafayette Hook and Ladder Company was assaulted by a gang of rowdies. One of the members was hit in the stomach with a brickbat and injured badly. The rest of the members were prevented from defending their companion when the gang at large drew pistols. Unfortunately, the identified assailant escaped punishment in a court of law. The firemen believed this was because "the testimony of the complainant, a Frenchman, was set at naught."[96]

Truly, they were tested. Although "bullied and attacked on the streets, and followed by their assailants to the very portals of their engine houses," although "the hot blood of a rightful indignation at the insults heaped upon them, has mounted to their cheeks," the firemen never forgot who they were. As the press reported, "the thought of their own unsullied reputation" prevented them from retaliating as they wished to do. Overall, the San Francisco firemen "displayed a forbearance which their best friends did not give them credit for," and they did so out of a sense of honor.[97]

Until 1856, in fact, the editor of the *Fireman's Journal* could with some truth report that "blows in anger" had never been exchanged among the firemen (although the editor himself had a year earlier been attacked by the chief engineer).[98] Neither competition, wagers, boys, nor rowdies could compel the "model fire department of the world" to fight, but politics could.

A highly contested 1857 election for chief engineer would provide the impetus for the "one blow struck in anger," which would, as warned, eat away at the department. A five-vote victory of one candidate over another in 1857 left the San Francisco department badly divided. Until January 1860, when the Supreme Court of California finally decided the contested election, the department had neither a consensus as to who was in charge, nor a strong leader to discipline disgruntled firemen. False alarms and other difficulties resulted. In December 1857 the San Francisco *Bulletin* began to report on the "Rowdyism in the Fire Department." After nearly every fire, firemen became "a little ugly." Generally this involved members of different companies squaring off, exchanging dirty looks and threatening remarks. In one example, an engine blocked the path of another company on its way home, "whether by design or not, we can not say," the *Fireman's Journal* reported. After an "unreasonable" delay, "sharp words passed." At that point, matters heated up quickly, at least by the standards of this department. "The foreman of Manhattan company, was observed to have his coat off, and to talk more than the occasion required. . . . Some one halloed out 'Three cheers for Jim Nuttman!'[one of the candidates] and there was a response, which was not calculated to calm the feelings of the companies towards each other. . . . There was considerable noise made, but all ended in smoke." On at least one occasion, blows as well as insulting remarks were exchanged, although examples of "smoke" were far more common.[99]

Sarcastic cheering, passive-aggressive engine placement, a foreman removing his coat: this was not rowdyism as practiced elsewhere in the country. The press recognized this fact but panicked nonetheless. "Heretofore, the Department of this city, with a few exceptions, has been a model for similar institutions in the Union. . . . They [the firemen] are of our quiet, orderly, law-abiding citizens, who have discountenanced all attempts at rowdyism or open violations of the peace."[100]

The restraint of the San Francisco firemen can be attributed to the deeply held belief in law and order among San Franciscans in the wake of the 1856 Vigilance Committee. The open antagonism in the fire department appeared to some to be the first step in the fall of the department and a return to the disorder that San Franciscans believed had plagued the city in the early 1850s. "If such a spirit is allowed to gain a foothold, all decent men will leave the Department in disgust, and it will fall into the hands and control of rowdies," wrote the *Bulletin*. Six months later, with no improvement apparent, the *Bulletin* was nearly hysterical with the possibility of disorder: "When it became evident that if the insurrection was not nipped in the bud, our streets might run in gore, our city be disgraced with such riots as have from time to time occurred in eastern cities . . . it was necessary to take decisive action." The city supervisors "have the benefit of the record of similar difficulties in eastern cities," they pointed out, "and should prevent the difficulties from occurring." The paper also suggested that "it is time for all good citizens, who wish bloody riots prevented, to interfere."[101]

Others agreed. One letter writer to the *Bulletin* advised, "In times of insurrection and rebellion, the first step is everything." He suggested that the entire department be abolished, while admitting that "riots, quarrels and disgraceful scenes are unknown among [the firemen]." In light of the developments in cities like Baltimore, where many of the members of the San Francisco department had served as firemen, it was perhaps not unreasonable to assume that unchecked riot was just around the corner. But as of yet, that riot had failed to appear.[102]

The first "disgraceful fight" took place in August 1860. "Fists, and even harder weapons were freely used, and numbers of bruised faces and bloody noses attested to the prowess of the rival combatants." Apparently that harder weapon was a fireman's trumpet, and the firemen's paper warned against using "the most dangerous of weapons . . . as sharp as an ax and three times as heavy." Three months later, the foreman of the Volunteer Engine Company was knocked down and beaten with a hose pipe and iron wrench during a fire by unidentified "members of other companies."[103]

The same tensions motivating these acts of violence appear to be at the heart of the dramatic 1865 firemen's riot in San Francisco, although there are no recorded episodes of fighting in between. Short-term hostilities had been building over several days as firemen collided at various false alarms and fires. The department picked an extremely bad time to finally riot. Sunday afternoon, on a street filled with citizens returning from church, "the quiet of a Sabbath afternoon was suddenly broken by shouts, curses, pistol shots, blows from spanners, billets of wood and paving stones, to the great terror of men, women and children, who fled from the disgraceful scene in the utmost consternation and confusion."

Between five and fifteen shots were fired as the Knickerbocker Fire Company, with assorted members of other companies, battled the combined forces of the Howard and Monumental companies. The participants were careful not to damage the fire engines but did much damage to one another. An assistant foreman was shot through the arm and clubbed on the head. Another fireman was shot in the foot. Several other firemen were hit with stones, clubs, and spanners. Chief Engineer Scannell immediately suspended the three companies involved in the fray.

This riot not only justified the warnings of the department's earlier naysayers, but furnished "the enemies of the Volunteer system with an unanswerable argument in favor of its early and entire abolition."[104] After nine years of condemnation for minor acts of violence, one riot was enough to finish off the fragile department. In 1866 the department was disbanded. The San Francisco Volunteer Fire Department, a group which neither sanctioned violence nor regularly engaged in it, was disbanded in the same manner and amid the same accusations as was the Baltimore Volunteer Fire Department seven years earlier.

And their reputation outlived them. In a report issued by the fire commissioners in 1867, the new, paid firemen of San Francisco were lauded in terms that clearly condemned the old volunteers and their behavior. "Intoxicating liquors, freely tendered, were refused by you: vigor, order and sobriety marked your conduct: that you deserve public commendation all will acknowledge: for ourselves we are proud of you."[105]

It is worthwhile to trace the career of Mose in San Francisco at this point. In 1851 the character Mose appeared at the Jenny Lynd Theater in San Francisco, and in 1857 Mose was cast in his own San Francisco adventure, *Mose in*

California.[106] To have seen the original production in New York in 1848 or to have known the actual Mose was a point of great pride among the New Yorkers in the department.[107] His presence is detectable in an 1856 advertisement for firemen's coats that "boys 'who runs wid der machine' " were advised to purchase. Letters from an old New York fireman to the *California Spirit of the Times and Fireman's Journal* in 1862 celebrate the dialect of the Bowery, "The Old White Ghost, 40 [Mose's company]," and the "occasional knock-down, when a butt [or hose] was not taken out quick enough."[108]

He is detectable, as well, in the fears of the press starting in 1857. When the first fights began between the firemen, Mose was blamed. "Even the least observant can readily see that this present unhappy disagreement grows out of a bold, high handed attempt on the part of the worst portion of the department, the 'Mose' and 'Dead Rabbit' class of ruffians—to gain the ascendancy and control of affairs," wrote a critic of the department. Not only was the noble Mose misunderstood by this critic, but so too were the San Francisco firemen.[109]

Clearly the figure of Mose was an important signifier among firemen and critics of firemen alike. But the reference was not at all consistent. In St. Louis, Mose provided an easy explanation for violence in the department as well as historical inspiration for the retrospective creation of that violence. In 1854 in Nashville, firemen, outfitted like Mose, carried a deified image of Mose in a parade. They were clearly not celebrating the "Mose" class of "ruffians" condemned in the San Francisco *Bulletin* in 1857.[110]

When the San Francisco *Fireman's Journal* claimed in 1861 that "Mose and Lize are not the representatives of the Fire Department of the present day," they were identifying yet another Mose, an idealized figure. "All the clap-trap about gallant red-shirts, saving the babies from immense heights and on ladders swaying like reeds, the prayers of the mother, the kisses of the sweetheart, is played out. . . . In 1861, we want something substantial."[111] The firemen, in rejecting Mose, were asking for political power. As I will discuss in chapter 4, this was as damaging to the San Francisco firemen as was that ruffian "Mose" class which was so feared in editorials and letters to the editor.

Some Conclusions about Fire Department Violence

The decline of the volunteer fire department in the public's eye was paralleled by the decline of Mose, who was reduced from a "robust drama-cycle" to "vestigial skit." Mose's principal actor identified the "era of steam fire-engines" as marking the demise of Mose the Bowery B'hoy, but in doing so, he mistook cause and effect. For a time in the 1850s, volunteer fire departments could, and sometimes did, support rowdy behavior. A visitor to Baltimore in 1855 observed that Baltimore's fire companies, perhaps the most violent in the nation, were "jealous as Kilkenny cats of one another, and when they come together, they scarcely ever lose an opportunity of getting up a bloody fight. They are even accused of doing occasionally a little bit of arson, so as to get the chance of a row."

Yet this same observer could also write that "when extinguishing fires, they exhibit a courage and reckless daring that cannot be surpassed and they are never so happy as when the excitement of danger is at its highest."[112] This was the era of Mose, the symbol of the fireman who was both a great fighter and a great firefighter. This was also an era when the masculine culture which bound firemen in Baltimore increasingly provoked conflict with the norms of the larger society.

The separation of fighting and firefighting, which reduced Mose to an anachronism, was fully accomplished by the "era of the steam-engine," or paid fire department. The strengthening of the police and decline of other rioting in Baltimore in the 1840s produced the impression that firemen had suddenly become violent in that city. In St. Louis, efforts at refining the city cast that department's behavior in an increasingly negative light. In San Francisco, violence was rooted out and condemned, even where it did not exist.

The masculine culture of the volunteer fire department legitimated some forms of violence in a period when personal violence was increasingly condemned by civilized urbanites. Although firemen in most American cities fought in the 1850s, most firemen appear to have kept their violence within certain boundaries understood by the group. Firemen of different cities did not share a uniform behavioral code, although in each of these cities the press portrayed their fire department as having devolved into an uncontrollable mob by the 1850s.

What this perception reflected was not the reality of violence among firemen or uniform changes in class and ethnic composition across departments, but a decreasing tolerance, on the national level, for the masculine culture represented by the character Mose. In Baltimore, firemen were certainly an uncontrollable mob, but not a working-class one, nor was their violence a new development of the late 1840s. San Francisco's fire department was far from an unruly mob: the department remained primarily low white collar through 1860, with a stable ethnic composition of one-third foreign born in a city where 50 percent were foreign born. In St. Louis, the most extensive riots expressed nativist hostility on the part of the firemen, yet these incidents had less of an impact on the reputation of the firemen than did lesser events that threatened the comfort of the polite and refined segments of the population.

In none of these cities was the behavior of the firemen what it appeared to be to readers of the urban papers, and in all three departments Mose was the figure who came to represent the volunteer firemen. For this reason, the paid fire department banished Mose from its ranks so thoroughly that not even his language remained. The paid firemen of Baltimore were ordered in 1859 to "above all, refrain from indulging in the use of vulgar, slang phrases."[113] The American volunteer fireman was celebrated for his violent masculine subculture on the stage, but he was ultimately destroyed by that same celebrated image. This was true even when, as in San Francisco, actual volunteer firemen were not noticeably violent. Municipal firefighters were not permitted to fight one another, to get drunk at fires, or to otherwise indulge in the excesses for which the volunteers had gained infamy. The public order of the later nineteenth century had no room for masculine pugilists like Mose, or for any version of the masculine honor code that supported the brotherhood of volunteer firefighters.

> HARRY: Mose, don't go in that manner. [*Points to* Audience] Remember there!
>
> MOSE: Oh yes—I forgot. [*To* Audience] Look here, ladies and gentlemen—don't be down on me 'cause I'm going to leave you—but Sykesy's got in a muss, and I'm bound to see him righted, 'cause he runs wid our machine, you know—and if you don't say no, why I'll scare up this crowd again to-morrow night and then you can take another GLANCE AT NEW YORK.[114]

By 1861, Mose was "played out" precisely because the audience could no longer stand to be "scared up" by a fighting fireman, even on the stage.

Chapter Four

SMOKE-FILLED ROOMS: VOLUNTEER FIREMEN AND POLITICAL CULTURE

> Whatever name we give them, and for whatever purpose they may be instituted, they will not fail to form themselves into factious assemblies, however short their meetings may be.
>
> —Emperor Trajan to Pliny the Younger, A.D. 103[1]

A ROMAN EMPEROR issued the first recorded warning about the dangers of the political fire department, an assessment that observers of antebellum urban volunteer departments frequently supported. Fire companies and politicians seemed to have a strange affinity for one another. By 1836, according to Philip Hone, the firemen of New York were "so courted for political objects that they appear to consider themselves above the law." In Cincinnati, firemen paraded a coffin through the city "advertising the fact that two councilmen held responsible for defeating an appropriation had signed their political death warrants." While Mose might be the nineteenth century's second most famous volunteer fireman, William Marcy Tweed, New York's notorious political boss, was probably the first. The contest between the fighting fireman and the political one was a close one. The voters and reformers who successfully challenged ward-based politicians in the 1850s questioned whether firemen were more enthusiastic about politics than they were even about rioting. By the late 1850s, volunteer fire departments were envisioned by reformers as the tools of professional politicians, as incompetent, corrupt institutions that were suffered solely for the votes they provided to certain interested parties.[2]

The image of the political fireman, like that of the violent fireman, had some basis in fact. Enormous numbers of urban politicians in the antebellum era were also firemen. It was said in San Francisco that "every man who was ambitious and wished to rise, unless his powers were exceptionally great, became a member of one or the other [fire] companies."[3] Firemen in Baltimore and St. Louis became the first mayors of those towns. Politicians have always joined fire companies as a means of gaining respect and proving their interest in the city. Benjamin Franklin, Aaron Burr, Thomas Jefferson, and George Washington all belonged to volunteer companies.[4] In the antebellum era, this continued to be true. The fire department was a springboard for politicians because the combative, agonal culture of the period embraced the civic virtue of the fireman. A politician who was also a firefighter had a leg up in a race, but not because he had a department backing him. A firefighter-politician already had tribute. By virtue of being a fireman, he had distinguished himself within an agonal political culture. As a fireman, he had already proven that he was a manly man and a virtuous citizen. As a firefighter, he was already elevated above the mass of potential candidates.

But fire companies were not the political factions that Emperor Trajan, antebellum reformers, and modern historians have understood them to be. Historians who claim that fire companies were "working class and lower class organizations" also claim that they were "politically powerful." In Philadelphia, according to Sam Bass Warner, "much of ward politics was organized around the fire companies."[5] But evidence elsewhere contradicts this assessment. While firemen sometimes joined together in order to protect their funding, they also feared the divisive effects of party politics and attempted to keep their homes free from the taint of political issues. As historians have pointed out, the two decades before the Civil War were marked by the steady increase of federal and state government workers nationwide and a corresponding national distrust of "professional politicians," especially among social elites. The rise of professional politicians led to a decrease in patrician political involvement, and republican liberalism gave way to a new vision of virtue and citizenship, a Christian capitalist order. By the 1850s, according to Louis Hartz, "businessmen were heroes and politicians were villains."[6]

Like other Americans, firemen distrusted professional politicians, even when some of them took politics as their paid work. As a brotherhood of men committed to protecting lives, they believed that political issues were beneath their notice. As one San Francisco fireman wrote in a letter to the *Fireman's Journal*, "Let not the polluted touch of the politician dim for a moment the brightness of that light. . . . Let not the politicians' tainted breath tarnish the jewel."[7] San Francisco's Knickerbocker Engine Company was typical in that it explicitly forbade, in their constitution and rule book, discussion of "any religious or political subject" under threat of fine or expulsion. In 1845, St. Louis's Phoenix Fire Company protested the absence of their president at the previous week's meeting because he was "attending a Democratic meeting that same evening." The company condemned any member's absence "for the purpose of accommodating a Political Party for the avowed object of a political meeting." Indeed, there is less discussion of political issues in the surviving minutes of firehouse meetings in Baltimore and St. Louis than there is of uniforms, parades, or social events.[8]

Firemen were ambivalent about politics and almost always failed to politically mobilize in the interests of specific candidates or issues, or even in their own interests. Despite the perception of critics, the potential political power of the volunteer fire department was always undermined by the competition of the volunteer firemen. Indeed, a close examination St. Louis's political history indicates that firemen were often politically divided even within companies. They competed for political ascendancy within companies, and as companies because their masculine agonal culture valued competition. Firemen competed on the level of elections just as they competed by racing one another to the scene of fires and by fighting. And firemen clearly valued their political independence. The example of St. Louis demonstrates that, however politically powerful individual firemen might be, fire companies were not factions, nor did firemen gain much from the game of politics.

Seventeen St. Louis Mayors

The St. Louis example is a telling one. Virtually all of St. Louis's antebellum mayors emerged from volunteer fire companies. Through their representatives in the City Council and mayor's office, firemen in this city were able to ensure their own funding and support throughout the 1830s, 1840s, and into the 1850s. But firemen appear to have supported virtually every party and political faction available to them. The fire department politicians of St. Louis hailed from the Democratic, Whig, Native American, and Know-Nothing parties. Firemen in St. Louis competed fiercely for office, and no politician was assured of victory because he had the support of the firemen. More likely than not, his opponent also had the support of firemen or was a fireman himself. While belonging to a fire company was virtually a precondition for office in St. Louis, there is no evidence that the fire companies themselves worked to get politicians elected.

St. Louis's first mayor was a fireman, as were the vast majority of his successors. During the tenure of the volunteer fire department, there were only two St. Louis mayors who did not receive the fireman's tribute. One of them served in the 1830s, when the local Democratic organization and the City Council were under the control of firemen; and the other served in 1855, the year in which the first serious proposal to professionalize the fire department was introduced.[9]

The tenure of fireman control over the top office in St. Louis, as well as over a consistently high number of City Council seats and positions in the State Legislature, might appear to indicate that the St. Louis Fire Department fulfilled the prophecy of Emperor Trajan. But a close look at some elections in this city indicates that, while firemen were certainly political, politicians drawn from fire companies seem to have deliberately competed with one another, whatever the greater interest of the firemen at large. Firemen ran against one another for office in a number of elections. Firemen of the same company ran for office for different parties, on incompatible platforms. And the department was finally disbanded by one of its own, Mayor John How, a volunteer fireman.

For a decade after statehood, the office of the mayor of St. Louis belonged to two high-profile Whig firemen, leaders of different fire companies. Dr. William Carr Lane founded and directed the second informal fire company in St. Louis, serving the southern portion of town.[10] He was not only a powerful mayor but the town's most popular and genial figure. He was a model urban citizen. As mayor he envisioned his powers broadly, borrowed widely for necessary improvements, and greatly expanded the scope of municipal government. He advised his colleagues to utilize every bit of power granted to them in the city charter. According to Richard Wade, he was "the shrewdest observer of urban problems in the West."[11]

Among Lane's first visionary steps was to arrange for the official organization of fire companies in 1825. The first ordinance authorized the citizens of each of St. Louis's three wards to form into fire companies of between fifty and seventy-five adult men, to be approved by the mayor and Board of Aldermen. As in other cities, the firemen were exempted from all military duty in time of peace. The following year the Phoenix Fire Company, St. Louis's third fire company, was admitted as a recognized but unpaid department of the city government.[12]

When Lane decided to step down from office in 1829, another fireman, Daniel D. Page, took over as mayor. Page, a member of the Phoenix Fire Company, helped organize a fourth fire company while in office, the Union Company. As mayor he also oversaw the admission of the Central Fire Company the same year.[13] After three years as mayor, Page decided to leave office. The next election is seen by historians as marking the end of traditional politics in St. Louis.

The election of 1833 pitted a Whig fireman, Bernard Pratte, against a Democrat named Samuel Merry who was not a fireman but already held the office of U.S. Receiver of Public Moneys. Pratte was a second-generation St. Louis fireman. His father was a member of the first St. Louis bucket brigade and president of the Phoenix Company. Bernard joined the Central Company.

Pratte was beaten by Merry, but the Board of Aldermen, the majority of whom would have preferred Pratte, investigated the legality of a mayor simultaneously holding a federal office, and they reported that he was ineligible for office. The aldermen (a majority of whom were firemen as well) maintained that Page would have to continue as mayor until another election was held a few months later. A minority of aldermen protested this decision on the grounds of popular sovereignty, and under the leadership of Hugh O'Neil, a North Ward political boss, they rallied the people of St. Louis to protest this decision and to condemn Mayor Page for "abusing the will of the people."[14]

What appears to be a straightforward case of Whig firemen hegemony in St. Louis unfolds quite unexpectedly upon closer examination. The first three Whig candidates for mayor—Lane, Page, and Pratte—represented three different companies from different sections of the city. Furthermore, the aldermen who presented the minority opinion, including O'Neil, were also firemen. More strangely, O'Neil was a member of the Central Fire Company, the same fire company that Bernard Pratte, the unsuccessful candidate, belonged to. In the 1833 election, O'Neil supported the non-fireman candidate against a member of his own company, and politically attacked the previous fireman-mayor who had admitted his company to the department. One of the aldermen in his corner, John Reilly, was a member of the Central Company with O'Neil, but another was actually a member of Lane's Union Company, and a third had a brother in the Union Company.[15]

In the first contested St. Louis election, which was also the first election to pit ward and class interests against each other, company allegiances appear to have played no role, and both sides were represented by firemen. In the second election of 1833, O'Neil's father was defeated by another non-fireman candidate, John Johnson. The Democratic fireman faction led by the junior O'Neil achieved a "stunning" victory on the Board of Aldermen, however. O'Neil was elected president of the aldermen, and his supporters took a majority of seats. Although a non-fireman was in office for the first time, the Board of Aldermen was controlled by an organization led by O'Neil which had both internal discipline and political power.[16]

Under O'Neil, the Loco-Focos managed to expand the St. Louis franchise, make more city positions elective rather than appointed, pave the streets of the North Ward, and get political appointments throughout the 1830s and into the 1840s. They introduced party politics to St. Louis and put the Whigs on the defensive. The party that claimed to be nonpartisan was forced to organize in response. The result was that "the organization and discipline of the St. Louis Democrats signaled the end of deferential politics and the beginning of a new era of professional politics."[17]

Between 1835 and 1841, this Democratic-controlled City Council (by 1839 bicameral) continued to battle against Whig mayors who were also fireman. As in the early 1830s, the mayors were drawn from different companies. Lane (who returned for three more years of rule in the 1830s) was from the South Fire Company and unsuccessfully attempted to stop legislation expanding the franchise and removing his power to appoint officials, including the constable. John Darby, an organizer and treasurer of the Liberty Hose Company, served first as a Whig alderman, and then as mayor for three years. He was elected to Congress in 1859.[18]

Darby was followed in office by John D. Daggett, a Whig and member of the Washington Hose Company who was victorious over his fellow Washington Hose member, George Maguire, in the race for office in 1841, and was in turn beaten by Maguire in 1842. The following year, 1843, saw another contest between members of the same company for the chief office in St. Louis. John M. Wimer, a Democrat and president of the Liberty Company, beat ex-mayor Darby handily. In 1844 Bernard Pratte again ran for mayor, after serving a term in the Missouri legislature, and returned the mayor's office to the Whig firemen and the Central Company. Pratte served for two years. In 1846 a Native American Party fireman, Peter G. Camden, took the office after two failed attempts. In the late 1840s, three Democratic firemen from different companies were mayors for one term each.[19]

Until 1850, then, the mayor's office was almost exclusively controlled by firemen, fairly evenly split between parties, and showed no particularly powerful political company. While a block of Democratic firemen controlled the City Council until 1838, Whig firemen served on the council as well, taking control of the City Council from 1839 to 1842, after which the Democrats came back in control.[20]

Clearly both the department and individual companies were split over support of a number of factions in St. Louis. There was no single firefighter "position" in St. Louis, nor does support for the fire department, or for individual companies, seem to have been at issue in any of these races. Furthermore, even individual companies were not consistent backers of candidates. As Amy Bridges has observed about fire companies in New York, since "none of these organizations was primarily political, they formed a shaky organizational base for the parties. Even when they acquired partisan allegiance, these organizations maintained autonomy and self-direction that made them, from a partisan point of view, unreliable." In New York, fire companies were successful at maintaining their "autonomy from partisan manipulation and city-council dominance." In St. Louis, Baltimore, and San Francisco, fire companies also held themselves above party politics, and companies proved willing and able to change their allegiance.[21]

If politicians did not gain institutionalized political support from participation in fire companies, why were so many politicians also firemen? What seems clear is that within the political culture of St. Louis, a man needed the honor and tribute of the volunteer firefighter to get elected in the first place. Through participation in a fire company, a politician could prove that he was brave, benevolent, and worthy of electing. The masculine culture of volunteer firefighting, and not institutional support, was the real springboard to political success in antebellum cities. In New York, according to Bridges, wealthy men joined fire companies in order to establish their civic virtue. Although she believes that patrician participation in the fire companies in that city ended in the early 1840s, career politicians continued the pattern of joining fire companies to prove their valor and citizenship. In New York, although the players changed, "the fire companies continued to provide an arena in which a man who wanted to be a political leader could demonstrate his courage and leadership capability."[22]

As always, the New York example has only limited explanatory power. In St. Louis patricians continued to participate in the fire companies long after

Bridges claims that they deserted New York fire brigades. Firemen-politicians were elite individuals through the 1850s. These firefighter-politicians were neither workingmen nor did they voice a workingmen's rhetoric. Although Democrats in St. Louis characterized Whigs as aristocrats, and Whigs suffered under that image, it is not easy to differentiate Whig and Democratic firemen-politicians in St. Louis. The city's municipal government was dominated by merchants and lawyers from urban backgrounds, and the firemen were no exception.[23] Although John Mering has argued that the Whig Party in Missouri was somewhat more upper class and affluent than the Democratic Party, the candidates for mayor show similarities beyond the important one of belonging to fire companies, and sometimes even the same fire companies. Most candidates from both parties had family or other connections to the elite of St. Louis and were financially successful businessmen or lawyers. John Wimer, a blacksmith and Democrat, was the only candidate of either party who worked at a trade. In St. Louis at least, Arthur M. Schlesinger Jr.'s observation that "unless fine criteria are used . . . both parties can be said to have recruited their leaders from the same social and economic strata" appears to hold true.[24]

St. Louis's merchant-politicians had more in common than elite background and membership in fire companies. Two positions appear to have been shared by virtually all firemen-politicians until 1850. The first position shared by Whig and Democratic firemen is a support for immigrants in St. Louis. The anti-Catholic, anti-immigrant Native American Party first entered a separate ticket in municipal politics in 1842 and elected a mayor in 1846. The successful candidate, Peter Camden, was reportedly a fireman, but his name appears to have been stricken from fire department records. He is unlocateable in any surviving source. Most other Native American Party candidates were not firemen.[25]

Firemen put aside their divisions to foil the Native American Party in previous elections. In 1845, Whigs and Democrats arranged for Whigs to abstain from City Council elections in return for Democratic support of the Whig mayoral candidate, Pratte. In 1846, they were unable to agree to cooperate. The Whig mayors of the 1840s (all firemen) were careful to distance themselves from that party or from any stigma of nativism. The Democratic firemen were also, not surprisingly, anti-nativist. Brian Mullanphy, a Union Fire Company member and Democratic mayor in 1847, was one of the city's biggest philanthropists for the relief and support of immigrants to St. Louis. From its beginnings, the St. Louis Fire Department contained an ethnically diverse membership, and firefighter politicians were wary of nativism. Even when firemen in St. Louis were beating up the Irish, their political leaders were careful to avoid the most virulent rhetoric of nativism.[26]

The second unifying issue among firemen-politicians was funding for the department. The firemen-mayors of St. Louis were all supportive of the fire department. As one fireman stated, "The question of finance was one which never presented any serious difficulty."[27] The firemen always received high levels of financial support from the municipal government. In 1839, the city purchased 2,000 feet of leather hose "for the use of the several companies," and in 1841 it granted each company three hundred dollars a year to "keep their engines and apparatus in repair." The city also gave the fire companies free lots and grants with which to build their houses in the 1840s. The aldermen also purchased hose and hooks and ladders for the volunteers.[28]

There appears to have been only one case when a company requested money from the City Council before 1849 and was turned down. The Union Company requested funds to buy a lot for a new house in 1845 and considered disbanding when the money was not forthcoming. Instead, they decided to describe their ill-treatment to the public in a published letter. They suggested that perhaps they should disband and dared the public to find firemen "more self denying and laborious than ourselves, that they may perform their duties more faithfully than we have done, and show more zeal and daring than we have shown, when life and limb have been put to the hazard, in the contest between the *King* and *Men of Fire*." Although they bemoaned their lack of "success in high places," their luck soon changed for the better. In early 1847 they purchased the lot, not long after one of their founding members, Brian Mullanphy, was elected mayor.[29]

While the department was supported with more ease and grace than were the departments in other cities, the price of municipal support, here as elsewhere, was increased regulation. The three hundred dollars bonuses were to be issued on the quarterly reports of each company to the mayor. In return for granting lots to companies and financing the building of engine houses, the city generally acquired the buildings and leased them back to the firemen for a dollar a year.[30]

Both of these issues would have damaging consequences for the firemen by the 1850s. By 1850 nativism had taken a firmer hold on the Whig Party, a development that would lead to the collapse of the party both in St. Louis and nationally in the mid-1850s. Luther Martin Kennett, a member of the Liberty Company (John Darby's company), served as alderman on the Native American ticket in 1845 and 1846. In 1850 he returned to the Whig ticket, and although the *Missouri Democrat* accused him of "having changed his forefathers so often there is no telling how long he will remain an American," he won election to the mayor's office three years in a row. In 1854, John How, a Democratic fireman, became mayor, and in 1855, fireman candidates from both parties were beaten by the candidate of the new Know-Nothing Party, Washington King.[31]

The rise of the Know-Nothing Party drove many Whig firemen into the Democratic Party and increased tensions between companies that contained strong Know-Nothing support, including the St. Louis and Liberty Fire companies and the majority of other companies that opposed the new anti-party

party's virulent nativism and reformist stance. The Know-Nothings blamed Irish Catholics for the excessive "political corruption" of professional politics and supported both temperance reform and limiting immigration to the United States. These policies found limited support in ethnically diverse fire companies, but its conspiratorial style appealed to many. These political difficulties were multiplied in the 1850s by the increasing sectional tension in the city. If the nonpartisan approach of the Phoenix Fire Company in 1845 was representative of the political tenor of the department in that decade, the fact that the Missouri Company openly allowed Democratic Party meetings in its house in 1857 indicates much about the increasing political fervor of the later period.[32]

Starting in 1852, city elections, here as in Baltimore, were marked by violence. The role of firemen in the election riots of 1854 to 1856, however, is even more ambiguous here than in Baltimore. Firemen were clearly not aggressors in the 1852 riots, although a member of the St. Louis Company was shot and killed. Newspaper reports of the riots of 1854 and 1856 do not single out the role of firemen or fire companies, although in the riot marking the 1854 congressional election of Thomas Hart Benton against Luther Kennett, firebells across the city rang out as a nativist mob battled the Irish.[33]

It has been observed that in the riots of 1854 and 1856, "it would be as easy to identify among the political rioters 'well-known' citizens' who were also volunteer firemen, as it would be to identify volunteer firemen among those who were called to check the riots." From the historian's perspective it appears much easier to identify firemen called upon to check the riots. An Irish-dominated militia company, the Washington Guards, was organized by and made up of members of the Union Fire Company in 1853, when that company first considered voluntarily disbanding in light of increasing "rowdyism" in the department. The city's most exclusive militia company, the St. Louis Greys, also contained members of the volunteer fire department. Both of these companies fought to maintain order during the rioting, and "the Washington Guards even fought against their own Irish countrymen."[34]

Increasing political tension had a damaging effect on the St. Louis Fire Department, and the question of funding finally did as well. After over twenty years of firemen in the mayor's office and City Council, St. Louis's department grew accustomed to getting what it wanted from the city. The destruction of much of the department hose and supplies in an enormous fire in 1849 was the impetus for the department to demand extensive support from the city government. Just two weeks after this fire, the firemen petitioned the City Council for an annual appropriation of fifteen hundred dollars per company. Although the mayor of the city was a Democratic fireman and the City Council also contained firemen, the council had more pressing funding to consider in the light of the seven million dollars' worth of property that was also destroyed in the 1849 fire.[35]

Like the Union Fire Company when it did not receive funding for its lot, the department again turned to the public for support. It protested the stingy appropriations of the City Council and promised the public that it would "dispense with the disagreeable task of begging from a portion of you the funds necessary to defray the current expenses," once the department received its due from the City Council.[36]

The *Missouri Republican* blamed the Democrats in power for allowing fire department debt to pile up, and for not meeting the demands of the department in 1849. This probably assisted the Whig nativist, Luther Kennett, in his victory in 1850. Under Kennett's administration the city partially met the firemen's demands, but in a manner that proved unsatisfactory in the long term. The city agreed to pay each company two hundred and fifty dollars quarterly on the approval of the new inspector of the fire department.[37]

Yet the money was still not in hand. In July 1850, the firemen, under the direction of the newly formed Firemen's Association, threatened to strike if the money was still not in evidence within twenty days. Kennett stood firm in the face of this threat. "I humbly concur," he wrote to the Firemen's Association, "that the council would lose sight of the respect due to the position they occupy if they are in any way influenced by the threat of closing doors intimated."[38]

The firemen had by now antagonized both Democrats and Whigs. Matters only worsened in the following year. The firemen asked the council to pay their debts, and Kennett demanded in return that the "companies one and all come under the supreme control of the City Government" and suggested that some members of the City Council were in favor of a paid department, like the one recently instituted in Cincinnati. In return for the money, the department agreed to ever-increasing public control.[39]

According to the *Missouri Republican*, the ordinances passed in 1850 and 1851 "imposed no disabilities or obligations inconsistent with the entire freedom and independence of the Company," but these ordinances in fact specified that improper company conduct could result in city control. The Union and Liberty companies attempted to hold out against the Faustian bargain offered by the City Council but eventually acquiesced, as "many men of pride," disgusted that their firefighting should be financially supported by the city, deserted the companies.[40]

As both the *Missouri Republican* and the *Missouri Democrat* reported increasing violence in the department and suggested that rowdies had infiltrated St. Louis's firefighting force, political pressure mounted to modify the excesses of the volunteer system. In what must have seemed a great betrayal of his firemen brethren, Democratic fireman John How became the first mayor to openly call for "the gradual abandonment of the Volunteer Fire Department and the establishment of a paid one."[41] Given that the City Council was at that time under the control of loyal firemen, his suggestion was little more than an empty gesture.

After the 1855 election of a Know-Nothing mayor, Washington King, and a City Council controlled by Know-Nothings, attempts to reorganize the fire department began in earnest. As in New York, reformers and nativists aligned in St. Louis to target corruption in the political system and urban disorder. The firemen should not have been surprised that King would suggest a municipal department after being accosted in the streets of St. Louis by some "savages" running with a fire engine. Even the Know-Nothings failed to overcome the "immense political influence" of the fire department, although they did begin to mobilize public support against the firemen.[42]

When fireman How returned to the mayor's office the following year, he finally disbanded the volunteers. Despite the active hostility of a majority of fire companies, How passed and approved a city ordinance providing for the organization of a paid fire department in April of 1857.[43]

The Limitations of Political Mobilization, or What Do Seventeen Mayors Really Buy You?

Individual firemen in St. Louis exerted an enormous amount of political power during three decades of St. Louis's history, but it is unclear that the firemen, as a group or in companies, were particularly influential. If the St. Louis press and voters never questioned the immense power of firemen in city politics, it was because the majority of politicians on both sides were firemen. Firemen seem to have represented virtually every political position available in antebellum St. Louis. The most powerful Democrats and Whigs of the period were firemen, and although there were no powerful Know-Nothing firemen, there was at least one powerful Native American Party fireman who ruled St. Louis in Whig disguise.

Yet despite the near hegemony of firefighter-politicians in this city, it seems easy to conclude that the political machinations of the firemen were more harmful than beneficial to volunteerism in this city. A St. Louis fireman in later life condemned "the poison of ward politics," which "had more than begun to contaminate" the fire department by the 1850s. By the 1850s as well, the department had the firm support of neither Democrats nor Whigs—nor their newspapers—after department demands for allocations in 1849 and 1850.[44]

The clearest advantage gained by the firemen through politics, the funding they received so easily from the City Council until 1849, has been identified by historians as the primary impetus for their eventual replacement by a paid department. The terms set for companies to receive funding "were not felt at the time to have their logical consequence." The logical consequence was that once the city was empowered to decide which company was entitled to funds, the department no longer had the full freedom granted to them in Mayor Lane's original fire department ordinance of 1825. It was only a matter of time before "the city increasingly came to look on the volunteer companies as a single tax-supported fire department."[45]

The other obvious benefit accruing to firemen from fire department hegemony in the city government appears to have been the extension of the life of their organization. For three years, St. Louis mayors unsuccessfully attempted to get rid of the volunteer fire department, apparently because of the political power of the firemen on the City Council. But what does it reveal that a Know-Nothing mayor, who was not himself a fireman and whose party controlled the City Council in 1855, was as ineffective at introducing a paid department in St. Louis as was a fireman-mayor with a Democratic-controlled City Council? It is questionable how important fire department allegiances actually were in St. Louis, even among mayors and City Council members who were themselves firemen. Even though San Francisco's volunteer firemen had very little political support in the state legislature (their governing institution), they also managed to stall the introduction of a paid department for several years.[46] The firemen's culture might support politicians, but politicians, even when firemen, didn't always support the firemen. Political independence came at a cost for volunteer firemen.

However damaging their political strategy was in the long term, in the short term St. Louis's firemen were able to use their representation in high political office to maintain their funding. In San Francisco and Baltimore, firemen were successful not even at that. In both of these cities, they were unable to mobilize enough votes to influence municipal and state governments to purchase the equipment for which they had lobbied. When the San Francisco firemen lobbied the state legislature for funding in 1856, in response to massive budget cuts imposed by a draconian Board of Supervisors, the reaction in the press was swift and unambiguous.[47] The fire department should have no hand in politics. Cried the *Evening Bulletin*, "Let the fire department, at least, be kept pure and untrammeled from politics, religion, or any other cause than that for which they were intended, and in which they have won laurels." The *Alta California* warned the firemen against the machinations of their "bastard organ, the *Fireman's Journal*." "You derive your support from the strength of public opinion, which has always been, and will always be, in favor while you contain yourselves strictly within the province of the objects of your organization: sink into the depths of the polluted maelstrom, and you will deserve, and not only deserve but receive the execration of every high-minded, honorable citizen of San Francisco."[48]

And according to the *Fireman's Journal*, some of these high-minded citizens were already irritated. Even the "staid old merchants and business men . . . now devoting their time, energy and means in procuring hose for a better efficiency of the fire department" were "annoyed" by the politicking of the department.[49]

Firemen were prevented from politically mobilizing in this city because professional politicians were especially demonized in San Francisco's political culture. The People's Party, which ruled San Francisco from 1856 to 1867, claimed to be nonpartisan and called for the best citizens of San Francisco to lay their successful businesses aside and take responsibility for running the city. The People's Party was decidedly elitist and assumed that "only those in the elite could have the background and the integrity to manage the city safely."[50] The fact that some firemen in San Francisco, as in other cities, were successful politicians in the Democratic Party meant that, in the rhetoric of the ruling anti-party People's Party, the entire institution was suspect.[51] An article in the *Evening Bulletin* on the issue of department funding in 1858 made clear the degree to which reform politics upset the norms of political culture. When some firemen were also professional politicians, volunteer firemen as a group lost their virtue.

The *Evening Bulletin* first commended the supervisors for their fortitude in standing up to the volunteer fire department on the issue of funding. The Board of Supervisors, in this age of enlightened People's Party rule, the paper argued, were praiseworthy precisely because they were businessmen, not politicians. The services that they rendered were "at a sacrifice of time, business and social comfort." They had "no official aspirations, no axes to grind, no friends to reward, and consequently act independently and promptly for the best interest of the city."

> How different would have been the result had the Board of Supervisors been composed, as of old, of political demagogues! . . . The members would have hesitated in their decisions—considered the necessity of appeasing the Fire Department, lest a few votes might be lost at some future election; the malcontents would have seen where their strength lay, and would have been bold and exacting in their demands, nothing would have been attempted by the authorities; insubordination would have been encouraged, riots would have followed, and the Fire Department be turned into a political tournament.[52]

Implicit in this comparison between the Board of Supervisors of old (the political demagogues) and the current enlightened and nonpartisan board is more than simply People's Party rhetoric, and the rather strange oversight of the sacrifice of time, business, and social comfort made by volunteer firemen. The *Evening Bulletin* also asserted that under an old regime, the fire department had been turned into a political tournament, and insubordination had been followed by riots. This terrifying picture had no basis in the past experience of the volunteer fire department in San Francisco, as detailed in chapter 3. The open antagonism during this 1857 to 1859 period led to fights, but it did not undermine the ability of the department to fight fires successfully. There are no reports in either the *Evening Bulletin* or the *Fireman's Journal* of buildings burning while firemen fought nearby, and the *Fireman's Journal* claimed in 1860 that the department had never been as efficient as in the previous three-year period.[53]

This fiction, of a fire department as full-fledged political machine and as a riotous and uncontrolled mob, would have had a resonance for the San Francisco public, despite the total inconsistency of the account with any actual experience of the department. In 1858, rashes of volunteer fire departments in the Midwest as well as on the East Coast were in the process of disbanding, and were accused of exactly these sins. New York's volunteer fire department was one of the departments in which malcontents had been "bold and exacting in their demands," insubordination was rife, and riots were legendary. San Franciscans were wary of political firemen, because the supposed political character of firemen, like their supposed violent character, preceded them. Any reader of San Francisco's newspapers in the 1850s was familiar with the political exploits of professional political firemen in eastern cities, and of course most San Francisco residents were recent immigrants from these very cities.[54] The reputation of political firemen was enough to undermine the virtue of San Francisco's firemen, even when firemen were clearly without political power. Within San Francisco's new political culture, firemen, as public servants, were expected to be above politics, and politicians could never be firemen.[55]

Baltimore's firemen met a similar fate at the hands of reformers, even though firemen in this city were even less politically effective than in San Francisco. Although historians have identified Baltimore's fire companies as "among the most powerful political organizations in the city," firemen had trouble both maintaining their funding and sustaining their organization.[56] A number of high-profile politicians of both the Democratic and Whig parties in this city were also firemen, but the department was slighted by both parties. Volunteer companies in this city never had enough money and were forced to rely on donations from the community to make up the difference. In a city ravaged by political divisions, the legislating of Baltimore's fire department from 1800 to 1858 is one of the few issues to reveal a high degree of nonpartisanship.[57]

Competition over resources contributed to the violent culture of the Baltimore firemen. The Union Fire Company complained to the Standing Committee that "members of other companies who have leisure time traverse the neighborhood of the location of our apparatus and succeed in getting subscriptions to their companies located in our section of the city, there by causing us to be very poor, while they have full and plenty of time to spare."[58]

This type of "turf" allegiance formed a basis for the majority of violent disputes that gripped the department. There were too many companies in too small of an area, and they were not only battling for the financial and emotional support of neighborhood residents, but for the right to do duty at fires as well. These territorial divisions took on the appearance of political divisions in the 1840s as associations of unskilled workers organized into Democratic and Whig political clubs on the same turf. These clubs generally met in taverns near the firehouses or in public rooms of the firehouses themselves.[59]

Firefighter violence in Baltimore was mostly nonpartisan until the 1850s—at least it is safe to say that common political allegiances never stopped two companies from fighting.[60] Reform efforts were also nonpartisan. The Democratic mayor and City Council in the 1840s worked together with Whigs to deal with violence in the department. In 1842, the City Council divided the city into three fire districts, each theoretically under the control of a marshal who was selected by the mayor. (In practice, the fire marshals were ignored by the fire companies and did nothing to promote order.) Democrats and Whigs on the City Council also joined together in 1848 to divide the city into fire districts, confining one company to each district.[61]

The rise of the Know-Nothing Party in 1854 ushered in a new era of political violence in the department and throughout Baltimore.[62] Fire companies aligned themselves with both the Know-Nothings and the Democrats in the 1850s, but as opposition to firefighter violence mounted in the 1850s, reformer and Know-Nothing mayor Thomas Swann's proposal to do away with the department met with bipartisan support. Firemen in Baltimore appear to have gained nothing for their supposed political power.[63]

Firemen, then, can be said to have been remarkably successful as political *individuals* but failures as political units. Not only did they fail to mobilize in their own interests when it mattered, but the fact that so many ward-based politicians were firemen helped damn the firemen by association in the 1850s. Both reformers and firemen condemned the connection between the two. In the 1870s, volunteer firemen in New York were quick to attribute the fall of their fire department *not* to their own rioting, or failure to fight fires, or choice of lifestyle, but to the evil influence of politics on their organization. In an editorial in 1878, the *National Fireman's Journal*, published in New York, advised the fire department of New Orleans to cease meddling in the politics of their city. "The New Orleans Department deservedly ranks high, but if politics plays a leading part in it, it is doomed to demoralization and destruction. Firemen have always been the losing party in the game of politics," the paper warned. As an example, they cited the experiences of New York:

> If it is demoralizing to a Fire Department to be controlled by politics, it is equally demoralizing to a city to be controlled by the Firemen. This can only occur where Volunteer Departments exist in full strength, as formally in New York. . . . Then

> the Firemen were all-powerful in politics, and no man thought of running for office until he had first placated the Firemen. It was because of the baleful influence they exerted upon the politics of the city that it became necessary to disband the Volunteers and inaugurate the Paid Department.

Upon examination of the political careers of three volunteer fire departments, it becomes difficult to disagree with their conclusion that "firemen have always been the losing party in the game of politics."[64] Although membership in a volunteer fire department might serve as a springboard to a political career, although it might appear to be a precondition for office in some cities, volunteer firemen proved unable to mobilize the potential power latent in their large organizations. Firemen held themselves above party and maintained their political independence from parties. Their competitive agonal culture further limited their effectiveness because firemen fought against one another in the political sphere for honor and resources, rather than fighting together. Although publicly associated with professional politicians, firemen were generally political amateurs. In the 1850s and 1860s it was a group of reformers, with the help of the insurance industry, who would prove to be the real professionals in the game of politics.

Chapter Five

INSURING PROTECTION: FIRE INSURANCE AND THE ERA OF THE STEAM ENGINE

> The merchant insuring his property, paying his premium on the amount insured, and taking his policy, must not suppose for an instant that the mere fact of going through a ceremonial of that description, is the real power which preserves him from loss.
>
> —*Fireman's Journal*, May 1856[1]

> The adaptation of a mighty agent to the extinguishment of fires . . . with such miraculous capacities, at once established a self-evident fact, that a legion of firemen was no longer needed.
>
> —Letter to Latta Engine Co., 1857[2]

As reports of riots, politicians, and corrupt firehouses increasingly demonized the masculine culture of volunteer firefighting—the stage was clearly set for the volunteer fire department's denouement. Their tribute relationship with the antebellum city had disintegrated, but as yet nothing had replaced the volunteer fire department as an object of the public's faith. What the *Fireman's Journal* identified as the "real power which preserves" citizens from fire was still in the hands of the fire department.

Until that final transference was made, municipal governments had no choice but to continue their uneasy standoff with the firemen. After all, paid departments were expensive—that Boston's paid department cost over $138,000 a year was repeatedly marveled at by San Franciscans in the early 1860s, while the "exorbitant" cost of Cincinnati's paid department (at $90,000 a year, three times that of the volunteer departments) fueled support for the status quo in St. Louis and Baltimore.[3] Even after appointing a commission to reorganize the fire department in 1858, Baltimore's mayor admitted that "the volunteer system is not so bad that it may not be borne with until something more decided is proposed."[4] Volunteer firemen were better than the unknown.

A viable alternative had to be in place before a municipal fire department could become a reality. In the 1850s that alternative rose from the ashes of the department. Two seemingly unrelated mid-nineteenth-century successes, fire insurance and the steam fire engine, would together form a seductive and reliable alternative to volunteer firemen. The individual heroics of the volunteer fireman were permanently replaced by the financial security of insurance and the seductions of technology. It was no coincidence that the first city to employ a fully paid department, Cincinnati, was the home of Alexander Latta, the manufacturer of the first quality steam engines, and also the home of a powerful board of underwriters that funded the manufacture of the first viable American steam engines. In 1852, insurance and steam engine interests offered a firefighting combination that Cincinnati found irresistible. Almost every other American city would likewise be seduced within the next two decades.[5]

The paid firemen were nearly superfluous in this equation. Although critics of the volunteer system championed paid forces that would perform in a more sober, orderly fashion than did their predecessors, they rarely argued that paid firemen would prove more skillful at fighting fires than their volunteer counterparts. Even while strongly in favor of a paid department, a joint committee of the Baltimore City Council had to admit to Mayor Swann that "your committee are of the opinion that volunteer intelligence, judgment and discretion are superior to hired ignorance," which was all that the city would be able to attract with the proposed hundred-dollars-a-year salaries. The skill of the individual volunteer, when he was sober and attentive, would not easily be replicated by new men. Nor could the valor of the individual volunteer fireman be faulted. But steam engines negated such concerns. The machine, it was promised, would substitute technology for human error and weakness. As a contemporary enthusiast reported, "It is time that steam, which is cheaper, be substituted for bone and muscle." The machine, and not the paid firemen, was the real replacement to the volunteer forces.[6]

And no group championed the steam engine—and paid forces—more vehemently or successfully than did fire insurance companies. Early steam engine development in England and America was funded by insurance companies, and the earliest paid fire companies were contracted by insurance companies in England after the great London fire of 1666.[7]

Insurance had undeniable sympathies with these enterprises. Insurance, after all, helped replace faith in the efforts of men to prevent damage with faith in the ability of money to negate the importance of damage. Fire insurance companies could not help but see a kin expression of their driving ideal in the paid department. If fires could be rendered impotent with dollars, should not firemen also be made reliable with money? Americans were increasingly integrated into the market in the antebellum period and made aware of the fact in a series of crippling depressions starting in 1837. Insurance represented money without contingency, safety through dollars that, it was increasingly evident, were not themselves normally safe. Insurance offered decreasing risk in a period when other risks became ubiquitous.

And the steam engine shared many of these advantages. Both the steam engine and insurance worked to ward off contingency, to reduce human intervention in processes like fire and the market, which were not themselves human. One was not insured by an individual, one was insured by a corporation. One was not protected from fire by men utilizing machines, but, it was increasingly believed, by machines driven and guided by men. The machine was privileged in this construction, as was the corporation. Ralph Waldo Emerson's observation that "things are in the saddle and ride mankind" accurately assessed the transformations in nineteenth-century firefighting as well as in society at large. Money, not man, became the key to security in the middle of the nineteenth century, and trust in experts, and expert systems, replaced faith in the bravery of the individual fireman.[8]

The increased value placed on the material interests of property owners in municipal governments in nineteenth-century America eventually undermined the position of volunteer firefighters within urban society. It also transformed the object of firefighting. Modern firemen have critiqued an "obsession over the years to limit destruction by fire in buildings which has resulted in a blurring of preferences—fire loss versus loss of life."[9] This obsession had its origins in the period of transition from the volunteer to paid systems. Although no manuals in the 1860s or 1870s argued that paid firefighters should value goods over human life, no longer was the protection of the citizen championed as the guiding principle of the fireman. Five of the fourteen "suggestions for firemen" made to the new Baltimore paid force in 1859 pertained to the best treatment of goods in a burning building, only one to saving the life of a person in said building.[10] Under the paid regime, the protection of property emerged as the new focus of firefighting efforts. No longer were poems published that honored volunteer firemen:

> No hireling of a city's purse,
> no clique to be obeyed,
> Their motto published to the world
> is "Voluntary Aid":
> Their fame is not of battle field—
> of deadly, mortal strife—
> But higher, nobler for than this—
> 'tis hope, 'tis human life![11]

The hirelings of the city's purse were made aware of their duties to property. They were advised, for instance, that "when fire is in the upper part of a building and the water thrown in has not reached the lower floor, instead of removing the goods below, it is better, (if it can be done,) to protect them with water-proof coverings, and get the water out from above by sweeping it down stairs."[12]

Of course, focusing on property was not always the wisest course for a firefighter or for a property owner to follow. According to Marcus Boruck, only months after institution of the paid fire department in San Francisco, the firemen were prevented by insurance agents and property owners from entering a burning building because those parties feared the potential damage water might do to the goods stored in the building. The result was a serious conflagration. This disaster, however, does not appear to have changed the relationship between the paid fire department and the insurance industry. As the nineteenth century wore on, the bond between the two would strengthen in San Francisco, as in other cities.[13]

Insurance agents, politicians, and property owners came to agree that volunteerism was an idealistic concept better suited to the Jacksonian era than the 1850s. For volunteerism to function as a guiding principle of interaction, all segments of the population had to believe that they were bound by ties of common interest. In the decades leading up to the Civil War, many city dwellers began seriously to doubt that this was true. The ties that bound the property owner with the fireman he did not know personally began to appear entirely insufficient to protect property. By the 1850s, urban elietes had internalized an ethic of self-control and self-discipline and demanded both stability and order in their society. According to Burton Bledstein, professionalism became a value in and of itself. "Amateurish, a new mid-century word, connoted faulty and deficient work, perhaps defective, unskillful, superficial, desultory, less than a serious commitment, the pursuit of an activity for amusement and distraction. The middle-class person required a more reliable institutional world in which to liberate individual energy than amateurs had previously known." Both internal ethic and social vision were incompatible with volunteer firefighting.[14]

But the transferal of trust from the volunteers to a paid force using modern equipment and protecting insured property was not accomplished without pain and difficulty, or without extensive effort on the part of reformers and insurance agents. Although historians would later read the transformation from volunteer to paid department as a natural if somewhat contested evolution, many contemporary observers (including firemen) saw nothing natural or evolutionary in the replacement. They recognized that the two systems represented radically different visions of labor, the individual, and of the city itself.

Insuring Protection

Before becoming the strongest foes of the volunteer firemen, fire insurance companies were among their staunchest supporters. These organizations originated in the sixteenth-century Low Countries and Germany. They flourished after the great fire of London in 1666, and by the eighteenth century, commercial fire insurance had spread through England.[15] America's first stock insurance company, the Insurance Company of North America, appeared in 1792.

By 1820, at least twenty-eight American stock companies were competing with more powerful British companies to insure buildings in East Coast cities from fire. A New York conflagration in 1835 proved a minor setback to this process, and insurance companies continued to multiply and expand in the 1840s and 1850s.[16]

Insurance companies were understandably anxious to support volunteer fire companies in cities where they offered policies. In their effort to minimize losses, underwriters were generous contributors to the volunteer fire companies of St. Louis and San Francisco. For years they could be counted on to provide money when other sources were insufficient to purchase new hose or updated equipment. They also contributed to the firemen's tribute in these cities. The insurance companies of St. Louis and San Francisco held banquets to honor their firemen. They serenaded Samuel Brannan, a leading San Francisco businessman and member of the Empire Engine Company to the familiar refrain of Schultze's celebrated "Fireman's March." They presented Chief Engineer Scannell with a gold-headed cane.[17] One San Francisco underwriter stated the nature of the relationship eloquently in 1856: "As the objects of underwriters and of the Fire Department are always the same, with this difference, that what we are paid for doing, the firemen do for nothing—it seems no more than reasonable that we should contribute for their benefit."[18]

But insurance companies also contributed adversely to the volunteer system. In early nineteenth-century Baltimore, insurance companies stimulated intercompany rivalry by placing their fire marks on buildings they insured and then rewarding the company that extinguished the blaze to the insured property.[19] Baltimore's insurance companies were also less generous than those elsewhere. Because early insurance companies in Baltimore "were successful, making money by insurance but contributing but little to the fire companies who 'put out all the fires,'" members of the department formed their own fire insurance company in 1826, the stock of which was held by firemen only. In 1846, Baltimore firemen started another fire insurance agency, which, like its predecessor, proved lucrative to its firemen stockholders.[20]

As long as both parties believed that the interests of the firemen and insurance companies were the same, all was well, but signs of friction emerged early in St. Louis and San Francisco. Theft of property at the scene of fires in St. Louis led in 1841 to the creation of fire wardens and property guards, "an association of gentlemen in the interest of the Underwriters," after pressure was put on the aldermen by insurance representatives. The fire wardens, employees of the insurance companies, had the authority to direct the volunteer firemen to salvage goods from burning buildings, an authority which firemen neither appreciated nor always recognized.[21]

In San Francisco, something close to extortion became the divisive issue between fire company and underwriter. Under the draconian measures of the 1856 Consolidation Act and the People's Party Board of Supervisors, the firemen repeatedly entreated the insurance agencies to provide them with support. This approach was advocated by Marcus Boruck, who recognized that "the security of the insurance agent is the volunteer fire department." They demanded ten thousand dollars from the combined agents in May 1856, and smaller sums of money with some regularity thereafter.[22] The agents capitulated to these demands, but always with substantially smaller contributions than those requested. After the ten-thousand-dollar request (for which the agents offered two thousand), the exasperation of the underwriters became increasingly apparent: "The undersigned desire to add, that the demands made upon them have been, of late, frequent and urgent; and that while they will ever be ready to respond to appeals like the present, they must beg to be excused from the constant applications to which they have been subjected for objects they cannot so fully approve and endorse."[23]

Neither of the reactions of the firemen was calculated to endear them to the insurance agencies. Many firemen considered it no more than their due that the insurance companies should contribute generously, and in good spirit, and remarked that "if the Insurance Agents contributed liberally to the support of the Department, in consideration of the service rendered by the latter to the former, there would not be so much complaint as there is, in regard to the wants of the firemen." In the mid-1850s, when all the insurance in San Francisco was provided by companies based in England or in eastern cities, the *Fireman's Journal* began to lobby for a firemen's insurance company like the one in Baltimore. Not only would the project provide generous profits to the firemen, insulating them from the parsimonious Board of Supervisors, but it might even spur them to greater efforts. "All know the losses to the Insurance Companies in San Francisco are, comparatively speaking, nothing. When the firemen have no other intent than to serve their fellow citizens, how much less would they be when they knew so great a responsibility rested on them," the *Journal* wrote.[24]

The proposal met with enthusiasm in the state press. Firemen would be able to provide insurance at lower rates than foreign agencies. "Many a citizen," wrote the Sacramento *State Journal*, "would much prefer paying that sum to parties of whose responsibility he has an opportunity to judge than three or four times that rate to agents of companies thousands of miles away." The *State Journal* encouraged firemen in Sacramento, Marysville, and Stockton, where "a large portion of the business men and property owners" were also firemen, to likewise start agencies.[25] "Our firemen would have the satisfaction of knowing that their generous and gratuitous services were rendered for the sole good of their fellow-citizens instead of for the benefit of capitalists in distant parts of the world," added an enthusiastic "citizen" in San Francisco.[26]

There were structural reasons why insurance in San Francisco was provided by foreign companies, however, which prevented the firemen from starting their own agency. A state law governing corporation formation contained a "personal liability" clause which held every director of a California corporation personally liable for the sum total of demands placed on the corporation. Foreign companies operated under looser constraints. A wealthy fireman and businessman in San Francisco offered his solution to this problem, the most threatening proposal yet to the insurance interests. He suggested that the city government combine with the firemen to start their own insurance department. The capital of the company would consist of city bonds, and the board of directors would be made up of fire department and city officials, together with businessmen and the president of the Chamber of Commerce, all of whom would serve without pay. In addition, a tax and security deposit was to be imposed on foreign insurance companies doing business in the state. His plan to municipalize insurance won approval primarily only among the firemen, and thus it died out in 1860.[27]

Was it surprising that, as the firemen soon discovered, insurance companies were lobbying in favor of a paid fire department? The firemen were not only surprised but outraged upon hearing of these machinations. "Having made MILLIONS out of the voluntary exertions of the firemen, they, too, are desirous to see the volunteer Fire Department disbanded and have intimated that they are ready to assist the city in purchasing steam engines, and supporting paid flunkeys who are too lazy to work otherwise."[28]

A committee appointed in the State Assembly in 1866 to decide on the wisdom of a paid department saw little need for debate. Within five minutes the majority had declared themselves in favor of paid firefighters. The strongest advocate for the new system, Mr. Ashbury, gave in its favor that "the Underwriters of this city, knowing what the result had been elsewhere, are strongly in favor of the Paid Department, and he understood, they would contribute $25,000 to establish it." The underwriters guaranteed that the paid system would result in lower insurance rates and offered to help finance the department. The business-minded political leadership of San Francisco gladly accepted their proposal.[29]

In other cities, as well, the interests and aid of the insurance companies played a pivotal role in the decision to switch to paid departments. Both the St. Louis and Baltimore committees appointed to consider paid departments highlighted the approval of the underwriters in their reports. In Cincinnati, the St. Louis committee reported, the paid system was "not only efficient in preserving property, but also in promoting public morality and increasing the profits of the insurance companies."[30]

And even in cities where the volunteer firemen were not working to municipalize fire insurance, insurance companies were wholeheartedly in favor of the new system. As one insurance agent from Cincinnati reported, even though a paid system cost several times that of a volunteer system, the cost to the insurance agents was *less*. Under a paid system, firemen would not look to the insurance companies for support, nor would an insurance company be expected to contribute anything to their upkeep, beyond whatever minor tax the city levied. The agent was effusive:

> As to the effect of the organization upon the insurance business, I believe I but utter the sentiment of my brother underwriters, in saying that it has been most beneficial. It has so materially diminished the losses, that the balance is largely on the right side of the ledger; and were the underwriters to-day called upon to pay the whole expense of the department, I believe they would cheerfully do so—were it just and right to demand it of them, and their business would warrant it,—rather than return to the old system, with its levies of black mail, riot and arson.[31]

Of course it would never have been considered just and right to demand that insurance agents pay for a city service, and so the insurance companies made a great profit from the change in service. They had fire protection without the personal responsibility of supporting a volunteer institution, they had lower rates produced by a more orderly firefighting force, and they had some of the trust once placed in the volunteer firemen.

Before the final collapse of the volunteer departments, insurance companies attempted to win the trust and security of the public by presenting competing claims to the volunteer fire forces. Warned one San Francisco advertisement:

> Almost every night a fire bursts out in some part of the city, and the cry the next day is, "John Smith's entire building and furniture was consumed last night, and not a dollar of insurance!" How easily "John Smith," or any other man, can protect himself against ruin by applying to the Builders' Insurance Company, for instance.[32]

But firemen were able to counter such attacks. They took exception to this advertisement's implication that every night a fire was allowed to destroy property in San Francisco. The more damaging injury for them in the long term, however, was one they consciously took no note of. Can one be protected from ruin, without being protected from fire?[33] The answer, of course, is yes, if you are insured. Insurance promoted itself as a power greater than fire. Fire insurance companies not only worked to overturn volunteer companies, but also promised to remove the sting from fire, allowing a subscriber to rise from the ashes financially intact.[34]

Insurance companies realized that more than simple financial stipends, and promises of a power greater than fire, were necessary to convince cities to institute paid departments. It was true that in every city volunteer firemen had alienated powerful segments of the population. Their behavior within the firehouse and masculine culture was threatening and offensive to the emerging middle class. Their behavior in the streets was not in keeping with the growing and widespread desire for urban order. The perception of fire departments as vehicles for corrupt professional politicians made firemen the enemies of reform politicians and their supporters.

But despite all this, volunteer firefighters still had the "motto of voluntary aid" on their side. Volunteer firemen were celebrated for protecting human life, but the protection of property called for a different savior. If man could best save man, perhaps property could best save property. As the underwriters of Cincinnati and St. Louis quickly concluded, steam, which helped create property, could also be its salvation. "Steam, whose restless power has been so extensively used in the fabrication, development and transportation of property," could perhaps be "compelled to aid in its preservation from fire."[35] For this reason they spent a great amount of money and time in the 1850s financing and popularizing the steam engine, the power greater than man to match their own power greater than fire.

A Mighty Agent

> Rendering into the Steamer all that is her due, we think we can safely say that we know one part of the fireman's duty she cannot perform nor can all the machinery invented by man on earth accomplish it. That to which we allude can only be fulfilled by the secret springs implanted in man by the God of nature—the great cylinder is the body; the piston which works it is the heart; the fluid which generates the motive power is the blood which flows through its complicated vessels. And the fires are kindled by the warm impulses which actuate the brave and the disinterested. The "Steamer" CANNOT SAVE LIFE![36]

As indicated by this quote from the first issue of the *Fireman's Journal*, firemen had an ambivalent relationship to technology. They fetishized it, and they abhorred it. After all, the essence of the volunteer firefighter culture was that a volunteer fireman was a man brave enough and strong enough to join with other like-minded individuals to combat fire. To "Men of Fire," tools were necessarily marginal. As volunteer firemen understood firefighting, the individual had to face and conquer the fire using his intelligence, strength, and bravery. The agonal struggle of volunteer firefighting demanded that "everybody had constantly to distinguish himself from all others, to show through unique deeds or achievements that he was the best of all."[37] Tools had little use in the individual struggle that drove and supported volunteer firefighting.

Yet Marcus Boruck was unable to express man's preeminence over engine without resorting to a crude machine metaphor. Boruck identified the essence of the superiority to lie in the "secret springs implanted in man by the God of nature," a slightly unusual expression for God's grace, it seems. Yet these "springs" were revealed to be not the bubbling evidence of God in man, nor Emerson's transcendental flow of nature through man, but *mechanical* springs. This was a telling pun. According to Marcus Boruck, God implanted a machine inside man superior to the steam engine. The components were the same, even down to the fire that both steamer and man carried within (unlike hand engines). But the fireman surpassed the steam engine in that his fire was kindled by warm impulses that "actuate the brave and disinterested."[38]

This argument may have had some force in comparison with paid firefighters, but Boruck measured the volunteers against their true foe, the steam engine, and found himself on fragile ground. A steam engine was nothing if not disinterested and as brave as a man insofar as it harbored no fears for its safety. If all that separated these two "machines" were the qualities of bravery and disinterestedness it would be an easy choice in favor of the steam engine, which manifested both qualities more consistently and absolutely.

The fact that firemen to some degree did identify with their machines helped initiate their downfall. They were never able to mount a successful campaign against steam engines, because firemen in every department were extremely anxious to use them and put "muscle against machine" to the test. Like other nineteenth-century Americans, firemen were fascinated and deeply attracted to the possibilities of new technology.[39] Despite the vociferous warnings of some, firemen in St. Louis, Baltimore, and San Francisco, with the backing of the insurance companies, were the first to invite the Trojan horse inside the gates of their institutions.

The first steam fire engine was built in London in 1829. The "Novelty," as it was named by its inventor, George Braithwaite, was a mechanical failure, as was the first American steam engine, commissioned by insurance agents in New York. The New York model could throw a stream of water 166 feet but was so large and ungainly that it was effectively useless. Also, it broke down repeatedly and was sabotaged by the New York firemen.[40]

Alexander Latta and his partner Abel Shawk, both of Cincinnati, built the first successful steam engine in 1852.[41] Latta had enormous faith in his engine but feared that it might meet the same fate as did the New York machine. He was working under incredible adversity, as he complained to an early visitor to his factory:

> You are, probably, not aware how bitter is the feeling of the volunteer firemen against this engine. They say it shall never throw a stream of water on a fire in this city; and I sometimes fear that I shall never live to see this grand idea brought into the service of the world. The recent riots show what a mob can do in our city. My steps are dogged. Spies are continually on my track. I am worried with all sorts of anonymous communications, threatening me with all sorts of ills and evils unless I drop work on this engine, and pronounce it a failure.[42]

Latta's paranoia was justified when the Cincinnati volunteers cut the hose lines and hurled stones at his engine when it was first put into action at a warehouse fire. A later improved model, the "Miles Greenwood," was purchased by the Boston Fire Department after it was successfully tested against hand engines by insurance agents in that city in 1855. It proved too large, however, to maneuver through the streets. Months after its purchase, Latta complained bitterly in a letter that "the steam engine has been standing in the city stables. . . . I don't ask any favors of the city of Boston as regards the engine, only to give it a fair chance." The city of Philadelphia also purchased the model, but "found itself in the position of a man who has won an elephant in a raffle." The enormous engine cost over twenty thousand dollars to repair in a three-year period.[43] "The old man's eyes flashed as he said: 'I'll never give up! . . . When it is finished, it will be heard from at the first fire, and woe to those who stand in its way.' "[44]

As Latta promised, he did not give up despite his many setbacks. With the backing of the insurance industry, he traveled from city to city, exhibiting and advertising his creation as the future of firefighting. This was the general manner in which new firefighting inventions were introduced in cities, and Latta was not the first to make enormous claims for his product. As a Boston publication for firemen, the *Fireman's Own Book*, concluded after reviewing the various futile anti-fire inventions of the last two centuries, "The world has long been of the opinion that a more ready way than that in general use might be found for extinguishing fires in buildings."[45]

In the 1840s there was a flurry of such inventions. Technological advancement was closely followed by the urban press and public throughout the 1840s and 1850s and reported in great detail. To this extremely optimistic generation, the possibility of a technological panacea seemed always around the corner. Fireproof doors, fireproof paint, and a "fire fort" that could "also be used to immense advantage in sundry movements incidental to warfare" were all optimistically reported on in the urban press, until they were tested and found wanting.[46]

Seemingly minor improvements on volunteer firefighting tools were also loudly trumpeted in the urban press during this period. Minor details of new fire bells, improved hydrants, new nozzles, and new hose were considered news by the regular press as well as firemen's journals. Antebellum cities agreed that "to procure, then, a cheap and good preventative against fire, is a desideratum which all must desire."[47]

The most influential of these inventions prior to the steam engine was the Phillips' Fire Annihilator (fig. 5.1), patented in England in 1841. Billed as a portable, "domestic" firefighting device which utilized chemicals to "annihilate" fire, it was one of the first innovations that promised not just to aid, but to supplant the fireman. This claim would later be made by boosters of the fire-alarm telegraph system and the steam engine. As one advertisement sanguinely proclaimed, "The time is not far distant when every house will have a 'Fire Annihilator,' and such a thing as a serious conflagration will be unknown in our country." The Fire Annihilator, like the later steam engine, was supported by insurance companies, taken from city to city, and tested in front of reportedly large crowds, including city leaders.[48]

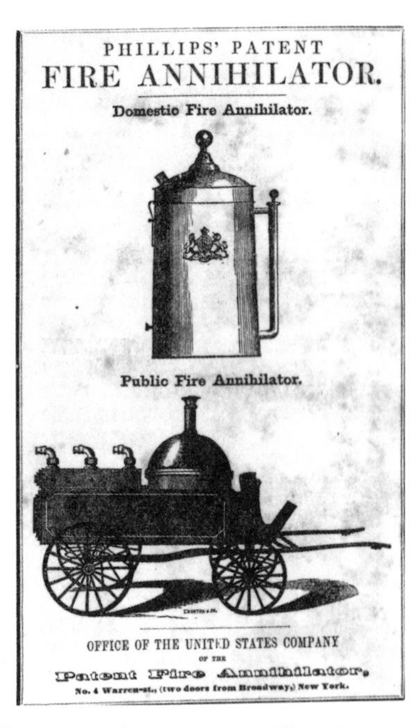

Figure 5.1. Phillips' Fire Annihilator. P. T. Barnum might manage the American office of the company, but even he couldn't make a success of the "portable Fire Annihilator."

It proved, however, to be an enormous disappointment. When tested in Baltimore it ran out of chemicals before the fire was fully extinguished. When exhibited in New York it failed to produce any effect on the fire whatsoever, but definitely enflamed the crowd that gathered to watch. "Upon this, in true New York 'spirit' which means rowdyism, the crowd charged upon the uncharged Annihilators, and demolished them, carrying still further their work of annihilation by 'smashing up' several machines that stood near, which had not been used. . . . Mr. Phillips' Annihilator is 'all gas' and Mr. Phillips had better 'stan' off de hose!' "[49]

A reporter for the *Alta California* pointed out in the defense of the inventor that "Mr. Phillips would have had a vast amount of annihilation to perform in overcoming this popular branch of public sentiment regarding the method of encountering a conflagration in New York." New Yorkers were not ready for this sort of "progress" in 1852, as the reporter explained. "Notwithstanding the rapid changes and improvements of this utilitarian age, works of science and strength would all fall short of supplanting the 'brakes' and the 'butt' in the affections of the New York b'hoys. Mose's occupation would be gone!"[50]

San Franciscans were likewise not ready for an alternative mythical protector. The *Alta California* did not recommend that the Annihilator make its way to San Francisco for a test, but the chief engineer insisted on testing it. It failed on the West Coast as surely as it had on the East. An orator addressing the San Francisco firemen the next year confidently stated that "there is no probability that the annihilator will succeed in annihilating the fire department, dispensing with the necessities of our existence, or even become a rival of whom it would be worth our while to get jealous, as we undoubtedly should, had its operations been entirely successful." Ironically, the Battersea factory that produced the Fire Annihilator burned to the ground in 1852.[51]

Future inventors would have to reckon with the legacy of the Fire Annihilator. The well-publicized failures of that invention convinced many that "science can not yet dispense with the firemen."[52] The public was not so gullible by the mid-1850s, and it was no longer interested in hearing about the "so-called 'Fire Annihilators,' which have, from time to time, been brought before the public, and proved failures." The press reported hesitantly about future inventions, including an unsuccessful sprinkler system invented in San Francisco in 1866 and the fire-alarm telegraph.[53]

The fire-alarm telegraph proved to be an important success. William F. Channing, a physicist, first publicized his invention in Boston in 1845, and in 1851 its City Council invested ten thousand dollars in the new invention. Other cities followed suit later in the decade; St. Louis purchased its own system in 1858. Channing envisioned his fire-alarm telegraph quite differently from the long-distance telegraph that had already begun to transform business communications. His system would work like the nervous system of the human body. It would "organize a single city or town so as to bring every subordinate part into relation with its center of government and direction . . . the whole being intelligently connected into a system by which the municipal body shall understand itself in every part, and shall have a common life and vital functions for its own essential purposes."[54] The fire-alarm telegraph, one of the first urban uses for the telegraph, replaced the watchtower system with a series of boxes throughout a city from which alarm of fire could be communicated to a central office. Wires, connecting the central office with the firehouses, would instantly communicate to the firemen the exact location of the

Figure 5.2. Automatic Signal Telegraph Company. Telegraph systems promised protection from both fire and criminal. Although they were expensive to install, by the late 1850s many large cities decided they were worth the investment. (Trade card from the Warshaw Collection, National Museum of American History, Smithsonian Institution, Photo 89-13496.)

fire. The alarm system also served to link the police stations of a city together, so that "riots and other disturbances may thus be nipped in the bud, often almost before their commencement." The fire-alarm telegraph system proved crucial in the move toward the complete policing of urban behavior. It was the perfectly conceived tool for a period of economic and political centralization on both an urban and a national level.[55]

The centralizing tendencies of this technology, evident in Channing's body metaphor, were also highlighted in advertisements at the time. An early ad for the American Police and Fire Telegraph noted that "popular disturbances and fires are kindred evils, equally sudden and violent, and alike demanding immediate resistance." A later ad for a more sophisticated telegraph condemned the firemen directly. The telegraph boxes, it claimed, "cannot sleep or move, get drunk or tell a lie."[56]

But firemen appear to have been strong boosters of this system in the 1850s and 1860s and do not seem to have viewed it as a serious threat to their organization. After a public display of the telegraph in St. Louis in 1856, the firemen of the city began vigorously to lobby for it and recommended its immediate adoption to the City Council. By February 1858, the system was in place in St. Louis, and the *Alta California* reported that "the rates of insurance there have fallen wonderfully since the inauguration of their present fire signals."[57]

An unsuccessful testing of the fire-alarm system in San Francisco in 1864—no one could determine whether or not the alarm had been struck, and if so, what was intended to be communicated—was followed by a full year of lobbying on its behalf by the *Fireman's Journal* before it was adopted in 1865. In Baltimore, the fire-alarm telegraph was not instituted until six months after the volunteer fire department was disbanded, but here too, the firemen repeatedly urged the city to employ the system. Firemen seem to have recognized the difference between the telegraph and steam fire engine. The fire-alarm telegraph system was not a technological change that directly required or facilitated organizational change in firefighting. It did not reduce the size of companies or transform actual firefighting, as would the steam engine.[58]

Discussion of the fire-alarm telegraph and its transformative effects was overshadowed by the simultaneous national introduction of the steam engine. Despite the failures of the Annihilator, the rioting of the Cincinnati volunteers against Latta's steamer, and the failures of steam equipment in Boston and Philadelphia, insurance companies continued to support Latta as well as other early manufacturers. The Cincinnati Equitable Insurance Agency contributed seven hundred dollars to the purchase of Cincinnati's first steam engine, and once Cincinnati's department was fully reorganized in 1854, it invited visitors from throughout the country to view the new department and machinery.[59]

Although a steam engine and paid department were not inseparable, a steam engine catalyzed the development of a paid department in two ways. It minimized both the number of men required to man a fire engine and the number of engines required in a department. A hand-pump engine required a minimum of fifteen men to drag the engine to the fire, pump the water through the engine, and control the hose. Thirty men could perform these activities more quickly and effectively than could fifteen. The average fire company had at least forty members.

One steam engine was commonly believed to pump more water than could three hand engines, in a shorter amount of time, and yet it needed only a small fraction of the men to operate it. Steam engines were too heavy for even thirty men to drag to a fire; they required the use of horses. Once at the fire, men were needed only to set up the machinery and direct the flow of water. These were jobs which ten men could successfully complete. Cincinnati boosters claimed that between one-third and one-tenth as many firemen could successfully man a department composed of steam engines compared to a department of hand engines. Experts in Baltimore and San Francisco estimated that between one hundred and one hundred and fifty paid firemen could operate steam-engine departments in those cities.[60]

The steam engine also required specialized and expensive knowledge to work. In the 1860s and 1870s, lengthy and technical handbooks covering the "running, care and management" of the new engines were published to guide firemen.[61] "The man in charge should be a practical engineer," advised one source.

> He should have a thorough knowledge of steam and steam machinery; should be capable, also, of adjusting all the different parts of his engine, and telling whether they are in order or not. He should fully understand the causes of deterioration in the boilers of this kind of machines [*sic*]. . . . He should have, if not a thorough, a tolerably good knowledge of hydraulics and hydraulic machines and should be capable of determining their capacity, and understanding the strains to which they are subjected when in use.[62]

Running a steam engine was a technical feat, as a three-page list of instructions to engineers in the same guide reveals. What this job, like increasing numbers of jobs in nineteenth-century America, demanded was *specialized* knowledge of the sort only a professional could acquire. This was no job for the part-time fireman, for the fireman who left his employment at the alarm of fire. A capable fireman would have to devote all of his time to understanding the machinery of the steam engine, and devote himself entirely to its upkeep. If a steam engine was to operate at all, it was necessary that some portion of the fire department would be paid, even if the department was not a "paid" department. Expertise had to be paid for. Strength and endurance, so celebrated by volunteer firefighters, were of relatively little importance in the use of steam engines. The strongest man, if not trained in the intricacies of the machine, would be powerless against the fire. The man who knew how to work a steam engine would have to be a professional.[63]

What the steam engine replaced was the old methods of firefighting. Men could fight the fire from a farther distance with a steam engine. The chances of burns were reduced by the greater power of the stream. The need for strength and agility in the face of fire were to a large degree replaced by a tool with which a few highly trained individuals could extinguish a fire from some distance. The mechanical technology of the steam engine in fact required an entirely different human technology of firefighting.

Insurance agents understood that steam engines really replaced volunteer firemen, not other engines. In their descriptions of these successful engines, firemen were invisible, and the engines received the praise once accorded to firemen: "Proceeding noiselessly to the scene of the destruction, we find it in a few minutes at work, and in as many moments more mastering the devouring element, and promptly extinguishing it. But should the fire be more stubborn from the combustible nature of the material, with untiring energy it works on, and limits it where it originated."[64]

Steam engine manufactures also measured their creations against firemen rather than against other engines. Miles Greenwood of Cincinnati compared his namesake engine to the violent volunteers. "To a delegation from Balti-

Figure 5.3. Illustration from 1854 of citizens admiring an early steam fire engine, with no firemen in sight. (From William T. King, *History of the American Steam Fire-Engine*, p. 19.)

more who asked about the merits of the steam fire engine, Greenwood replied, with characteristic terseness, 'It never gets drunk. It never throws brickbats, and the only drawback connected with it is that it can't vote.'"[65]

Of course there was no reason why the men operating these machines might not get drunk. But Greenwood and the insurance agents were so entranced by the promise of this machine that they constructed a technological fantasy in which the steam engine was freed from the limitations of man. The steam engine operating itself was the vision they promoted. To Americans alienated by the excesses of the firemen's masculine culture, the replacement fantasy of the tireless, perfect machine proved extremely attractive.

But volunteer firemen were not all as quick as the Cincinnati rioters to recognize the threat posed by these new machines. Firemen's culture celebrated technology, and many firemen wanted to see and test the steam engine. Once a steam engine was tested in Baltimore, in early 1858, five companies applied to the City Council for funds to help them purchase one. "A steam engine would be a great honor," the Pioneer Hook and Ladder Company concluded, but a prohibitively expensive one. "In view of the circumstances of the Company and the fact that other companies are also endeavoring since we began to procure a steam fire engine, the standing committee would hereby recommend the Company to withdraw their application from the city council."[66]

The steam engine's first real break resulted not from actions of the insurance agents, but within the volunteer firemen ranks. The Union Fire Company of St. Louis, the only company that had refused to accept the thousand-dollar stipend offered the firemen of that city in 1852, voluntarily disbanded and sold its equipment in order to buy St. Louis a steam engine in 1855. The conditions under which the Union Company disbanded guaranteed its immortality in name if not in organization. The new steam engine would carry the name of the company, and "said name must be perpetuated in the department for all time." Ironically, it was the "political influence" of this company which, according to a department historian, forced steam "on the city and the country."[67]

In San Francisco, Marcus Boruck was an early and strong antagonist of the introduction of steam engines in the city. He tried to explain to his fire department that "it cannot be otherwise that a steam engine carries with it the paid system; either the whole or a part of the company having her will be *paid* for being firemen."[68] When members of the San Francisco Volunteer Fire Department Board of Delegates expressed interest in 1855 in testing a steam engine in their city, Boruck dissuaded them by pointing out how expensive the engines were, and by guaranteeing that any current engine in the department could beat it.[69]

When the *Evening Bulletin* published flattering reports of steam engines in other cities, Boruck countered with equally unflattering reports of steam-engine performances, reasons why they were inappropriate for San Francisco, and further information on the cost of these engines' purchase and upkeep. A correspondent named "Dix" from New York assured readers that more than performance was at stake when steam engines entered a fire department. "Fire Engines are, as they ought to be, below par," he stated, and their use stripped firemen of their very honor and manhood. "If there is any absurdity that equals a sailor on horseback, it is a fireman, in full rig, in a similar position, and all who witnessed the folly of firemen on horseback dragging a 'steam squirt' in the Brooklyn procession, will not fail to remember it all their lives." The strongest objection this fireman could think to make was not technological but cultural. He criticized not the machine itself, but the impact of the machine on the appearance of the firemen.[70]

By 1860, however, the *Alta California* reported that the insurance agents of that city had "signified their willingness to assist" in the purchase of a steam fire engine for the Pennsylvania Fire Company, and Boruck left all restraint behind. "Steam engines have made difficulty in every volunteer department where they have been tested," he wrote. "Paid firemen are expected to submit to insults, volunteers *will* not."

> The great object sought to be attained in Cincinnati, by the organization of steam engines, was the prevention of incendiary fires, the criminals being firemen. In St. Louis, for the same reason. In New Orleans for the same reason and to prevent riots. In Baltimore and Philadelphia to abolish the hordes of fighting blackguards

> who infested those departments to their disgrace. . . . As to a Steam Engine contributing so much to the security of property and reducing the rates of insurance, particularly in this place, is all bosh, and it is an insult to this department to say to the contrary.[71]

Boruck maintained that the steam engine was promoted by those who wished to get rid of volunteer firemen and their behavior. The steam engine might be able to rid a department of arsonists, rioters, and criminals of all sorts, but it could not make property more secure or lead to the reduction of insurance rates. What use was there for it in San Francisco, where firemen were peaceful and law abiding?

In other words, as he printed two weeks later, "If the firemen of this city wish to see a paid Fire Department organized on the ruins of the present system, let them sit calmly by and permit the introduction of Steam Engines." He called to the department as a whole to stop the purchase of the steam engine by the foolish Pennsylvania Company. "Let them assist in the establishment of steam engines in our midst and at that moment the volunteer system breathes its last, and all that the firemen have worked for—honor and glory—will have been lost."[72] Boruck recognized that the steam engine would provoke the fall of the volunteers. He paid tribute to his fellow firemen in order to convince them:

> The excuse given by the company named is that the introduction of a steam engine into San Francisco, with its *paid* firemen, is to *further enhance the protection of property in this city*. Who have protected San Francisco thus far against the ravages of fire, and brought her to her present position of splendor, in her public buildings and edifices, but the volunteer firemen? And now forsooth comes Pennsylvania 12, to insult that band of brave men, by saying they intend to introduce steam engines.[73]

The *California Spirit of the Times and Fireman's Journal* also reprinted an item from another fireman's journal in Boston, the *Fireman's Friend*, in which in a battle between "steam and muscle" "the Steamer came off, as usual—second best."[74] In actuality, early steam engines were not perfect. The enormous "Central" steam engine in St. Louis often reached fires after the volunteer companies had already extinguished flames. Baltimore's first steamer, the "Alpha," arrived in May of 1858.[75] Although two more fire companies purchased steamers several months before the Baltimore department was shut down in 1858, they also met with limited success, arrived at fires late, broke down, and were sometimes not even brought out.[76]

Although the Baltimore press claimed that "the great mass of the citizens are favorable to steam fire engines, and will protect them," the firemen chose to take out their hand engines instead of steamers at several large fires, apparently because of fear of attack by other firemen and their supporters not favorable to steam engines.[77] A trial of an improved Latta engine in that city in late 1858 was successful, but the city chose not to purchase the engine despite the offer of financial aid from insurance companies because, although the City Council had passed an ordinance reorganizing the department, the mayor had not yet signed it into law. According to the *Sun*, "The re-organization of the fire department [was] still resting in doubt."[78]

And the usefulness of the steamers was still in some doubt as well, even in cities that had already invested in them. Although the Baltimore *Sun* proclaimed in July 1858 that "with a few more steam engines properly managed no fear of an extensive fire need be entertained," six months later hand engines still fought successfully side by side with the steamers, and the city refused for the time being to purchase more. St. Louis's department continued in a volunteer state with just one steam engine for two years.

Just before the Pennsylvania Company's steamer was due to arrive in San Francisco, a flurry of articles appeared in the *Alta California* and *Evening Bulletin* on the subject. The optimistic *Alta* embraced America's shining technological future. It supposed that "everybody entertaining the progressive ideas of the ages, will not dispute that steam has, eventually, got to take the place of hand labor in fire engines." But the *Evening Bulletin* was still skeptical: "We feel pretty well assured that in a very large portion of the city of San Francisco, those machines would prove unavailable . . . [and] their services valueless except in exceptional cases." Their views suggest the alternative visions of society that grounded this debate. The *Alta* looked toward a future made secure by technological progress. The *Evening Bulletin* held on to a vision of the masculine and heroic individual as the salvation of the city. Within this second vision, the machine would only be useful on select occasion, to be determined by the wise firefighter.[79]

When the engine finally arrived from Philadelphia in September 1860, the city was in a state of extreme anticipation. The company advertised the formal trial of the machine in the local papers. On the fateful day, the engine was slowly dragged by the formally dressed company members to the appointed spot on a busy corner. A rope was stretched across the street to protect the firemen from the eager crowd of spectators. "With 130 pounds of steam on, the word was given for the pipeman to make ready, and away shot the water," reported the *Alta California*. Only moments after water was produced, however, the "strong Brannan hose, double riveted, burst." The company's embarrassment was acute, their public humiliation total. A second trial was not held for six months.[80]

The ignominious performance of the first San Francisco steam engine had a dramatic effect on the debate over steamers in San Francisco by decreasing the vehemence on both sides. Marcus Boruck had met the steamer, and emerged with something like empathy for the embarrassed Pennsylvania Company and their extravagant and ridiculed engine. When the engine was re-tested, in front of a much smaller crowd, he attempted to celebrate the engine's success along with the Pennsylvania Company. "We must confess we were pleased with her performances," he wrote, and also pleased that the Board of Supervisors had resolved to "apply to the Legislature for authority to purchase the engine in question."[81]

In July 1861 he concluded that he had overreacted. By then, three steam engines had entered the department, one owned by a company, one by the city, and one by a private citizen, and the department remained, as before, a voluntary organization. Now that the extremely expensive technology was in place and his organization did not appear to be threatened, he looked to justifications for the use of the steam engine. "We however, never doubted the usefulness of steam engines, and our principal opposition arose from the fact, that we were fearful a paid department would spring from the introduction of steam. We see no indication of that now." He reported favorably about the attempts of the Stockton Fire Department to purchase a steam engine, and on the credible record of successes of the Philadelphia steamer over the next year.[82]

It was just as Boruck let down his guard and steamers came into general use that his fears were realized. The Board of Supervisors began debate on a bill to replace all hand engines with steam engines, under the control of the Board, with the promise that the insurance companies would reduce their rates by half if the bill passed. Three steam engines were almost a quorum necessary to support a paid department in a city the size of San Francisco, and the city already owned outright the Pennsylvania Company's steamer. The city also owned many of the volunteers' firehouses, which the companies leased from the city.

In San Francisco it was not unusual for the Board of Supervisors to subsidize expensive equipment by "purchasing" the item and leaving it in the hands of a company. It was in this manner that the city came to possess many of the department's firehouses. What Boruck and the Pennsylvania Company did not realize was the qualitative difference between the city owning a hand engine, which could not be operated without a large group of firemen, and the city owning a steam engine, which could be worked by as few as four or five firemen. By purchasing a steam engine, the city effectively purchased a fire company. The men were relatively easy to acquire. Since only six steam engines, with their greater pumping capabilities, were needed to protect all of San Francisco (as opposed to fourteen hand engines), owning one steam engine was the equivalent of owning one-sixth of a paid fire department.

By purchasing the other two steamers already in San Francisco and then acquiring just three more whose purchase would be aided by the San Francisco underwriters, nothing would stand between the city and the institution of a paid fire department except public opinion. Although the *Evening Bulletin* had been skeptical about the promises made for steam, it had never been the friend of the volunteer fire department and had condemned the behavior and politics of the volunteers for years.

Suddenly the *Evening Bulletin* began to impress upon the public the advantages of steam, and of its "natural" counterpoint, the paid department. The two departments the paper chose to illustrate the advantages of this system were, coincidentally, Baltimore and St. Louis. In Baltimore, "since the substitution of steam fire engines in this city, the losses by fire have been reduced almost to nil." This was complemented by vast increases in insurance subscriptions in that city, "up to $120,000,000, while the absolute losses by fire do not exceed $15,000 and this in a city of at least 220,000 inhabitants!" Nor was Baltimore an exception. "All the insurance agents urge the purchase of the steam-fire engines as of the utmost importance in saving the destruction of property."[83]

But it was the experience of St. Louis that presented the strongest argument for change. The advantages of St. Louis's paid department over volunteer departments like San Francisco's were not identified in its men but in its steam engines and telegraph alarm, "co-workers against the destroying element." Here, finally, was the system that permanently removed fear of fire:

> When a fire breaks out, it creates no particular alarm, for every one feels confident that it will not be permitted to extend beyond the building on fire. As an instance: a large audience, composed of the most respectable ladies and gentlemen, was sitting one evening in the Library Hall, listening to a public lecture. . . . The working of the fire engines was heard. Before the lecture was through the fire was seen bursting through the roof of the building, in full view of the audience. So confident was that audience that the fire would be extinguished promptly by those who were employed to put it out . . . that not one in ten persons left their seats to concern themselves about the matter. It was felt to be no part of their business to put out the fire, as they knew they could render no assistance, and so kept their seats.[84]

In St. Louis, safety had been attained through a paid fire department manned by professionals with modern equipment. The final vestiges of volunteerism were gone from St. Louis, along with fear of the most potent danger of the early nineteenth-century city. The promise made by steam engine boosters in Cincinnati, which helped convince St. Louis and Baltimore to switch to paid forces, appears in this article to have been fulfilled. Thanks to the steam engine, wrote a Cincinnati insurance agent in 1857, "The alarm of fire carries no feeling of terror to the citizens, and the occupants of a burning roof may be sure of the safety of the lower part of the building, if he knows the steam-engine can reach the fire."[85]

The lecture audience, the reader is told, was confident that "the fire would be extinguished promptly by those who were employed to put it out." In clear view of a fire, they rested in their seats, because "it was felt to be no part of their business to put out the fire." Not only were these ladies and gentlemen reassured by the steam engines and telegraph alarm (as well as the unspoken probability that the burning building was insured), but also by the fact that the proper people, people who were *employed*, would put out the fire. There was no chance that these firemen might not appear when the firebell rang. Firefighting was their *job*. If they were disorderly, they could be fired. If they were inefficient, they could be replaced by the city. They were experts in firefighting, employed, like other Americans, at the job in which they were most skilled.

Professionalization and payment had at some point before 1858 replaced selfless volunteerism as the guarantor of service. No doubt the rise of fire insurance, which also promoted payment as assurance against loss, played at least a suggestive role in this process. It is interesting to note how often supporters of paid departments argued that labor should be paid for, even when the volunteers were willing to do that labor without payment. State Assemblyman Frank McCoppin of San Francisco declared that he "was in favor of paying for labor generally, and also in favor of the Paid Fire Department," when casting his vote on the new system in 1866. In 1858 the mayor of Baltimore also declared that it was necessary to pay firemen to fight fires. "It would hardly be expected that any class of men would bring themselves under the obligations of an oath to do that which they are asked voluntarily to assume, and from which they can hope to derive no manner of profit or emolument."[86] Neither of these men believed that the volunteers already received sufficient payment in adulation, a sense of community, and personal satisfaction for their services as currently rendered. This was because leadership in society had passed into the hands of professional men—business leaders who were "modernizers as well as moralizers." Professionalism, and middle-class Christian capitalism, replaced the republican values of agonal political culture. For the new leadership, only money could guarantee an oath, and only money could adequately reward.[87]

American industrialization was largely responsible for this shift. Professionalization was increasingly embraced in America in the decades before the Civil War. The rapid expansion and integration of the economy led to new business and commercial activities. The growth of cities, rising volumes of trade, and improvements in transportation all contributed to the creation of hundreds of specialized and previously unknown firms. New technologies of production and the rise of factories contributed to the transformation of manufacturing. Within cities like San Francisco, St. Louis, and Baltimore, an entire new class of middle managers was created to coordinate increasing numbers of employees carrying out very particular jobs. The organizational and technical challenges inherent in these management positions encouraged a new sense of professionalization among white-collar employees. This was matched in other professions, like medicine, which worked to protect and elevate its membership through standardized training. Throughout society in the 1840s and 1850s, employment became increasingly specialized, and professionals began self-consciously to identify with others practicing their occupation.[88]

Volunteer firefighting, which upheld not the skill of the paid expert, but selfless sacrifice, thus became suspect. "That a service so important to the welfare of society," marveled one critic of Baltimore's volunteer department, "so closely allied to the taxable resources of a large city, and so essential to the preservation of the property and the very lives of its people, should have been, for so long a time, performed entirely by volunteers, without fee or reward, save in the applaudings of conscience, and the occasional approval of others, is of itself a fit subject of remark."[89]

Fire in St. Louis was no longer the business of gentlemen, and so they kept their seats while those who were "employed" or paid did the work. Fire insurance also played a role in this transformation. As early as 1825 Josiah Quincy, the mayor of Boston, recognized that fire insurance led to alienation of citizens from firefighting. Increasingly, he noted with some worry, neighbors would not turn out to aid the firemen. "Why is this? If you ask the owner, and he answers truly, nine times in ten it will be, 'I am insured; why should I keep fire-buckets? Why subject myself to the rules and customs of fire clubs: or why turn out to fire at all? I go to the expense of protecting myself. I ask no protection of others, and I mean to incur no voluntary expense, and much more, will not incur the risk of health and life in protecting them.' "

But this, Quincy recognized, "is the practical language of men in all great cities."[90] With the combined recommendations of insurance support, political and social fears of the volunteers, and the great promise seemingly held by the steam engine, the bells began to toll for the urban volunteer fire department. "The time has probably come for this city to take steps for establishing a paid Fire Department," concluded the *Bulletin* and *Alta*, papers that only two years before had concluded that paid firefighting was prohibitively expensive in San Francisco. "The steam fire engines will just as surely supersede the hand machines here, as the railway cars will drive off the omnibuses," predicted the *Bulletin*.[91]

The underwriters had the force of expertise and money behind them. They were the professionals in the business of fire. As they grew in capital they also grew in civic influence. On the eve of the replacement, the *Alta California* summed up the underwriter arguments in favor of paid firefighting, and why those arguments could no longer be denied.

> The Underwriters everywhere favor the Paid System. In this city they unanimously passed a resolution in favor of it; they sent representatives to lay facts and figures before the delegation at Sacramento; they have offered to contribute a considerable sum towards the establishment of the Paid System. They are experts in fire matters; they have studied everything connected with the causes, risks and

> management of fires; they know the experience of other cities and the opinions of men in their business throughout the world; their opinions in regard to a matter of fire policy or fire risk should be regarded as authoritative. . . . Firemen work for excitement, and must keep up to the artificial standard of honor which has been established among them, and which, unfortunately, is entirely inconsistent with the interests of property.[92]

Volunteer standards of honor upheld by firemen in San Francisco could not compete with the expertise and financial stake of the underwriters. The transition process in St. Louis and Baltimore was similar to that of San Francisco. In all three cities the introduction of a few steam engines paved the way for the total replacement of the volunteer forces with the financial support of the insurance industry. Once the new technology was introduced, it was impossible to remove. In St. Louis, the early purchase of the Union Fire Company engine and a visit from Mr. Latta of Cincinnati was followed two years later, in September 1857, by a proposal on the part of the Board of Engineers to order three new and improved Latta engines. Once a fire-alarm system was in place, the underwriters of the city successfully proposed to supply the rest of the six steam engines necessary to support a paid department.[93] "With the telegraph completed and the addition of the three new steamers the Department was greatly strengthened, and by its systematic, orderly and effective work rapidly gained the confidence of the general public. The Board of Underwriters of the city took a deep interest in its welfare, and gave it their hearty support from its inception."[94] The confidence of the general public was gained. The telegraph produced quicker responses by the firemen to alarms. The steam engines performed impressively. The small bands of paid firemen followed the directions of their engineers in an orderly and nondisruptive manner. The firefighting system emerged like a machine itself—systematic, orderly, and effective.

This process was repeated nationally. According to the author of a steam engine handbook in 1876, the transition from volunteer to paid department was almost always made *after* a quorum of steam engines was in place. The technology facilitated the transformation.[95]

In Baltimore, which had no fire telegraph but in late 1858 had three steam engines in partial use and two more on order, Mayor Thomas Swann vetoed a proposal for a mixed fire department—volunteer companies and paid employees working together. He had the backing of the insurance industry, which assured him that a department, half-paid and half-volunteer, could not function. The conflict of interests between the volunteer and paid firemen would be too great. They assured him that in Cincinnati, "so great is the attachment of the Insurance Companies, and the mercantile and mechanical interests generally to the Paid Department, that, we doubt not, they would agree to pay the entire expenses of the same rather than permit it in any manner to be seriously affected or interfered with." He also had a quorum of needed steam engines already in place and could safely urge a single municipal department at an initial cost of fifty thousand dollars on the city of Baltimore.[96]

The civic influence and authority of the insurance industry would only increase in the second half of the nineteenth century. "By what right, or under what authority, do the insurance companies attempt to interfere in the management of the Fire Department?" grumbled a St. Louis fireman in 1879 as the underwriters attempted to depose the department's chief engineer.[97] He had apparently not been following the growth of insurance in his city closely. The rights of the underwriter continued to grow as both firefighting and the business of insurance became increasingly schematized. Fire insurance companies continued to study and to fund improvements in fire engines and firefighting itself.[98] Fire underwriters threatened municipal authorities with the withdrawal of their policies if stringent fire codes were not enacted. According to Jon Teaford, "by the close of the 1890's the national board [of Fire Underwriters] had assumed such authority that it virtually dictated the standards of fire protection and prevention in America's municipalities." [99]

As a result, insurance was vindicated—and not primarily because fire losses decreased.[100] The true victory for the insurer was the minimization of chance in the destructiveness of fires, the increasing legitimacy of "risks" to be codified and insured at the appropriate rate. An 1879 publication for firemen reveals the close relationship that evolved between the underwriters and new professional firemen's organizations like the National Association of Fire Engineers and State Firemen's Associations, in the years following the institution of paid departments. These associations "are doing much to encourage an interest in fire matters, and to disseminate useful information relative to the best means of organizing and perfecting Fire Departments," stated the 1879 *Fireman's Journal*, itself an example of these efforts. By including information on the equipment, water supply, and other facilities of the nation's fire departments, "these tables will show them [insurance companies] to what points it is necessary to direct their efforts for securing better Fire Protection, and will also indicate those localities wherein a wise policy dictates the withdrawal of their agencies or a curtailment of the volume of their business."[101] This *Fireman's Journal*, despite its title, was not designed for firemen but was primarily intended for the eyes of the insurance industry. Or perhaps the term "fireman" now meant not the man that physically fought fire, but the man who insured against fire. This new "fireman" was the authority, as the *Alta California* pointed out, in all matters pertaining to fire and its control. Insurance had successfully undermined traditional firefighting to the point where the terms had become indistinguishable.[102]

Another *Fireman's Journal* was eventually directed to the eyes of these replacement "firemen" as well. When Boruck's paper joined with the *California*

Spirit of the Times in 1858 to become the *California Spirit of the Times and Fireman's Journal*, it introduced a weekly column for underwriters, under the heading "Insurance." In the 1870s it made a final transition, in keeping with the true "spirit of the times." The *California Spirit of the Times* traded the fire department for the new god of insurance, just as had San Francisco and almost all other large American cities by that time. Boruck was once the most eloquent spokesman for the interests of the volunteer fireman in America. But by the 1870s he had deserted the firemen for a better risk. Marcus Boruck became editor of the *California Spirit of the Times and Underwriters Journal*.[103]

Chapter Six

DELUGED AND DISGRACED

> In the summer of 1858 we had been dead several months, but not yet buried. In the killing process I well remember the heartsick feeling when the Washington engine made her first run up Fourth street behind a pair of red sorrel horses driven by a red-faced "lager beer" German. . . . To see that beautiful engine, the pride and joy of boys and old men, hauled through the streets at a very slow trot like a dray, was humiliating. And we were sure the old beauty felt her disgrace for she refused to throw a decent stream, when the hired "firemen," after a long delay, got to work, and on going home she had a melancholy look as if she would never be herself again. How could the old machine, after years of petting and varnishing by loving hands, and after dancing through the streets behind a long line of clean-limbed athletes, feel or look otherwise than a tramp when trudging mournfully along behind those spavined red sorrels.[1]

Captain W. P. Barlow, once a proud St. Louis volunteer, thus expressed the shared dismay of his volunteer brethren when faced with the travesty that was paid firefighting. The first transition months were the hardest. In both St. Louis and Baltimore, during the six-month period after the paid fire departments were instituted, volunteer companies were essentially lame-duck protectors of their cities. They remained in operation while steam engines were on order and the paid department was organized. There was no such grace period in San Francisco. For better or worse, once the paid department was instituted, the volunteers could immediately experience the disorientation of watching others perform their jobs.

Volunteer firemen had to tend to a variety of practical issues during this period, including the disposal of land and property. Whether the firemen owned their houses, or the city owned them, volunteer firemen, as firemen, could no longer occupy them. They either had to vacate or sell their houses or, as one company in St. Louis preferred, burn their own houses down. Individual companies and whole departments had to decide how best to bid their firefighting days good-bye, to which end they held picnics, balls, and, in San

Francisco, a wake. Each individual had to consider whether to retire with grace or violence. And amid these difficult decisions, they had to watch paid firemen, or "hirelings," do their job. "It was hard to part with that which had been their pride, and which had been long years accumulating to go into hands of others and in which they could have no share," explained a St. Louis volunteer firemen years afterwards. "For the romance of 'running wid de mashine' is sunk when one does it for his daily bread."[2]

To volunteer firemen, paid firefighting was not only less romantic than volunteer firefighting, but an essentially less noble activity that reflected on the character of the city itself. "Do you think, sir," asked a Boston fire captain when his department was reorganized, "that the citizens of Boston will ever submit to be prohibited from assisting a fellow-townsman in distress? Such sorts of laws may be obeyed in despotic countries or in cities where the inhabitants do not feel for one another; but this is not the case, nor ever will be in Boston."[3]

Why would a city in which the inhabitants cared for each other need to resort to paying firemen? The volunteers wondered at the breakdown of community signified by such an institution at the same time as they plotted revenge against the new system. Although the majority of paid firemen were drawn from the ranks of the volunteer forces, there was no love lost between the old and new firemen. Volunteers and paid men were not on good terms, for the most part, during the transition period. All cities reported verbal and physical abuse against the "hirelings." In St. Louis, Baltimore, and San Francisco, "the men who had left the volunteers were regarded as traitors and were hooted and jeered at whenever they appeared on the streets."[4]

The volunteers did not believe that paid firemen would approach their duties with the same dedication and spirit that volunteers had done. Under a volunteer system, Marcus Boruck wrote,

> the members of a Fire Department have reputation, honor and fame to attain, a spirit of emulation actuates them to be prompt to respond to the well known call upon them, whereas under the paid system, the fact of being distanced in running to a fire, and being beaten in getting water upon it, makes no impression. No disgrace can possibly be connected with it. They are working for just so much, and as long as they give a *quid pro quo*, time or achievement is but an after consideration.[5]

The volunteers doubted that such hired hands even deserved the title "firemen," as the use of quotation marks around the title in Captain Branson's manuscript indicates. Apocryphal stories circulated among the volunteers of paid firemen who refused to turn out at fires, and hired firemen who unnecessarily delayed getting to work and approached their duties with a lackadaisical attitude.

A Boston correspondent to the *Fireman's Journal* mocked the incompetence, laziness, and servitude of the paid firemen in that city in his description of an alarm of fire:

> On inquiring of the watchman where the firemen were, the former answered, "'Sleep, I 'spose," and went on his way. Pretty soon a tall specimen of a man made his appearance, and asked if there was a fire, or whether it was a false alarm. The tall stranger turned out to be one of the belated firemen, and leisurely proceeded to unlock the house, saying at the same time, "I guess I'll unlock the house and wait till the captain comes, and see whether it is best to go out or not," and added that he felt "real tired," and hoped it was a false alarm. By this time lurid flames lit up the sky.[6]

None of the other firemen even appeared until the captain had arrived and had yelled for their presence. A short while later the incompetent group struggled to work the steamer, while a petulant hoseman complained about his wages. "I ain't going to get wet all through and most choked to death with smoke and not get any more pay than you fellows do, no how you can fix it up." The correspondent assured his readers that this was one of the most efficient companies in Boston.[7]

Volunteer firemen generally agreed that firefighting, while certainly work, was not labor in the sense that paid work was understood. Those who would only "work" the engine for money, the volunteers agreed, must be naturally "lazy." To be a paid fireman was to lose dignity as well. As Marcus Boruck pointed out, paid firemen were "expected to submit to insults, volunteers *will* not."[8] Paid firemen were repeatedly described by volunteers as less "manly" in bearing and appearance and, as the comments of Captain Barlow indicate, not "American." Barlow acknowledged with a slur that the paid fireman driving his engine was a "red-faced 'lager beer' German." This observation was less reflective of the ethnic composition of the new St. Louis force (for both the volunteers and paid forces contained a large German contingent) than it was of the alienation volunteers felt from men fighting fires for pay.[9]

By transforming community responsibility to paid labor, these "firemen" denied one of the activities of which the volunteers were most proud, and which they believed best represented their status as men and as Americans. "It is a fact that the volunteer firemen is distinctly American, and no country on the face of the globe can produce his counterpart," asserted one badly informed volunteer after the firefighting transition.[10] Volunteers worked not for pay, but for community recognition. For this betrayal, the paid "firemen" were nothing less than un-American. They were "lager-beer Germans" and Hessians.[11] In violent Baltimore, and in St. Louis, the volunteers threw rocks and stones at the paid men; in San Francisco the restrained volunteers were content to jeer and insult the paid men.[12]

Paid firemen were but one of several travesties volunteers perceived in the new system. The second generation of steam engines was less awkward and more effective than those purchased in the mid-1850s by cities like Cincinnati, Boston, and Philadelphia, but they were still enormously heavy and required the use of horses for transport. Baltimore's steam engine "Deluge," purchased for the paid company residing in the Independent Fire Company's old headquarters, weighed 8,600 pounds, slightly more than most steam engines.[13] The horses were a particular irritant to the volunteers, men who had celebrated their strength by dragging engines up steep hills, across cities, and even around tracks in formalized contests. The volunteers had ridiculed suggestions that their own hand pumps be horse-drawn in any other circumstance than a parade, although horses would have allowed the firemen to reach fires faster. The masculine subculture of the volunteer fire department had effectively prevented the use of horses in volunteer fire companies across the country. As a Sacramento fireman with the nom de plume "Machine" pointed out when a volunteer company had considered using horses to drag its engine, "if the same enthusiasm existed in that company that there did a year ago, horse power would be no *whar*."[14]

The volunteers had no illusions that the paid firemen had "enthusiasm," but they were horrified that horses had helped to replace them, and worse, that those same horses were now living in their firehouses. San Francisco's Pennsylvania Company arrived late for the first test of their steamer because of the difficulty of getting the engine up the street without the help of horses. Volunteers in Baltimore frequently didn't use their steam engines because they wanted nothing to do with owning horses. They refused to bring horses into the privileged space of the firehouse, because the firehouse was their home. To bring horses into that space would turn it into a stable.[15]

In St. Louis, horses were actually stabbed and killed by the volunteers after usurping the position of the "clean-limbed athletes." It is not clear if it was the horses or German driver that caused Captain Barlow to imagine that his old engine felt like a "tramp." His company clearly felt that a "woman's" honor had been insulted and called for recompense. The lady of the firehouse was "humiliated" and "in disgrace." His company restrained their protest to slurs and "remarks about raising their wages," but other companies felt it necessary to seek vengeance against the animals that had replaced them.[16]

If the horses drew a steam engine rather than the "pride and joy of boys and old men," it was yet another source of irritation to the old volunteers. Firemen attempted to match "muscle against steam" even after the real battle had been fought and lost. Captain Dave Risley, a popular member and secretary of the St. Louis Missouri Fire Company, was one of the first to take on the steamer. He badly injured himself when traveling with members of the Union Fire Company to Cincinnati to investigate purchasing one of the engines. When the steamer was demonstrated for the St. Louis firemen, Risley was shocked that four men were employed in directing the stream of water and "informed Chief Greenwood that in St. Louis one good man such as he himself gloried in being, was all-sufficient for the purpose."

Risley was thrown "all over the street like a dishrag" by the powerful steam engine, but his story ended on a positive note. While he was recuperating in a Cincinnati hospital, the ladies of Cincinnati presented him with an embroidered ruffled shirt "in appreciation of his daring venture." Risley kept the shirt, a public acknowledgment of his manly gesture against the machine, until his death. Like John Henry, who lost his life with a hammer in his hand, Risley had failed—but he failed nobly. His manliness was respected and rewarded, even in the face of a greater power.[17]

A later attempt at matching men against machine did not end with so much honor to the men. Captain Barlow remembered that his company, while "dead, but not buried," raced with their old "Hunniman tub" to a fire against the steam engines. "I suppose the engine knew it was her last chance for glory, for she threw a stream, as the boys declared, to beat any blasted old steamer in the world, and did it willing and easy like." The firemen knew it was their last chance for glory as well: "Like well-drilled soldiers we arose, each hand clasping a 'dornick' or brick bat." But the fight did not come off due to the timely interference of "a lot of portly council men and aldermen in black broadcloth and silk hats."

These firemen were not rewarded for their valiant efforts, as Risley was. They were shamed by the aldermen, and Captain Barlow makes it absolutely clear that the embarrassment they suffered was what finally "buried" the volunteers. Of one of his fellow firemen, Barlow wrote that "as Ben's teeth slowly protruded through his lips the Corpse of the St. Louis Volunteer Fire Department got both feet into the grave." An organization which survived on tribute was finally killed by its opposite—the pity and disgust of observers. "Our courage, heroes of a hundred battles that we were, painfully oozed away."[18]

Although the volunteers attacked paid firemen and horses, it was the new technologies that were the primary recipients of volunteer violence in this period. Paid firemen were not immune to the love of the machine that marked the volunteer period. John Klumker, chief engineer of a Florida paid department, praised the Silsby Manufacturing Company for creating his steam engine, "Louise." "Our people thought she was one of the prettiest little engines in the States, and thought she was too beautiful to do any hard fire service," he wrote.[19] Volunteer firemen generally hoped to prevent Louise, and others like her, from seeing hard fire service, but not because of their beauty. Even after the steam engine had proven competent, some firemen tried to keep it from duty through force. Firemen "harassed and impeded the work of the steamers at every opportunity." In San Francisco and St. Louis, false alarms and tampering forced the city to stop use of the expensive fire-alarm telegraphs for some time, while in Baltimore and St. Louis, as in Cincinnati and New York, volunteers attacked the steam engines in the streets.[20]

Despite these examples of violence, the majority of firemen in all cities accepted the transition to steam quietly, if not without misgivings. A New Orleans correspondent to the *Fireman's Journal* reported that the disbandment of that department was accomplished peacefully, despite the fact that "for twenty years its members have volunteered their services, to save life and property, without money and without price, and now that a few dollars may be saved in their support, they are thrust aside without so much as a 'we thank you.' " The New Orleans men festooned their engines with black crape and signs announcing the "death" of the companies, and marched through the town to the tune of "The Girl I Left Behind Me."[21]

Most companies sold out, or moved out, and donated a portion of their profits to the city without resorting to violence against paid firemen, horses, or technology. The Mechanical Company of Baltimore, after being forced out of its house by the mayor, expressed regret when learning of its fate. "Talking, contracting, receiving, examining and waiting for one year, the Mechanical Fire Co. # 1 nearly 100 years old died. Kicks the bucket. Gives up the ghost."[22] Yet the members faced their demise with resignation: "The Steam Fire Engine 'John Cushing' was placed in the House formally occupied by this company. All the machinery of this company was removed and the premises were given over to the city for the use of Steam Engine No. 4 of the new paid department. And the old and honored Mechanical Fire Co. No. 1 after battling against the devouring element for a period of over 96 years goes out of service forever."[23]

Other Baltimore companies acknowledged what had passed by presenting each member of the company with a memento, like a bedstead or silver horn, or by creating "active" associations that would carry on the fire company in name, if not in firefighting duties. The Baltimore Fire Department set up an Aged Men's Home for the future care of old, worthy and "strictly moral and temperate" volunteer firemen, funded by donations from firemen in the relief fund.[24]

Suggestions that some of the volunteer fire department resources might, like individual company resources, be presented to the city or the new, paid department were met with hostility by the firemen. Their written statement on the matter reveals some of the resentment felt by the firemen toward the city and the shabby way in which years of "sacrifice" had been repaid.

> The Department is not the creature of the Corporation of Baltimore, and its Vitality is not in any ways dependent upon the will of the latter. For twenty-five years or more, its members have toiled, not only without fee or reward, but at the

> sacrifice of time, and money, and health, and life, for the preservation of the property of their fellow citizens, and now when they have been bowed out of service . . . they desire *of their own accord—in their own way* to which they are not committed or determined, to make a proper disposition of their own monies.[25]

Once properly buried, volunteer firemen could still enjoy a lengthy afterlife. For some years, the exempt firemen of San Francisco volunteered their firefighting expertise in case of an emergency. Volunteer departments in almost every American city set up veterans organizations, complete with uniforms, relics, and apparatus which they exhibited in parades. In 1890, one hundred and fifty old firemen still met regularly in Baltimore. In Philadelphia, between two and three hundred volunteer veterans gathered together on a monthly basis. In 1888, the New York Veteran Volunteer Fireman's Association traveled to San Francisco to meet the over one hundred active volunteers in that city's Exempt Firemen's Association. At the start of the twentieth century, there were still eighty active members of the San Francisco organization.[26]

San Francisco volunteers buried a stuffed figure in fireman's uniform on the night that their organization ceased to exist. In St. Louis this "virtual" burial was repeated in actual form. St. Louis's association, formed in 1888, contained a membership representing every fire company of the volunteer department. Although the organization attempted various charitable activities in St. Louis, it was eventually reduced to its primary purpose, "to attend in a body as far as possible the funerals of its deceased members."[27]

Paid firemen did not fulfill the promise of a nonpolitical, moral, orderly firefighting force. As one fireman explained, "Experience seems to show . . . that without *selection* there is little difference whether the men be volunteers or paid."[28] Critics continued to complain about firemen who were untrained in the basic skills of their occupation, morally lax, or not committed to firefighting. The Silsby Steam Engine Company claimed that its engines were so well made that even drunk firemen, now all paid, could not permanently damage them, and published a testimonial to that effect.[29]

Selection was limited in these departments because wages paid to the firemen were not particularly high (between twenty and forty dollars a month), and appointments were regularly made on a political basis.[30] In Baltimore only one fireman in each company was expected to be on full-time duty; the rest were expected at the alarm to "leave their several occupations and hasten to participate in extinguishing the flames."[31] In San Francisco the wages of the majority of paid firemen were significantly below the standard of living. Rather than increase the firemen's salaries, however, the stingy legislature determined to employ only paid firemen who already held another full-time occupation. This created serious problems for the firemen and the department, as the chief engineer of the San Francisco Paid Fire Department explained in his first annual report to the Board of Fire Commissioners in 1867:

"Many of the men are so situated in their business that to leave it to attend a fire in the daytime they are liable to be discharged by their employers; and in some cases, this has been done. Their pay, as firemen, is so meager that, rather than risk a discharge from employment they prefer to neglect their duty as firemen; consequently, we often have not sufficient force to manage a line of hose at a fire of any magnitude."[32]

Volunteer firemen had faced a similar quandary. Transformations in the work place in the Jacksonian period made it increasingly difficult for laborers and clerks alike to desert their business at the alarm of fire. The pace of the workshop had once allowed for regular breaks. Both journeymen and shop owners participated in refreshments and conversation, and both could leave work aside to fight a fire. As the scale of the average workshop increased, and as white-collar employees mediated a growing distance between boss and worker, the increased pace and transformed relationships of the work place prohibited the disruption of volunteer firefighting. The increasing difficulty workers faced in the 1840s and 1850s in deserting their labor at the ring of the fire bell unquestionably diminished the status of the volunteer companies.[33]

But paid firefighting only worsened the situation, because men who could afford to desert their labor without angering foremen or employers were uninterested in joining an organization that received its payment in dollars rather than in community respect and tribute. As the St. Louis volunteer had said, "The romance of 'running wid de mashine' is sunk when one does it for his daily bread." Paid firefighting did not unite men of different ages and occupations as had volunteer firefighting. Of the 150 members of San Francisco's new, paid fire department, 88 percent were blue-collar workers, and only one fireman was a merchant. Thirty percent of the paid men were between twenty-one and twenty-three years old.[34]

Like San Francisco's paid department, Baltimore's was far more working class than the volunteer department had ever been. Of the 78 of 129 members of the new department locatable in either the 1858 city directory or the 1860 census, only two members were merchants, and both of them were foremen of paid companies. Seventy-eight percent of the paid firemen were blue collar, and were almost all of the white-collar members were clerks. These paid firemen were younger than members of the volunteer companies, on average, and were almost exclusively native born.[35] Ironically, the fire departments of Baltimore and San Francisco came to resemble Wilentz's working-class organization only *after* they were professionalized.

While reformers upheld the importance of "paying for labor generally," they did not find it necessary to pay very much. Firemen in Providence received seventy-five dollars a month, and paid firemen in Cincinnati earned about a dollar a day for their efforts.[36] A Baltimore fireman bemoaned the paid fireman's quandary. "Very few [businesses] are willing to employ men who are liable at any moment to be called to fire duty," he observed. As a result, a large portion of each department was composed of "call-men," reserve firemen who (theoretically) appeared when called, received little money, and in practice, performed nearly as poorly as the volunteers suggested. On at least one occasion in the 1860s, a Baltimore steam engine arrived at a fire with only one fireman in tow, the driver. Until the call-men arrived, the steamer stood idle. Into the last decades of the nineteenth century, firemen in all three of these cities protested nearsighted funding policies such as this one, which crippled the effectiveness of paid departments.[37]

The paid departments of San Francisco, St. Louis, and Baltimore all turned to urban political machines in the second half of the nineteenth century for support and aid. A national convention of chief engineers, which met in Baltimore in 1873, took as a main focus the "importance of separating the departments from political influence."[38] A fireman's handbook in 1872 likewise argued that "it is time that all political effects should be forever banished from fire departments; as nothing but injury to the service has ever yet resulted from any connection between these two."[39] San Francisco's paid department in the late 1870s and 1880s showed more unity and support of certain Democratic politicians than the fractured and independent volunteer firemen ever had.[40]

The politicized professional fire department did not come about by accident. Like the newly organized Baltimore Municipal Police Department, the members of which were recruited largely from Know-Nothing clubs, the paid fire department eventually also became a "valuable patronage machine." Mayor Swann ignored the committee appointed to plan the paid department, which advised that the paid firemen should "not be liable to removal therefrom by reason of any political consideration whatever." The mayor appointed the five member Board of Commissioners, which was in charge of appointing the department members. The new law also arranged for the chief engineer to be picked by the mayor and City Council. Under a sweeping Democratic victory in 1867, the paid department was again reorganized and placed under even closer control of the mayor, who was able to appoint a new Board of Commissioners for each term he served. In Baltimore, the paid fire department was almost entirely under the control of the mayor, and the firemen complained that politicians regularly "fleeced" them. By the late 1860s, critics of Baltimore's paid department also claimed that the municipal firemen had become as violent as their predecessors.[41]

In all three cities, fires were still scenes of potential disorder, but with vastly improved methods employed to control it. The paid system removed the public from the firefighting process in several ways. It separated firemen from non-firemen by paying them, by utilizing equipment too complicated for non-firemen to understand, and by standardizing firefighting methods and behavior according to preset guidelines. In the interests of safety, the public was increasingly distanced from the actual fires as well. During the first year of the paid department in both San Francisco and Baltimore, paid firemen began to use ropes to cordon off the crowd from a scene of fire. During the first year of San Francisco's paid department, the chief engineer occasionally used a stream of water to control a too enthusiastic crowd, fighting the public with the same tool used to fight the fires. The fire-alarm telegraphs proved useful for this purpose as well. One foreign observer found it ominous that "since the paid department had replaced the volunteer, squads of policemen make their appearance in the streets whenever there is a fire." This distancing effectively completed the municipalization of firefighting; a service that had once been entirely voluntary was completely removed from the participation of the public.[42]

Professional firefighting was increasingly distanced both from public participation and public observation. Yet at the very moment that professional firefighters distanced themselves from the public physically, they refined their behavior at fires so as to produce the appearance of order. The attitude and behavior of paid firefighters, whom Anthony Giddens would call "systems representatives" in the expert system of fire protection, became crucial factors in maintaining the trust of the property owners.[43]

But paid departments were an improvement over the volunteer system, as even the staunchest volunteers eventually came to admit.[44] Steam engines and the fire-alarm telegraph were far more efficient than hand pumps and a watchtower. Paid departments were more effective at reaching fires, and putting those fires out. After the transition to a paid department, daily papers enthusiastically reported fires at which "there was no noise or confusion, no rioting or rowdyism,—a few men, acting in concert under the direction of competent officers, with the aid of the fire alarm telegraph and the steam engines, proved more efficient in battling against the flames lighted by accident or the torch of the incendiary, than thousands of willing and daring firemen could have been with only the machinery of the old department."[45]

In all three cities, losses from fire decreased with the advent of the new system. Because of the basically unpredictable nature of fire and fire damage, comparative figures are often misleading indicators of efficiency. Long-term trends, however, support what every contemporary observer maintained—fires caused less damage under paid departments. In St. Louis, which had an unusual number of fires in the final year of the volunteer department, losses dropped from $1,302,000 to $211,000 over a twelve-month period.[46] Enormous losses in San Francisco in the first months of the paid department obscured the efficiency of the new system for some time, but within three years losses were well below volunteer levels.[47] Losses in Baltimore dropped by 50 percent over a five-year period of paid service, as did absolute numbers of alarms and fires. Average losses per fire decreased in the 1880s and 1890s nationwide. In the future, urban fires would rarely extend beyond a single building. Insurance rates in all three cities dropped between 20 and 50 percent. By the close of the century, American firefighting and fire technology were superior to that of any European nation.[48]

The volunteers believed they were killed by the paid fire departments, but they were wrong. The volunteer departments were dead, if not buried, even before the steam engines stepped in to deliver the final blow. Volunteer firemen had broken their promise to urban dwellers. The protection they offered their cities was limited and finally not worth the tribute demanded. The volunteer firemen had to form their own celebratory organizations before their final burials because urban citizens were no longer willing to do that celebrating for them.

The first anniversaries of the paid departments of these cities must have been particularly dour events for the volunteers. Great urban parades marked the occasions without a note of regret over the passing of the old system. Enthusiasm over the wisdom of reformers and bright hopes for the future of the municipal order were the overwhelming expressions of the day. The firemen were gone, so much so that in a lengthy description of St. Louis's anniversary parade, the *Republican* not only failed to mention the old volunteers, but limited its parade description to the fine appearances of the steam engines and horses. Paid firemen were as invisible as volunteers.

Volunteers had marched proudly and to loud acclaim in their parades years earlier. But not the paid firemen. In the pageantry of paid firefighting, the men were but ignoble figures, mere wage earners in the employment of the city. Clearly the hopes of the urban populace rested elsewhere. At the end of this St. Louis parade, a gift presentation took place, just as had always been done in the volunteer parades. But one difference in this gift presentation marked the distance the municipality had traveled since those times. Here was the traditional virtuous woman ready to offer tribute to the valiant protector, in clear sight and with the approval of the city. The reader can imagine the loud cheering of the gathered citizens as the tribute was made, and as, in the words of the reporter, "a pair of horses was presented to the Deluge by a lady." But who was this "Deluge," the privileged recipient? Deluge was not a fire company, paid or otherwise. On the first anniversary of the death of the St. Louis Volunteer Fire Department, our lady, and the city with her, paid tribute to none other than a steam fire engine.[49]

Conclusion

ONE LAST EULOGY

ONLY A FOOL would mourn the death of volunteer firefighting, since volunteer firefighting is clearly alive. Only a small minority of American firefighters are paid. In fact, volunteer departments purchase about 80 percent of the firefighting equipment sold in the United States. Firefighters in small towns and rural areas are as actively hostile to municipalization today as their predecessors were 150 years ago. Volunteers continue to find camaraderie, brotherhood (and sisterhood), and public honor in their unpaid work, and maintain that paid firefighters wouldn't work as hard.[1]

But in urban America, the experiment of volunteer fire protection proved a conspicuous failure, and volunteerism was deemed untenable by the start of the Civil War. In cities across the nation, voters and reformers ignobly banished firemen from positions they filled without salary. They forbade them from regularly endangering their lives for the benefit of property owners. They no longer allowed them to risk their welfare in the interests of the city. As scores of men fought and died in warfare of a different sort, reformers concluded that only individuals chosen by the city, and compensated with a salary, could endanger their lives by fighting fire.

Why did this happen, and what does the strange career of the volunteer fire department reveal about nineteenth-century America and the values of nineteenth-century Americans? In the early nineteenth century, citizens cherished volunteer firemen for their sacrifice. The press offered them tribute, the public hung heroic images of them in their homes, politicians used the honor offered to firemen for their public service as a springboard for office. Men of different occupations found in volunteer firefighting not only a classless brotherhood, but a basis for respect and honor separate from their paid work. Within the republican-liberalist political culture of the antebellum city, the fireman was not defined by class but by his civic virtue. Through his citizenship he won the respect and honor of his peers. In popular representations of the Jacksonian period, the volunteer fireman was celebrated both as a model of civic virtue and as an ideal of masculinity.

Yet by the 1850s, volunteer firemen had alienated politicians, reformers, and property owners. In San Francisco, St. Louis, and Baltimore, volunteer firemen fell from the positions of honor they had occupied in the Jacksonian period. They lost their status as model urban citizens, although in many cases their behavior had changed very little. The early-nineteenth-century vision of the volunteer fireman was of a classical warrior who distinguished himself in the public realm and enabled the contemporary polis to practice its republican ideals. Yet by the 1850s, reformers uniformly, and in many cases unjustifiably, condemned firemen for corrupting urban political structures.

In the 1820s, thousands of people openly celebrated the masculinity of the fireman. They cheered while firemen held contests of strength, endurance, and speed and when they paraded through the city. Wealthy citizens contributed large sums of money for the purchase of elaborate firehouses. Yet firemen were universally condemned by reformers only thirty years later for corrupting the morals of children within these houses, and for endangering the safety of decent citizens outside them. Reformers concluded that firemen were disorderly, immoral, politically corrupt, and beyond the reach of decency or law. Yet the ideals of the volunteer firemen had not changed.

But the city had. If the modern city is characterized "by the separation of work and community, in space and by role, for all social classes," then the decline of volunteer firefighting also charts the rise of the modern city.[2] In the fireman's city, men of different classes worked at firefighting in the name of the community, and found a community with other firemen. In the modern city, men would find their value in their paid work and turn to their biological families as the basis of their community. In the fireman's city, men could leave their paid work, or their homes, for the more important work of volunteer firefighting and the alternative homes of the firehouse. In the modern city, a man could not drop work for firefighting and his home was rarely still within hearing of the fire bell. In the fireman's city, there was enthusiastic competition, and in the modern city, there was professional order.

The great irony of the transformation is that firemen were active participants in the rise of the modern city. Volunteer firemen upheld a notion of citizenship that elevated and embraced volunteer firefighting and reassured these volunteers that they were the best citizens—because of their combative spirit and because they were willing to drop everything in order to man a fire pump as someone else's property burned down. Yet by protecting that property, they ensured that a different definition of citizenship would emerge, and that their own would come to seem increasingly archaic.

Republican liberalism fell to a Christian capitalist order in part because the city was made safe from fire. Firemen provided the stability and order that allowed for the growth of professionalism. And with that transformation, the volunteer fireman fell from grace. Once a man's citizenship was based in his business success and not his service to the city, firemen lost their tribute. With the loss of their tribute, firemen found that their classless masculinity, which celebrated physicality and brotherhood, was impossible to sustain. In the modern city, masculine ideals were divided by class, and urban firefighting was done by professionals.

In 1860 Marcus Boruck proudly stated that "paid firemen are expected to submit to insults, volunteers *will* not."[3] What he noted, and what I have argued in these pages, is that the combative, agonal spirit of the polis disappeared from antebellum firefighting. It also, and not coincidentally, disappeared from urban political culture by the start of the Civil War. When firefighting took the protection of life as its guiding principle, it demanded a constant state of individual struggle and readiness to go to war against fire, much as political life was understood by romantic republicans.

Indeed, the tribute literature of the early city constantly honored and praised volunteer firemen for such struggles and readiness. Once the object of firefighting switched to the protection of property and not life, fire needed only to be contained, not eradicated. By the 1850s, everyone except the volunteers agreed that fire was contained best not by individuals, but by networks of paid firemen, zoning regulations, and fire insurance. The agonal struggle of the individual against fire was replaced in the mid-nineteenth century by systems of control over fire damage. The paid fireman, integrated as he was into a web of proscribed behavior, was expected to submit to insults because he *could not* be damaged by them in the way the individual volunteer could. Like the body of the condemned man at the center of Michel Foucault's *Discipline and Punish*, the paid fireman and paid fire department were increasingly governed by a "network of relations" resembling "a perpetual battle" more closely than "a contract regulating a transaction or the conquest of a territory." The contract of the paid fireman replaced the conquest of fire as the reigning metaphor of firefighting.[4]

By the start of the Civil War, the qualities of service, of selflessness, of strength and vigor—the qualities that volunteers championed and believed made them better firemen—no longer defined the preeminent urban citizen. The model citizen was still willing to sacrifice for his beliefs, but he was increasingly the man of family, the man of stability and restraint, the private man, and not the public one.

The model citizen was the insurance agent who offered to remove the sting of fire with money, not with individual heroics. The model citizen had increasingly become the man of business—in other words, the man who paid his obligation to the community through his personal attention to work, the man too busy with the real business of life to waste his energies at the firehouse. Firefighting was transformed from an offering to the health of the city into labor, to be paid for and to be guaranteed by pay. Volunteerism was replaced by responsibility to family and work in a changing ideal of urban citizenship by the 1850s.

What was lost in this transformation was not good firefighting, whatever the volunteers may have believed. What was lost with professionalism was a culture that subsumed class differences within the discourse of manhood and sacrifice. And what was lost with professionalism was one more arena for individual investment in the community. Volunteer firefighting provided ample cause for alarm, but the order that replaced it would set off yet other alarms.

OCCUPATIONAL SCALE USED FOR QUANTITATIVE ANALYSIS

Because my original quantitative work was on San Francisco, I created this occupational scale with San Francisco in mind. I wanted a scale that would in some way reflect perceived differences in status in San Francisco in the mid-nineteenth century, and one which would also facilitate comparison with the work of other social historians. This five-category scale is based on the model developed in Stephan Thernstrom's *The Other Bostonians* (Cambridge, Mass., 1975, 289–302), with some specifics in laborer categories drawn from Philip Ethington's *Public City* (Appendix, 422–423). Distinctions between high- and low-white-collar categorization were made in line with Peter Decker's *Fortunes and Failures: White Collar Mobility in San Francisco*, partially to allow comparisons between his conclusions and my own, and partially in recognition of the depth in which he has studied the San Francisco merchant class. For comparative purposes I used this same scale to analyze firemen in Baltimore and St. Louis.

I have added to the "low white collar" category individuals whom I have designated "artisan proprietors," in keeping with the categories in Don Harrison Doyle, *The Social Order of a Frontier Community* (Urbana, 1978, 261). I use this category much more narrowly than Doyle, however. Only those artisans clearly listed in city directories as shopkeepers or proprietors rise in this study to low-white-collar status. Due to the unreliability of census information on wealth, I have chosen to ignore reported income as a basis for constructing this category, even when census returns reported that an artisan had a great deal of real property.

The greatest difficulty of classification in San Francisco or in any other city during the mid-nineteenth century cannot, of course, be addressed by (or within) a quantitative model. Part of my argument in this book is that class had a very different meaning to individuals in antebellum cities than it did in later periods, one which is in a crucial sense impossible to reconstruct. Would a day laborer in San Francisco, where day laborers were highly paid and difficult to find, have a different perception of himself (and his public status) than the one generally accorded by a five-category scale? Such essential information is entirely missing from this scale. Because I strongly believe that individuals did not find their identity in their paid occupations, I recognize that it is somewhat disingenuous of me to "class-ify" these firemen in the first place. I offer this classification as suggestive only, and have tried not to draw any "conclusions" based solely on quantitative analysis.

The following lists include most of the occupations listed for San Francisco and Baltimore volunteer firemen in either the 1860 census or in city directories.

High White Collar. Attorney, Broker, Comedian, Dealer, Distiller, Editor, Gentleman, Importer, Judge, Manufacturer, Merchant, Physician, Professor, Publisher.

Low White Collar. Accountant, Agent, Auctioneer, Bakery Keeper, Bath House Keeper, Barkeeper, Billiard Saloon Keeper, Bookkeeper, Builder, Chemist, Clerk, Collector, Contractor, Dealer, Engineer, Farmer, Fruitener, Government Employee/Official, Grocer, Hotel Keeper, Inspector, Insurance, Jeweler, Music Hall Keeper, Laundry Keeper, Market Keeper, Master Mariner, Teller, Property-Man, Proprietor, Real Estate Agent, Restaurant Keeper, Salesman, Saloon Keeper, Secretary, Shipmaster, Stables Keeper, Storekeeper, Superintendent, Writer (Newspaper).

Skilled Labor. Baker, Barber, Blacksmith, Boatmaker, Bootfitter, Bootmaker, Brewer, Bricklayer, Brickmason, Butcher, Cabinet Maker, Carpenter, Carriage-Painter, Confectioner, Cook, Cooper, Coppersmith, Foreman, Gardener, Hair Dresser, Hatter, House Painter, Iron Machinist, Leveler, Mechanic, Melter, Painter, Pantry Man, Paperhanger, Pattern Maker, Pinker, Plumber, Policeman, Printer, Sailmaker, Sashmaker, Shipcaulker, Shipjoiner, Shoemaker, Stevedore, Tailor, Tanner, Tinner, Tinsmith, Undertaker, Upholsterer, Wheelwright.

Semiskilled. Bellringer, Drayman, Driver, Hackman, Mariner, Policeman, Porter, Soldier, Special Policeman, Stage Driver, Teamster, Waiter, Watchman, Writer (Academic).

Unskilled. Day Laborer, Laborer, Waterman.

NOTES

INTRODUCTION
BEGINNING AT THE WAKE

1. Throughout this work I will use the one-word term "firefighting" rather than the standard two-word "fire fighting." I do so because I am interested in documenting a specific nineteenth-century practice of fighting fire. The two-word spelling is organized around and emphasizes the object, fire, not the manner in which the fire is fought.

2. Harry C. Pendleton, *The Exempt Firemen of San Francisco* (San Francisco, 1900), 27–28.

3. Philadelphia finally formed a paid department in 1871.

4. Ernest Earnest, *The Volunteer Fire Company, Past and Present* (New York, 1979), 74, 108–109; New Orleans correspondent to the *Fireman's Journal*, January 5, 1856.

5. *Missouri Republican*, February 18, 1858.

6. William T. King, *History of the American Steam Fire-Engine* (Boston, 1896), x; also see *Alta California*, July 29, 1858.

7. Edward Edwards, *History of the Volunteer Fire Department of St. Louis* (St. Louis, 1906).

8. It would be impossible to list all of the works that fall into this category, since virtually every nineteenth-century city had some chronicler of its volunteer firemen. Some of the better heroic portraits include: Arthur Wellington Brayley, *A Complete History of the Boston Fire Department from 1630–1888* (Boston, 1889); Charles A. Burdett, *The Gloucester Fire Department; Its History and Work from 1793 to 1893* (Gloucester, Mass., 1892); J. Albert Cassedy, *The Firemen's Record* (Baltimore, 1891); Augustine F. Costello, *Our Firemen: A History of the New York Fire Department* (New York, 1887); H. H. Easterbrook, *History of the Somerville Fire Department from 1842–1892* (Boston, 1893); Leonard Bolles Ellis, *History of the Fire Department of the City of New Bedford, Massachusetts, 1772–1890* (New Bedford, 1890); Clarence H. Forrest, *Official History of the Fire Department of the City of Baltimore* (Baltimore, 1898); Thomas R. Lynch, *The Volunteer Fire Department of St. Louis, 1819–1859* (St. Louis, 1880); Pendleton, *The Exempt Firemen of San Francisco*; George W. Sheldon, *The Story of the Volunteer Fire Department of the City of New York* (New York, 1882); Charles E. White, *The Providence Fireman* (Providence, 1886).

9. Anthony B. Lampe, "St. Louis Volunteer Fire Department, 1820–1850: A Study in the Volunteer Age," *Missouri Historical Review* 62(3) (1967–1968): 237.

10. See especially Anthony B. Lampe, "St. Louis Volunteer Fire Department, 1820–1850: A Study of the Volunteer Age" (Ph.D. diss., St. Louis University, 1966), and his article, "St. Louis Volunteer Fire Department, 1820–1850: A Study in the Volunteer Age," 235–259. Lampe actually quoted from an address to the first class of VISTA by Lady Bird Johnson, the First Lady in 1965, in his article in order to make the contemporary implications of volunteer firefighting totally clear. Lampe concluded, "The St. Louis Volunteer Fire Department, 1820–1850, put meaning behind the statement: 'My neigh-

bor needs me. I will do something.' The volunteer's actions spoke—he needed no words. He left us his deeds over which to ponder" (p. 237).

11. Andrew Neilly, "Violent Volunteers: A History of the Volunteer Fire Department of Philadelphia, 1736–1871" (Ph.D. diss., University of Pennsylvania, 1959), was the earliest and most influential of this group. Also significant were Stephen F. Ginzberg, "The History of Fire Protection in New York City, 1800–1842" (Ph.D. diss., New York University, 1968); Richard B. Calhoun, "From Community to Metropolis: Fire Protection in New York City, 1790–1875" (Ph.D. diss., Columbia University, 1973); Kathleen J. Kiefer, "A History of the Cincinnati Fire Department in the Nineteenth Century" (M.A. thesis, University of Cincinnati, 1967).

12. Sean Wilentz, *Chants Democratic: New York City and the Rise of the American Working Class* (New York, 1984), 259; Bruce Laurie, "Fire Companies and Gangs in Southwark: The 1840's," in *The Peoples of Philadelphia: A History of Ethnic Groups and Lower-Class Life, 1790–1940*, edited by Allen F. Davis and Mark H. Haller (Philadelphia, 1973), 82–83; Bruce Laurie, *Working People of Philadelphia, 1800–1850* (Philadelphia, 1980), 58.

13. Laurie, *Working People of Philadelphia*, 58–61, 153–155; Wilentz, *Chants Democratic*, 259–263.

14. See, for example, Susan Davis, *Parades and Power: Street Theater in Nineteenth-Century Philadelphia* (Berkeley, 1986), 144–147; Christine Stansell, *City of Women: Sex and Class in New York, 1789–1860* (Urbana, Ill., 1987), 90. Ira Katznelson, *City Trenches: Urban Politics and the Patterning of Class in the United States* (New York, 1981), 51.

15. Steven J. Ross, *Workers on the Edge: Work, Leisure, and Politics in Industrializing Cincinnati, 1788–1890* (New York, 1985), 167–169.

16. Eric H. Monkkonen, *America Becomes Urban: The Development of U.S. Cities and Towns, 1780–1980* (Berkeley, 1990), 105–108.

17. David R. Johnson, "Police and Fire Protection," in Mary Kupiec Cayton et al., *The Encyclopedia of American Social History*, 3 vols. (New York, 1992), 3: 2169–2170. His source on antebellum firefighting is an article by Richard Calhoun.

18. Steven A. Riess, "The City," in Mary Kupiec Cayton et al., *The Encyclopedia of American Social History*, 2: 1259–1275.

19. Popular histories of firemen and firefighting have appeared from time to time and have drawn from different departments in their accounts. With the exception of Rebecca Zurier's architectural history of firehouses, these have not generally been analytical works. Rebecca Zurier, *The American Firehouse: An Architectural and Social History* (New York, 1982). See also William Draper Brinckloe, *The Volunteer Fire Company* (Boston, 1934); Donald J. Cannon, *Heritage of Flames* (New York, 1977); Paul Ditzel, *Fire Engines, Fire Fighters* (New York, 1976); Earnest, *Volunteer Fire Company;* Margaret Hindle Hazen and Robert M. Hazen, *Keepers of the Flame: The Role of Fire in American Culture, 1775–1925* (Princeton, N.J., 1992); Robert S. Holzman, *The Romance of Firefighting* (New York, 1956); and Dennis Smith, *Dennis Smith's History of Firefighting in America: 300 Years of Courage* (New York, 1978).

20. William Cronon, *Changes in the Land: Indians, Colonists, and the Ecology of New England* (New York, 1983), 48–51, 118–119; Stephen J. Pyne, *Fire in America: A Cultural History of Wildland and Rural Fire* (Princeton, N.J., 1982), 6–19, 45–59.

21. A survey taken in London in 1979 found that attempts by laypersons to fight fires were in inverse proportion to the seriousness of the fire, as they perceived it. The

more serious the fire, the more likely that laypersons would contact the fire department and immediately evacuate the building. The surveyors considered the behavior of individuals who attempted to fight fires themselves to be less desirable than those who immediately contacted the fire department and then left the building. Peter G. Wood, "A Survey of Behavior in Fires," in *Fires and Human Behavior*, edited by David Canter (New York, 1980), 83–95. A 1975–1976 study in America drew similar conclusions: J. L. Bryan, *Smoke as a Determinant of Human Behavior in Fire Situations*, Report from Fire Protection Curriculum, College of Engineering, University of Maryland, College Park (mimeo). Cited in Wood, "Survey of Behavior in Fires," 94–95.

22. Monkkonen, *America Becomes Urban*, 98–103; Roger Lane, *Policing the City: Boston, 1822–1885* (New York, 1975), 26–38; Philip J. Ethington, "Vigilantes and the Police: The Creation of a Professional Police Bureaucracy in San Francisco, 1847–1900," *Journal of Social History* 21 (Winter 1987): 197–228; Eric H. Monkkonen, *Police in Urban America, 1860–1920* (Cambridge, U.K.: 1981); David R. Johnson, *Policing the Urban Underworld: The Impact of Crime on the Development of the American Police, 1800–1877* (Philadelphia, 1979). One could argue that vigilantes were volunteer policemen, of course.

23. Paul Robert Lyons, *Fire in America!* (Boston, 1976), 9.

24. Jon C. Teaford, *The Municipal Revolution in America: Origins of Modern Urban Government, 1650–1825* (Chicago, 1975), 52–54; Glen E. Holt, "Volunteer Fire Fighting in St. Louis, 1818–1859," *Gateway Heritage* 4 (Winter 1983–1984): 3.

25. Keith Reginald Gilbert, *Fire Engines and Other Firefighting Appliances* (London, 1966), 4–8.

26. Baltimore *Sun*, August 26, 1843; Cassedy, *The Firemen's Record*, 53.

27. Frank Soule, John H. Gihon, and James Nisbet, *The Annals of San Francisco; Containing a Summary of the History of the First Discovery, Settlement, Progress and Present Condition of California, and a Complete History of all the Important Events Connected with Its Great City: to which are added, Biographical Memoirs of Some Prominent Citizens* (New York, 1855), 409.

28. With the exception of 1856, when 1,026 men voted. *Fireman's Journal*, November 29, 1856; Pendleton, *Exempt Firemen*, 11. *The California Spirit of the Times and Fireman's Journal* reported the number of members eligible to vote at the department elections each year.

29. David D. Dana, *The Fireman: The Fire Departments of the United States, with a Full Account of All Large Fires, Statistics of Losses and Expenses, Theaters Destroyed by Fire, and Accidents, Anecdotes, and Incidents* (Boston, 1858), 359.

30. Urban promotional literature of the late nineteenth and early twentieth centuries used the superiority of urban services as a major selling point. See, for example, Walter Williams, *The State of Missouri, an Autobiography* (Columbia, Mo., 1904), 250–256.

31. Perhaps boosterism arose from the eighteenth-century belief in an inelastic money supply, and the belief that the successes of one city to attract commerce and early manufacturing would necessarily mark the equal decline of another city in these areas. In *The Politics of Individualism*, Lawrence Frederick Kohl identifies skepticism toward the creation of wealth as a unifying characteristic of Jacksonian Democrats, stemming from their "pessimistic" worldview. Whigs, in contrast, believed that huge amounts of wealth could be created. Lawrence Frederick Kohl, *The Politics of Individualism* (New York, 1989), 186–201.

32. Excellent discussions of boosterism can be found in David Hamer, *New Towns in the New World: Images and Perceptions of the Nineteenth-Century Urban Frontier* (New York, 1990), and William Cronon, *Nature's Metropolis: Chicago and the Great West* (New York, 1991), 34–46. See also Lawrence H. Larson, *The Urban West at the End of the Frontier* (Lawrence, Kans., 1978), 79. For different perspectives on St. Louis's nineteenth-century boosterism, see George Lipsitz, *The Sidewalks of St. Louis: Places, People and Politics in an American City* (Columbia, Mo., 1991), 93–95; Jeffrey Scott Adler, *Yankee Merchants and the Making of the Urban West: The Rise and Fall of Antebellum St. Louis* (Cambridge, U. K., 1991); Williams, *The State of Missouri.*

33. *Missouri Republican*, January 19, 1841.

34. George McCreary, *The Ancient and Honorable Mechanical Company of Baltimore* (Baltimore, 1901), 67.

35. "A Loyal and Liberal Fire Company," *Alta California*, November 19, 1862.

36. *Alta California*, April 26, 1860.

37. Walter B. Stevens, *St. Louis, the Fourth City* (St. Louis, 1909), 155–156. The Franklin Library cost $4,000 to open to the public and maintain from 1859 to 1866. Lynch, *Volunteer Fire Department*, 48.

38. McCreary, *Ancient and Honorable Mechanical Company of Baltimore*, 80; John Calvin Colson, "Fire Company Library Associations of Baltimore," *Journal of Library History* 21(1) (1986): 166–170.

39. *Alta California*, February 2, April 26, 1860; May 25, 1861.

40. Colson, "Fire Company Library Associations of Baltimore," 163.

41. St. Louis Firemen's Fund Association Minute Book, June 1, 1841–January 3, 1871, vol. 15 of the Missouri Historical Society (MoHS) Volunteer Firemen Collection. On the rise of mutual aid societies in eighteenth and early nineteenth-century America, see Conrad Edict Wright, *The Transformation of Charity in Postrevolutionary New England* (Boston, 1992); Patricia Ferguson Clement, *Welfare and the Poor in the Nineteenth-Century City: Philadelphia, 1800–1854* (Rutherford, N.J., 1984); Steven C. Bullock, *Revolutionary Brotherhood: Freemasonry and the Transformation of the American Social Order, 1730–1840* (Chapel Hill, 1996), 193–195; On the later development of ideals of public assistance in the later nineteenth century, see Theda Skocpol, *Protecting Soldiers and Mothers* (Cambridge, Mass., 1992).

42. Forrest, *Official History*, 49; Baltimore *Sun*, August 25, 1843. Forrest quotes a 1825 report from Mayor Small that the upper apartment of a Fell's Point firehouse was rented out to a school for $120 a year (p. 46). Missouri Fire Company No. 5 minutes, vol. 8, January 8, 1857, MoHS Volunteer Firemen Collection.

43. Monkonnen, *America Becomes Urban*, 89–110.

44. *Missouri Republican*, January 19, 1841.

45. Charles F. T. Young, *Fires, Fire Engines and Fire Brigades* (London, 1866), 483.

46. Alexis de Tocqueville, *Democracy in America*. The Henry Reeve Text as Revised by Francis Bowen and Further Corrected by Phillips Bradley. Abridged with an Introduction by Thomas Bender (New York, 1981), 102.

47. The phrase "era of associations" is drawn from Mary Ryan, *Cradle of the Middle Class: The Family in Oneida County, New York, 1790–1865* (Cambridge, U.K., 1981), 105–144.

48. Baltimore *Sun*, November 20, 1851.

CHAPTER ONE
PAYING TRIBUTE

1. Dana, *The Fireman*, 65–66.

2. Harry T. Peters, *Currier and Ives, Printmakers to the American People* (New York, 1942), 2.

3. A. K. Baragwanath in *Currier and Ives Chronicles of America*, edited by John Lowell Pratt (New York, 1942), 122

4. *Fireman's Journal*, April 7, 1855.

5. Baragwanath, in *Currier and Ives Chronicles of America*, 123.

6. Walton Rawls, *The Great Book of Currier and Ives' America* (New York, 1972), 3–50; John Tagg, *The Burden of Representation: Essays on Photographies and Histories* (Amherst, Mass., 1988), 34.

7. Henry Maguire, "Disembodiment and Corporality in Byzantine Images of the Saints," in *Iconography at the Crossroads, Papers from the Colloquium Sponsored by the Index of Christian Art, Princeton University, March 23–24, 1990* (Princeton, N.J., 1993), 75–90; Bryan Jay Wolf, *Romantic Re-Vision: Culture and Consciousness in Nineteenth-Century American Painting and Literature* (Chicago, 1982).

8. See, for example, Donatello's "St. George" (c. 1415–17, Bargello, Florence) and Gorgione's "The Virgin and Child with St. Liberalis and St. Francis" (1500–1505, Church of Castelfranco) in Frederick Hartt, *History of Italian Renaissance Art* (New York, 1969), 137–139, 530; Byzantine Icons in Muśee Rath, *les Icones dans les collections suisses* (Berne, 1968), nos. 12, 127; David and Tamara Talbot Rice, *Icons* (Dublin, 1968), 38–40, 48–50; Maguire, "Disembodiment and Corporality in Byzantine Images of the Saints," 76–77; Albert C. Moore, *Iconography of Religions: An Introduction* (Philadelphia, 1977), 262.

9.. On Romanticism in antebellum culture, see David S. Reynolds, *Walt Whitman's America* (New York, 1995); John B. Halsted, *Romanticism* (New York, 1969); Lawrence W. Levine, *Highbrow/Lowbrow: The Emergence of Cultural Hierarchy in America* (Cambridge, Mass., 1988), 13–81; Barbara Novak, *Nature and Culture: American Landscape Painting, 1825–1875* (New York, 1980); Jenny Franchot, *Roads to Rome: The Antebellum Protestant Encounter with Catholicism* (Berkeley, 1994), 38–40, 101–102; Anne C. Rose, *Voices of the Marketplace: American Thought and Culture, 1830–1860* (New York, 1995), 60–89.

10. See Hartt, *History of Italian Renaissance Art*, for representations of halos.

11. Sermon to volunteer firemen, in the *National Fireman's Journal* 7 (1881): 266.

12. "Fires and San Francisco Firemen," *Alta California*, January 1, 1854.

13. On hyperbole in nineteenth-century journalism, see Kenneth Cmiel, *Democratic Eloquence: The Fight over Popular Speech in Nineteenth-Century America* (New York, 1990), 111.

14. "To the Union Fire Company," Baltimore *Sun*, July 16, 1838.

15. Oration by Frank Pixley, in the *Second Anniversary of the Organization of the Fire Department of San Francisco, 1853, Programme of the Procession; Address; Treasurer's Annual Report of the S.F. F. Department Charitable Fund and List of Officers and Members of the San Francisco Fire Department* (San Francisco, 1853), 10; "Fires and San Francisco Firemen," *Alta California*, January 1, 1854.

16. Edward Pollock, "Tribute to the Firemen," *Fireman's Journal*, September 13, 1856.

17. "Fires and San Francisco Firemen," *Evening Bulletin*, December 15, 1856; J. W. De Frewer, "The Fireman's Call. Lines respectfully dedicated to the Members of the Fire Department of San Francisco, California," *Fireman's Journal*, September 8, 1855.

18. Hannah Arendt, *The Human Condition* (Chicago, 1958), 41 (emphasis in the original). I thank Philip Ethington for introducing me to *The Human Condition* as a framework for thinking about citizenship in the antebellum city.

19. Tocqueville, *Democracy in America*, 416.

20. Baltimore *Sun*, November 20, 1851.

21. Philip J. Ethington, *The Public City: The Political Construction of Urban Life in San Francisco, 1850–1900* (New York, 1994), 43–85. On republicanism, see Gordon S. Wood, *The Creation of the American Republic, 1776–1787* (New York, 1969), 46–90; Drew R. McCoy, *The Elusive Republic: Political Economy in Jeffersonian America* (Chapel Hill, N.C., 1980); Daniel T. Rodgers, "Republicanism: The Career of a Concept," *Journal of American History* 79(1) (June 1992): 11–38; James T. Kloppenberg, "The Virtues of Liberalism: Christianity, Republicanism, and Ethics in Early American Political Discourse," *Journal of American History* 74(1) (June 1978): 9–13.

22. Ethington, *Public City*, 2–24, quote on 57.

23. "To the Union Fire Company," Baltimore *Sun*, July 16, 1838.

24. Count D., "Lines to the Fire Department," *Fireman's Journal*, April 7, 1855.

25. Arendt, *The Human Condition*, 41.

26. On the gendered nature of republicanism, see Ruth H. Bloch, "The Gendered Meanings of Virtue in Revolutionary America," *Signs* 13(1) (1987): 37–58; Ethington, *Public City*, 60–62, 70–72. On the public sphere in antebellum America, see Ethington, *Public City*, 33, 58–85; Jurgen Habermas, *The Structural Transformation of the Public Sphere: An Inquiry into a Category of Bourgeois Society* (Cambridge, Mass., 1989); Craig Calhoun, ed., *Habermas and the Public Sphere* (Cambridge, Mass., 1992); Arendt, *The Human Condition*, 38–78. I use the term guardedly: I don't envision the public sphere as an arena of free communication as Habermas does, but as a more limited communicative arena where men competed for honor in the nineteenth-century city.

27. "Fires and San Francisco Firemen," *Alta California*, January 1, 1854.

28. Baltimore *Sun*, April 1, September 11, 1844; November 21, 1846. See also the Baltimore *Sun* of August 5, 1843; June 1, September 4, 1849.

29. *Missouri Democrat*, September 23, October 14, November 20, 1856.

30. Sacramento *Union*, March 5, 1860.

31. *Alta California*, November 23, 1853; July 12, 1854; November 24, 1863.

32. Baltimore *Sun*, November 18, 19, and December 8, 1851.

33. Ibid., September 23, 1844.

34. *Alta California*, April 7, 1866.

35. Ibid., April 22, 1863.

36. Baltimore *Sun*, September 11, 1844.

37. *Alta California*, October 12, 1861.

38. *Fireman's Journal*, June 16, 1855; *Alta California*, June 14, 1855.

39. *Alta California*, May 4, 1863.

40. *Evening Bulletin*, June 26, 1857.

41. *Missouri Republican*, April 19, 1841.

42. Edward Pollock, "Tribute to the Firemen," *Fireman's Journal*, September 13, 1856.

43. Baltimore *Sun*, November 20, 1851.

44. "The Fireman," reprinted from the *Sacramento Age* in the *Fireman's Journal*, February 28, 1857.

45. Dana, *The Fireman*, 65, 368–366; L. E. Frost and E. L. Jones, "The Fire Gap and the Greater Durability of Nineteenth-Century Cities," *Planning Perspectives* 4 (1989): 338–341; Larson, *The Urban West at the End of the Frontier*, 78–79.

46. Soule, Gihon, and Nisbet, *The Annals of San Francisco*, 331.

47. *Alta California*, November 12, 1863.

48. Oration by Frank Pixley, *Second Anniversary*, 13.

49. Lynch, *Volunteer Fire Department*, 87.

50. Dana, *The Fireman*, 178.

51. Carl Smith, *Urban Disorder and the Shape of Belief* (Chicago, 1995), 26–28.

52. Johan Goudsblom, *Fire and Civilization* (London, 1992), 176–177.

53. Holt, "Volunteer Fire Fighting in St. Louis," 4; Roger Lotchin, *San Francisco 1846–1856: From Hamlet to City* (New York, 1974), 174–176. Most Canadian cities suffered from the same dangerous lack of zoning through the mid-nineteenth century. John C. Weaver and Peter DeLottinville, "The Conflagration and the City: Disaster and Progress in British North America during the Nineteenth Century," *Social History* (Canada) 13(26) (1980): 442–443.

54. Edwards, *History of the Volunteer Fire Department of St. Louis*, 46.

55. Oration by Frank Pixley, *Second Anniversary*, 13.

56. Goudsblom, *Fire and Civilization*, 132–135; Pyne, *Fire in America*, 32–33. For an excellent description of fire as satanic, see Smith, *Urban Disorder and the Shape of Belief*, 48–49.

57. Stephen J. Pyne, "Firestick History," *Journal of American History* 76 (March 1990): 1141.

58. Gaston Bachelard, *The Psychoanalysis of Fire* (Boston, 1964), 98.

59. Ibid., 111

60. *Alta California*, January 1, 1854.

61. Fire's anthropomorphic qualities are reflected in myth as well as contemporary methods of fire response. Pyne, *Fire in America*, 33; *Missouri Democrat*, July 18, 1855.

62. *Alta California*, January 1, 1854.

63. Oration by Frank Pixley, *Second Anniversary*, 14.

64. *Alta California*, September 13, 1860.

65. "Disastrous Fire—Twenty Five Buildings Destroyed—Heroic Exertions of the Firemen—Incidents, Etc., Etc.," *Alta California*, June 10, 1865.

66. *Missouri Republican*, January 19, 1841.

67. Tocqueville, *Democracy in America*, 409–410.

68. E. L. Godkin, "The Newspaper and the Reader," *Nation*, August 10, 1865, 165–166, quoted in Ethington, *Public City*, 21. The power of the newspapers could also work against the firemen, as became abundantly apparent to them in the 1850s.

69. Hazen and Hazen, *Keepers of the Flame*, 126–127; Robin L. Einhorn, *Property Rules: Political Economy in Chicago, 1833–1872* (Chicago, 1991), 15; Sam Bass Warner, Jr., *The Private City: Philadelphia in Three Periods of Its Growth* (Philadelphia, 1968);

Michael H. Frisch, *Town into City: Springfield, Massachusetts, and the Meaning of Community, 1840–1880* (Cambridge, 1972).

70. Even Einhorn's ultra-privatized, "segmented" Chicago provided for firehouse construction. Although the city "relied on volunteers who received subsidies from neighbors who wanted fire protection," the government also provided subsidies. Einhorn, *Property Rules*, 16, 149–151; George D. Bushnell, "Chicago's Rowdy Firefighters," *Chicago History* 2(4) (1973): 232–241; St. Louis Firemen's Fund, *History of the St. Louis Fire Department* (St. Louis, 1914), 164.

71. Forrest, *Official History*, 46. This was not an expensive house. The Sansome Hook and Ladder house, in San Francisco, cost $24,000 to build and over $5,000 to furnish. The Sansome, known as the "White Kid" company because of the wealth of its membership, privately funded this extravagance, however; *Alta California*, April 26, 1860. Fire engines ranging in price from $4,500 to $8,500 were paid for by the Common Council under section 3 of the state law governing volunteer fire departments, which specified that every company, once admitted, "shall be furnished with engine and house"; *Fireman's Journal*, May 5, 1855; February 23, 1856.

72. William Murray, *The Unheralded Heroes of Baltimore's Big Blazes* (Baltimore, 1969), 2.

73. *Fireman's Journal*, August 4, 1855. Rebecca Zurier discusses in detail the changes in architectural styles accompanying the transition from volunteer to paid departments. She notes that "the signs, statues, weathervanes and identifying mascots which had graced older stations were early casualties. Even the tower, which in the past had served the function of making the fire station stand out from the buildings around it . . . was now treated as a simple shaft—or eliminated altogether in favor of drying racks"; Zurier, *The American Firehouse*, 81.

74. Zurier, *The American Firehouse*, 65.

75. *Fireman's Journal*, November 17, 1855. Also see *Fireman's Journal*, August 11, 1855; St. Louis Fire Department, *Justifiably Proud* (Marcelline, Mo., 1977), 47; Edwards, *History of the Volunteer Fire Department of St. Louis*, 120.

76. *California Spirit of the Times and Fireman's Journal*, April 28, 1860.

77. "Magnificent Gifts to the Howard Engine Company," *Alta California*, June 22, 1861.

78. Baltimore *Sun*, November 20, 1851.

79. *Evening Bulletin*, June 19, 1857.

80. *Fireman's Journal*, November 17, 1855.

81. Edmond M. Gagey, *The San Francisco Stage: A History* (Westport, 1950), 15. Louis J. Stellman, *Sam Brannan: Builder of San Francisco* (New York, 1953), 151; Plays with firemen themes were also popular in the 1850s. One surviving example is Samuel D. Johnson, *The Fireman. A Drama, in Three Acts* (Boston, 1856). See also Richard M. Dorson, "Mose the Far-Famed and World-Renowned," *American Literature* 15 (November 1943): 288.

82. Hazen and Hazen, *Keepers of the Flame*, 40, 144: *Alta California*, December 3, 1860.

83. Letter from "Yoruck," *Fireman's Journal*, December 1, 1855.

84. Bachelard, *The Psychoanalysis of Fire*, 111.

85. Dana, *The Fireman*, 15–16.

86. Ethington calls this group-interest-based political culture "pluralist liberalism," and argues that it emerged in San Francisco after the Civil War. My argument is somewhat different. I see the important transformation occurring in the 1850s with the rise of the businessman, not with the rise of interest-group discourse, but I agree with him that the republican liberalism that embraced volunteers for their heroic individual efforts collapsed in the 1850s. Ethington, *Public City*, 198–207.

87. Charles T. Holloway, ed., *The Chief Engineer's Register and Insurance Advertiser, containing a Full Account of the Organization of the Baltimore City Fire Department, also The Laws of the State of Maryland and the Ordinances of the City of Baltimore etc.* (Baltimore, 1860), 96.

Chapter Two
Manly Boys and Chaste Fire Engines

1. David Leverenz, *Manhood and the American Renaissance* (Ithaca, N.Y., 1989), 138; Nina Baym, *Novels, Readers and Reviewers: Responses to Fiction in Antebellum America* (Ithaca, N.Y., 1984), 210.

2. *California Spirit of the Times and Fireman's Journal*, September 17, 1859. After Jupiter removed fire from the earth in an attempt to punish mankind, Prometheus climbed to the heavens with the help of Minerva and stole the fire back from the chariot of the sun, returning it to man; Hesiod, *Theogony*, 510, 550.

3. On San Francisco figures, see the Inter-University Consortium for Political and Social Research, Study 00003: Historical Demographic, Economic and Social Data: U.S., 1790–1970 (Ann Arbor, Mich.: ICPSR), http://icg.fas.harvard.edu/cgi-bin/brown/newCensus.pl. Thirty-nine percent of San Francisco's firemen locatable in the eighth census were married; see the appendix for more information on this figure. On St. Louis, see Adler, *Yankee Merchants and the Making of the Urban West*, 96; Inter-University Consortium for Political and Social Research, Study 00003. On Baltimore, see Sherry H. Olsen, *Baltimore: The Building of an American City* (Baltimore, 1985), 90, 119.

4. See Michel Foucault, *History of Sexuality,* vol. 1: *An Introduction* (New York, 1990), 17–35, for a discussion of the relationship between discourse and power. For two differing views of the implications of gendered fiction in the antebellum era, see Ann Douglas, *The Feminization of American Culture* (New York, 1977), and Gillian Brown, *Domestic Individualism: Imagining Self in Nineteenth-Century America* (Berkeley, 1990).

5. Edwards, *History of the Volunteer Fire Department of St. Louis*, 122–210; Phoenix Fire Company No. 7 minutes, October 1, 1844.

6. Laurie, "Fire Companies and Gangs in Southwark: The 1840's," 71–87. Membership lists in the Franklin Fire Company minutes, 1856, in the MoHS Volunteer Firemen Collection.

7. Lotchin, *San Francisco 1846–1856,* 103.

8. "Constitution et reglement interieur de la compagnie," Lafayette Fire Company, 1854 (Bancroft Library); Peter R. Decker, *Fortunes and Failures: White-Collar Mobility in Nineteenth-Century San Francisco* (Cambridge, Mass., 1978), 110–111; Frederick J. Bowlen, "Firefighters of the Past: A History of the Old Volunteer Fire Department of San

Francisco from 1849–1866" (unpublished manuscript, Bancroft Library), vol. 4, 130; James Andrew Baumohl, "Dashaways and Doctors: The Treatment of Habitual Drunkards in San Francisco from the Gold Rush to Prohibition" (Ph.D. diss. School of Social Welfare, University of California at Berkeley, 1986), 79.

9. This information is based on an examination of all members of the department identifiable in the 1860 census. For more information on my quantitative method, see the appendix.

10. There is some evidence that African Americans acted as firemen in Baltimore as well, although it is not clear that the "coloured men in the habit of working our Fire apparatus" in Baltimore's Mechanical Company in 1836 were actual members, as Batteurs was. This company waited on the mayor in order to prevent the arrest of the "coloured men" at late-night fires (Mechanical Company minutes, December 3, 1846). The Pioneer Hook and Ladder Company in Baltimore also appears to have employed African Americans. In 1858, a "Colored Boy" dragging their engine to a fire was shot by some rowdies. The company members pursued the assailants and brought the individual to their company doctor, "who extracted the ball, and we are glad to state that the wound was not dangerous" (Pioneer Hook and Ladder Company minutes, March 17, 1858).

11. Their president, H. Cobb, was born in Gurnsey but was educated in Belgium and France. A bilingual auctioneer, Cobb later became president of the California Board of Education. Jerry MacMullen, "The Company of Hooks and Ladders," *Westways*, May 1962, 14–16. For a contrary view on the "character" of departments, see Baumohl, "Dashaways and Doctors," 79.

12. "Constitution and By-Laws of the Knickerbocker Engine Company," 1854 (Bancroft Library); Decker, *Fortunes and Failures*, 209.

13. These conclusions are based on only a small fraction of firemen from only four companies and are only suggestive. Of 90 firemen identifiable in the census (out of a total sample of 427), 22 were foreign born. Eleven firemen were born in Ireland, one was born in England, and 10 were born in one of the German states.

It seems clear to me that foreign-born firemen are underrepresented in this sample. Firemen with Irish names seem to have been harder to locate in the census than other firemen, in part because their names were often too common to search. (When two or more individuals in the city of Baltimore had the same name I rejected that name for my data.) Even firemen with distinctive Irish and German names were hard to locate, perhaps because they had higher mobility rates than native-born firemen. I feel more comfortable basing my assertions about heterogeneous fire companies on the diversity of names in fire company lists than on the results of this census work. Firemen drawn from McCreary, *Ancient and Honorable Mechanical Company of Baltimore,* Mechanical Company membership list of 1858, no honorary members included; Pioneer Hook and Ladder Company membership list of 1859, from the Peale Museum Collection, no contributing or honorary members included; New Market roster of 1857, from the Peale Museum Collection, no contributing members included; Deptford Company membership roster of 1858, from the Peale Museum Collection, no contributing members included. Names cross-referenced in Ronald Vern Jackson, *Baltimore, Md., 1860 Census Index* (Salt Lake City, 1988), and the 1860 census returns for Baltimore.

14. Of course, firemen might have moved between 1859, when the department was disbanded, and 1860, but it seems likely that some high correlation would remain

between residence and firehouse. But of the 123 members of four fire companies (out of a total sample of 427 members) locatable in the 1860 census for Baltimore, there appears to be very little if any correlation between residence and firehouse. Firemen of different companies lived in the same ward, and firemen from the same companies lived in different wards. Of course, this sample is a small one, and those members locatable in the census might be exactly the kinds of firemen (family men, high-status professionals, older men) who would be least likely to choose a firehouse based on neighborhood association. The transient firemen might have left town by 1860 and thus don't show up in this sample. For information on the sample, see the previous note.

15. Helen Holdredge, *Firebelle Lillie: The Life and Times of Lillie Hitchcock Coit of San Francisco* (New York, 1967), 90. Maps and analysis of spatial diversity in other San Francisco fire companies can be found in Amy S. Greenberg, "Cause for Alarm: The Volunteer Fire Department in the Nineteenth Century City" (Ph.D. diss., Harvard University, 1995), 178–189.

16. Decker, *Fortunes and Failures*, 201, 203.

17. Ibid., 214–215.

18. Ibid., 204–205; The symbol '55 after a name in the captions of maps 2.1, 2.2, and 2.3 means that that name was located in the company roster in 1855 as well as in 1860.

19. Decker, *Fortunes and Failures*, 210–215.

20. Coleman lived in New York temporarily during the Civil War.

21. This sample is probably biased in favor of older firemen, who were probably more stable (and likely to still be in Baltimore a year after the department disbanded). Statistics based on 90 firemen from four companies (out of a total sample of 427) locatable in the 1860 census. Firemen drawn from McCreary, *Ancient and Honorable Mechanical Company of Baltimore,* Mechanical Company membership list of 1858, no honorary members included; Pioneer Hook and Ladder Company membership list of 1859, from the Peale Museum Collection, no contributing or honorary members included; New Market roster of 1857, from the Peale Museum Collection, no contributing members included; Deptford Company membership roster of 1858, from the Peale Museum Collection, no contributing members included. Names cross-referenced in Jackson, *Baltimore, Md., 1860 Census Index*, and the 1860 census returns for Baltimore.

22. Ryan, *Cradle of the Middle Class*, 144. See also Warner, *Private City*, 61–62; Don H. Doyle, "The Social Functions of Voluntary Associations in a Nineteenth-Century American Town," *Social Science History* 1 (Spring 1977): 338–43.

23. "The Association will settle all cases of riot, affray, quarreling or disagreement among firemen, in which the character of the department is involved." St. Louis Firemen's Association minutes, March 6, 1851.

24. Letter from Voluntary, Sacramento, in the *California Spirit of the Times and Fireman's Journal*, March 12, 1859.

25. St. Louis Volunteer Firemen Collection, box 1, series 1; *California Spirit of the Times and Fireman's Journal*, March 26, October 1, 1859. Advertisements in the back of John B. Hall's *The Fireman's Book* suggest that some popular firemen's publications, including, *The Fireman's Book* itself, were marketed to the volunteer firemen in several cities. Perhaps there was a shared firefighting literature in the antebellum period. Unfortunately, few examples of these popular publications have survived. John B. Hall, *The Fireman's Own Book: Containing Accounts of Fires Throughout the United States, As*

Well as Other Countries; Remarkable Escapes From the Devouring Element; Heroic Conduct of Firemen in Cases of Danger; Means of Extinguishing Fires; Accounts of Firemen Who Have Lost Their Lives While on Duty; Together with Facts, Incidents and Suggestions, Interesting and Valuable to Firemen and Citizens Generally. (New York, Philadelphia, Boston, 1850).

26. *The Pickwickian*, published by "Daughter, Julius and Pickwick" in New York, 1856. In the Pioneer Hook and Ladder Collection 662, of the Maryland Historical Society (MdHS) Manuscripts Division.

27. Lynch, *Volunteer Fire Department*, 80–82.

28. *Fireman's Journal*, June 23, 1955 (emphasis in the original). What exactly occupied the thoughts of the Stockton insane was not specified.

29. Ibid. And the exchanges became *more* extravagant. When the Stockton boys made their visit to San Francisco in 1856, they "carried off Assistant Engineer Capprice, Foreman F.E.R. Whitney, C. Walsh . . . and others, conveying them prisoners to Stockton." *Fireman's Journal*, July 12, 1856.

30. Olson, *Baltimore*, 119.

31. Adler, *Yankee Merchants*, 96.

32. Stephan Thernstrom, *The Other Bostonians: Poverty and Progress in the American Metropolis, 1880–1970* (Cambridge, Mass., 1973), 9–28; Stanley Engerman, "Up or Out: Social and Geographical Mobility in the United States," *Journal of Interdisciplinary History* 3 (Winter 1975): 469–489. Statistics on San Francisco in Ethington, *Public City*, 47–48; Decker, *Fortunes and Failures*, 171; St. Louis statistics in Adler, *Yankee Merchants*, 97.

33. Adler, *Yankee Merchants*, 96.

34. *True Californian*, June 30, 1856, quoted in the San Francisco *Fireman's Journal*, July 5, 1856.

35. Colson, "The Fire Company Library Associations of Baltimore," 166–169; Baltimore *Sun*, August 24, 1848.

36. Andrew Jackson Downing, *The Architecture of Country Houses* (New York, 1850), 25. On the increasing significance of interior decoration as a sign of the decorous and virtuous home, see Elaine S. Abelson, *When Ladies Go A-Thieving: Middle-Class Shoplifters in the Victorian Department Store* (New York, 1989), 51–59; John F. Kasson, *Rudeness and Civility: Manners in Nineteenth-Century Urban America* (New York, 1990), 169–181; Gwendolyn W. Wright, *Building the Dream: A Social History of Housing in America* (New York, 1983), 73–89; Katherine V. Snyder, "'Luxurious Bachlerdom': Domesticity, Consumer Culture, and Single Manhood in 1890s New York," unpublished paper delivered at the Organization of American Historians Annual Meeting, March 1996. On consumption generally, see Thorstein Veblen, *The Theory of the Leisure Class: An Economic Study of Institutions* (1899) (New York, 1931), and Pierre Bourdieu, *Distinction: A Social Critique of the Judgment of Taste*, trans. Richard Nice (Cambridge, Mass., 1984).

37. The literature on the domestic sphere is immense. See especially Katherine Kish Sklar, *Catherine Beecher: A Study in American Domesticity* (New Haven, 1973), and Ryan, *Cradle of the Middle Class*.

38. The manuscript of Captain W. W. Branson, quoted in Edwards, *History of the Volunteer Fire Department of St. Louis*, 281.

39. Holdredge, *Firebelle Lillie*, 90. This is an insupportable claim, but, like much of *Firebelle Lillie*, has value insofar as it indicates what was popularly believed about the fire department.

40. Lori Merish, "'The Hand of Refined Taste' in the Frontier Landscape: Caroline Kirkland's *A New Home, Who'll Follow?* and the Feminization of American Consumerism," *American Quarterly* 45(4) (December 1993): 487.

41. Laclede Fire Company records, March 1, 1853, meeting. Vol. 6 in the MoHS Volunteer Firemen Collection.

42. Phoenix Fire Company No. 7 minutes, February 10, 1845, in ibid., vol. 11.

43. *California Spirit of the Times and Fireman's Journal*, March 26, 1861; *Fireman's Journal*, October 27, 1855; letter from Protection, Sacramento, December 21, 1859, in *California Spirit of the Times and Fireman's Journal*, December 24, 1859.

44. Mechanical Company Ledger, November 17, 1844, MdHS, Manuscripts Division.

45. Anthony Rotundo, *American Manhood: Transformations in Masculinity from the Revolution to the Modern Era* (New York, 1993), 82–91. On women's same-sex relationships, see Carol Smith-Rosenberg, "The Female World of Love and Ritual: Relations between Women in Nineteenth-Century America," *Signs* 1 (1975): 1–29.

46. Based on those firemen locatable in the 1860 census. See appendix.

47. This sample is most likely biased in favor of married firemen, who were more stable and more likely to still be in Baltimore a year after the department was disbanded (and thus to appear in the census). Statistics based on 90 firemen locatable in the 1860 census, out of a total sample of 427. Firemen drawn from McCreary, *Ancient and Honorable Mechanical Company of Baltimore,* Mechanical Company membership list of 1858, no honorary members included; Pioneer Hook and Ladder Company membership list of 1859, from the Peale Museum Collection, no contributing or honorary members included; New Market roster of 1857, from the Peale Museum Collection, no contributing members included; Deptford Company membership roster of 1858, from the Peale Museum Collection, no contributing members included. Names cross-referenced in Jackson, *Baltimore, Md., 1860 Census Index*, and the 1860 census returns for Baltimore.

48. *Fireman's Journal*, August 4, 1855.

49. Karen Halttunen, *Confidence Men and Painted Women: A Study of Middle-Class Culture in America, 1830–1870* (New Haven, 1982), 92–123; Kasson, *Rudeness and Civility*, 147–181; Mark C. Carnes, *Secret Ritual and Manhood in Victorian America* (New Haven, 1989), 143–146, 152–156

50. *California Spirit of the Times and Fireman's Journal*, November 19, 1859.

51. Mechanical Fire Company documents, November 29, 1856; Pioneer Hook and Ladder Collection, October 22, 1854; Mechanical Fire Company, February 11, 1840; recordbook of the Washington Hose Company of Baltimore, 1815, 1835, Enoch Pratt Free Library.

52. Baumohl, "Dashaways and Doctors," 85–96. On temperance reform, see W. J. Rorabaugh, *The Alcoholic Republic: An American Tradition* (New York, 1979); Ian R. Tyrrell, *Sobering Up: From Temperance to Prohibition in Antebellum America, 1800–1860* (Westport, Conn., 1979), 191–206; Paul E. Johnson, *A Shopkeeper's Millennium: Society and Revivals in Rochester, New York, 1815–1837* (New York, 1978); Paul Boyer, *Urban Masses and Moral Order in America, 1820–1920* (Cambridge, Mass., 1978), 77–84.

53. The *Pickwickian*, March 2, 1856, 2 (emphasis in the original). On the YMCA, see Rotundo, *American Manhood*, 72–73; David I. Macleod, *Building Character in the American Boy: The Boy Scouts, YMCA, and Their Forerunners, 1870–1920* (Madison, Wis., 1983); Joseph Kett, *Rites of Passage: Adolescence in America, 1790 to the Present* (New York, 1977), 199–201.

54. Thirty-three of 46 members of this company in 1859 were locatable in either the 1860 census or the 1858 city directory. Of these 33 members, 55 percent practiced white-collar occupations. Pioneer Hook and Ladder Company membership list of 1859, from the Peale Museum Collection, no contributing or honorary members included. List cross-referenced with William H. Boyd, *Baltimore City Directory*, 1858; Jackson, *Baltimore, Md., 1860 Census Index*; and the 1860 census returns for Baltimore. On the library, see Forrest, *Official History*, 275–276.

55. Ethington, *Public City*, 33, 57–59.

56. Blumin, *Emergence of the Middle Class*, 2; Barton J. Bledstein, *Culture of Professionalism: The Middle Class and the Development of Higher Education in America* (New York, 1976), 8–13. On the impact of the Second Great Awakening on culture, see Paul Johnson, *Shopkeeper's Millennium*.

57. Melville quoted in Leverenz, *Manhood and the American Renaissance*, 19. Leverenz provides an excellent analysis of the transformations in masculinity in this period in his close readings of Frederick Douglass's autobiographies. Between the 1845 *Narrative* to the 1855 *My Bondage and My Freedom*, Douglass rewrote his fight scene with the slave breaker Covey to redefine his masculinity along class lines; 108-134. In the second version he emphasizes his self-control and Covey's humiliation: "He shows that he is more Christian, more self-disciplined and more manly than his bullying master"; 109.

58. Decker, *Fortunes and Failures*, 109; 1860 figures based on firemen locatable in the 1860 census or 1860 city directory. See appendix.

59. Forrest, *Official History*, 53.

60. Based on membership lists for the New Market, Friendship, and Independent Fire companies, cross-referenced with the *Baltimore Directory and Register for 1814–1815* (Baltimore, 1814). Of the 206 members of these three companies, 111 were locatable in the city directory. These companies might be unusually high- or low-status companies within the department, but I have no evidence that this was the case in 1814. New Market membership list from the Peale Museum Collection; Friendship Fire Company, membership record, MdHS MS 373, 1798–1822; Independent Fire Company list, MdHS MS 354, in the Federal Fire Company Records (misnamed). For my classification scale, see the appendix.

61. Of 427 firemen belonging to four fire companies in 1857–1859, I was able to locate 219 in either the city directory of 1858 or in the 1860 census. This sample could be biased in any number of ways: these four fire companies might not be representative of the entire department, and the firemen who showed up in the city directory or the census might be higher-status firemen than those who did not show up. These statistics (like all statistics used in this book) are thus meant to be suggestive rather than conclusive. Firemen drawn from McCreary, *Ancient and Honorable Mechanical Company of Baltimore*, Mechanical Company membership list of 1858, no honorary members included; Pioneer Hook and Ladder company Membership list of 1859, from the Peale Museum Collection, no contributing or honorary members included; New Market roster of 1857, from the Peale Museum Collection, no contributing members included; Deptford Company membership roster of 1858, from the Peale Museum Collection, no contributing members included. Names cross-referenced in Jackson, *Baltimore, Md., 1860 Census Index*, and the 1860 census returns for Baltimore. For my classification scale, see the appendix.

62. Don Piatt, *Some Historical Notes Concerning the Cincinnati Fire Department* (Cincinnati, n.d.), 1.

63. William R. Gentry, Jr., quoted in Lampe, "St. Louis Volunteer Fire Department, 1820–1850: A Study in the Volunteer Age," 236.

64. Stuart M. Blumin, *The Emergence of the Middle Class: Social Experience in the American City, 1760–1900* (New York, 1989); Anthony E. Rotundo, "Body and Soul: Changing Ideals of American Middle-Class Manhood, 1770–1920," *Journal of Social History* 16(4) (1983): 23–38; Ryan, *Cradle of the Middle Class*; Carnes, *Secret Ritual and Manhood in Victorian America*.

65. Blumin, *Emergence of the Middle Class*, 193.

66. Doyle, "The Social Functions of Voluntary Associations," 338–343; Baumohl, "Dashaways and Doctors," chap. 1.

67. Laclede Fire Company Records, September 3, 1857; on the appeal of fighting among the working class, see Elliot J. Gorn, *The Manly Art: Bare-Knuckle Prize Fighting in America* (Ithaca, N.Y., 1986).

68. *Fireman's Journal*, November 29, 1856.

69. Blumin, *Emergence of the Middle Class*, 213–215. On the growth of sports among middle-class men, see Rotundo, *American Manhood*, 239–244; Clyde Griffen, "Reconstructing Masculinity from the Evangelical Revival to the Wanings of Progressivism: A Speculative Synthesis," in *Meanings for Manhood: Constructions of Masculinity in Victorian America*, edited by Mark C. Carnes and Clyde Griffen (Chicago, 1990), 189.

70. Baltimore *Sun*, November 20, 1851; *California Spirit of the Times and Fireman's Journal*, June 11, 1859.

71. Phoenix Fire Company No. 7 minutes, May 18, 1846; James Henry Harris, in the *National Fireman's Journal*, August 3, 1878.

72. Clyde W. Park, *The Cincinnati Equitable Insurance Company* (Cincinnati, 1954), 91.

73. Jim Burger, *In Service: A Documentary History of the Baltimore City Fire Department* (Baltimore, 1976); Kenneth B. Perkins, "Volunteer Fire Departments: Community Integration, Autonomy and Survival," *Human Organization* 46(4) (1987): 345.

74. Dana, *The Fireman*, 16.

75. Letter from Machine, Sacramento, October 9, 1855, in the *Fireman's Journal*, October 13, 1855 (emphasis in the original).

76. Baltimore *Sun*, November 20, 1851; *Alta California*, May 6, 1862; May 5, 1863. On "the bone and sinew of the city," see the *Missouri Democrat*, May 4, 1842. Robyn Cooper argues that the fireman remained the "supreme model of manhood" in turn-of-the-century Britain and America; see Cooper, "The Fireman: Immaculate Manhood," *Journal of Popular Culture* 24(4) (Spring 1995): 138–170.

77. Wilentz, *Chants Democratic*, 53–60, 258–261; Elliot Gorn, " 'Good-Bye Boys, I Die a True American': Homicide, Nativism, and Working-Class Culture in Antebellum New York City," *Journal of American History* 74(2) (1987): 408. For a subtle reading of class and the appeal of firefighting among artisans, see Ric Northrup Caric, "Blustering Brags, Dueling Inventors, and Corn-Square Geniuses: Processes of Recognition among Philadelphia Artisans, 1785–1825," *American Journal of Semiotics*, forthcoming.

78. Wilentz, *Chants Democratic*, 96.

79. Amy Bridges, *A City in the Republic: Antebellum New York and the Origins of Machine Politics* (Cambridge, U.K.: 1984), 76.

80. Of course, the semiskilled and unskilled members would be less likely to appear in the city directories, so the company may have had more members from these catagories. Independent Fire Company statistics based on 30 of 61 members in 1814, 43 of 88 members in 1838, and 40 of 109 members in 1856 locatable in city directories. Independent Fire Company list of 1814, MdHS MS 354, in the Federal Fire Company records (misnamed). Independent Fire Company membership rosters of 1838 and 1856 from the Peale Museum Collection. Names cross-referenced in James Lakin, *The Baltimore Directory and Register, for 1814–1815* (Baltimore, 1814); Richard Matchett, *Matchett's Baltimore Director* [sic] (Baltimore, 1837 and 1855). For my classification scale, see the appendix.

81. Statistics based on 36 of 74 members locatable in the1814 city directory and 69 of 163 members locatable in the 1858 city directory, or 1860 census. New Market rosters of 1814 and 1857, from the Peale Museum Collection, no contributing members included. The 1814 list cross-referenced with the *Baltimore Directory and Register, for 1814–1815* (Baltimore, 1814); 1857 names cross-referenced in Boyd, *Baltimore City Directory*, 1858, Jackson, *Baltimore, Md., 1860 Census Index,* and the 1860 census returns for Baltimore. For my classification scale, see the appendix.

82. Membership list in Franklin Fire Company minutes, 1856; St. Louis Firemen's Association minutes in the MoHS Volunteer Firemen Collection. Class analysis of firemen is admittedly difficult. Records are incomplete, many men on rolls did not fight fires regularly, some wealthy men joined companies in order to be relieved of jury duty, and many members, especially unskilled laborers, do not appear in the census. But when large portions of locatable firemen were not working class by any stretch of the imagination, it seems impossible to maintain that these were working-class organizations.

83. Mark C. Carnes, "Middle-Class Men and the Solace of Fraternal Ritual," in *Meanings for Manhood*, edited by Mark C. Carnes and Clyde Griffen (Chicago, 1990), 48; Doyle, "The Social Functions of Voluntary Associations," 347.

84. Jon Kingsdale, "'The Poor-Man's Club': Social Functions of the Urban Saloon, Working Class," *American Quarterly* 25 (October 1973): 472–489. On the crisis in masculinity in general during this period, see Paul E. Johnson and Sean Wilentz, *The Kingdom of Matthias* (New York, 1994).

85. Adler, *Yankee Merchants*, 64, 47.

86. *Fireman's Journal*, August 23, 1856.

87. Ibid., November 10, 1855; April 19, July 14, December 13, 27, 1856; *Alta California*, December 12, 1853.

88. *Fireman's Journal*, June 6, 9, 1855.

89. See, as examples, Tocqueville, *Democracy in America*, 455–470; Frances Trollope, *Domestic Manners of the Americans* (New York, 1948), 99; Michel Chevalier, *Society, Manners, and Politics in the United States* (Boston, 1839), 433.

90. Cmiel, *Democratic Eloquence*, 90–93.

91. Baltimore *Sun*, November 20, 1851.

92. Letter from "Twenty Years Active," *California Spirit of the Times and Fireman's Journal*, February 8, 1862; *Fireman's Journal*, July 5, 1856.

93. Lillie Hitchcock Coit, the famous "firebelle" of the Knickerbocker Company of San Francisco, was made an official member of the company in the 1860s after years of

running to fires with the company as a "mascot"; Missouri Fire Company No. 5 minutes, September 1, 1853; vol. 8, MoHS Volunteer Firemen Collection.

94. Nancy Cott, *The Bonds of Womanhood: 'Woman's Sphere' in New England, 1780–1835* (New Haven, 1977); Ryan, *Cradle of the Middle Class*; Merish, "'The Hand of Refined Taste' in the Frontier Landscape," 485–523.

95. *Fireman's Journal*, October 13, 1855 (emphasis in the original).

96. Missouri Fire Company No. 5, July 1, September 9, 1858; *Missouri Democrat*, November 27, 1855.

97. *Fireman's Journal*, April 5, December 22, 1855 (emphasis in the original).

98. Letter from Ben Adhem, Sacramento, *California Spirit of the Times and Fireman's Journal*, February 12, 1859.

99. Herbert Asbury, *Ye Olde Fire Laddies* (New York, 1930), 140.

100. *California Spirit of the Times and Fireman's Journal*, August 29, 1859.

101. Baltimore *Sun*, November 20, 1851; *California Spirit of the Times and Fireman's Journal*, October 29, 1859.

102. Mary Ryan, *Women in Public: Between Banners and Ballots, 1820–1880* (Baltimore, 1990), 28.

103. *California Spirit of the Times and Fireman's Journal*, September 17, 1859; March 15, 1862; Edwards, *History of the Volunteer Fire Department of St. Louis*, 81.

104. Edwards, *History of the Volunteer Fire Department of St. Louis*, 90–91.

105. Stellman, *Sam Brannan*, 160–163.

106. Tom Lynch, "St. Louis: The Volunteer Fire Department, 1832–1858," *National Fireman's Journal*, July 27, 1878.

107. Reprinted from a "Boston paper" in the *Fireman's Journal*, June 9, 1855.

108. *Fireman's Journal*, October 27, 1855. See also Asbury, *Ye Olde Fire Laddies*, 164; *California Spirit of the Times and Fireman's Journal*, February 8, 1862.

109. *Evening Bulletin*, May 27, 1858.

110. Ryan, *Women in Public*, 27; Halttunen, *Confidence Men and Painted Women*, 38.

111. Rotundo, *American Manhood*, 178; Leverenz, *Manhood and the American Renaissance*, 137.

112. *Alta California*, March 12, 1854; Franklin Fire Company minutes, 1856.

113. Alexander Bonner Latta and E. Latta, *The Origin and Introduction of the Steam Fire Engine Together with the Results of the Use of Them in Cincinnati, St. Louis and Louisville, For One Year, also, Showing the Effect on Insurance Companies, etc.* (Cincinnati, 1860), 24.

114. John T. Scharf, *History of St. Louis City and County* (Philadelphia, 1883), vol. 1, 795–796.

115. Tom Lynch, "St. Louis: The Volunteer Fire Department, 1832-1858," *National Fireman's Journal*, August 3, 1878.

116. On parenting of boys, see Rotundo, *American Manhood*, 46–53; Blumin, *Emergence of the Middle Class*, 179–191; Ryan, *Cradle of the Middle Class*, 161.

117. Holloway, *Chief Engineer's Register*, 100. On the increasing power of middle-class women in reform movements in the antebellum period, see Ginzberg, *Women and the Work of Benevolence*, 11–35.

118. Kett, *Rites of Passage*, 5; Theodore Dwight, *The Father's Book* (Springfield,

Mass., 1834); Catherine Beecher and Harriet Beecher Stowe, *American Woman's Home* (Hartford, 1991), 300; Rotundo, *American Manhood*, 26–30.

119. Beecher, *American Woman's Home*, 285. On women and child rearing, see Linda Kerber, *Women of the Republic: Intellect and Ideology in Revolutionary America* (Chapel Hill, 1980), 189–231; Ryan, *Cradle of the Middle Class*, chap. 4; Jan Lewis, "Mother's Love: The Construction of an Emotion in Nineteenth-Century America," in *Social History and Issues in Human Consciousness: Some Interdisciplinary Connections*, edited by Andrew E. Barnes and Peter N. Stearns (New York, 1989); Ruth H. Bloch, "American Feminine Ideals in Transition: The Rise of the Moral Mother, 1785–1815," *Feminist Studies* 4 (1978).

120. Beecher, *American Woman's Home*, 300; Kett, *Rites of Passage*, 31.

121. A final irony: after the disbanding of the volunteer departments, the old engines became obsolete. Many ended up in veteran firefighter organizations or were sold to small towns. Some of the finest decorative panels, however, were removed from the engines. Herbert Asbury relates that "it became the custom to present them to expectant fathers, who made them into cradles." Perhaps only at this point did the chaste lady of the firehouse give way to the mother of the boy. Asbury, *Ye Olde Fire Laddies*, 142–143.

Chapter Three
Fights/Fires

1. Benjamin A. Baker, *A Glance at New York . . . As Performed at the Principal English and American Theaters* (New York, 1857), 17.

2. Boss Tweed, a slightly less fictional New Yorker, is more famous.

3. Dorson, "Mose the Far-Famed and World-Renowned," 288–289; Reynolds, *Walt Whitman's America*, 103–104.

4. Dorson, "Mose the Far-Famed and World-Renowned," 290–291.

5. Baker, *A Glance at New York*, 31.

6. Ibid., 9, 24.

7. British attempts to "fireproof" their theaters in the eighteenth century included installing a "fire screen" in the Drury Lane Theater. Elaborate stage displays contributed to the flammability of these buildings. David Hartley, *Proposals for the Security of Spectators in Any Public Theater against Fire* (London, 1792); Sally Holloway, *London's Noble Fire Brigades* (London, 1973), 12; C. V. Blackstone, *A History of the British Fire Service* (London, 1957), 87; David Grimsted, *Melodrama Unveiled: American Theater and Culture, 1800–1850* (Berkeley, 1987), 79; Robert Vole, "When Men Were Men and Firemen," *American History Illustrated* 17(3) (1982): 33–35.

8. Baker, *A Glance at New York*, 19. The choice of casting a volunteer fireman in this role was partially based on "precedents of plays with urban or fireman themes," according to Dorson, "Mose the Far-Famed and World-Renowned," 288.

9. Mose's only unrespectful observer seems to be David Grimsted, who argues in *Melodrama Unveiled* (p. 194) that "all low-comedy stereotypes were presented on stage with some condescension as well as much affection. Yet the groups condescended to were apparently those who most enjoyed the low-comedy characters. The New York toughs made a hero of Mose." He credits this seeming contradiction to the "amorphousness of American life." More likely, Mose's viewers were unaware of the condescension noted by Grimsted.

10. Hazen and Hazen, *Keepers of the Flame*, 147–149; Dorson, "Mose the Far-Famed and World-Renowned," 290–291.

11. Dale T. Knobel, "A Vocabulary of Ethnic Perception: Content Analysis of the American Stage Irishman, 1820–1860," *Journal of American Studies* (Great Britain) 15(1) (1981): 52; Dorson, "Mose the Far-Famed and World-Renowned," 288. The real Mose was a printer, not a butcher like the Mose character.

12. Dorson, "Mose the Far-Famed and World-Renowned," 295. The wariness of the Louisville audience about this hero of "humble life" reflects the class divisions which David Grimsted argues were beginning to make themselves felt in the theater in the 1850s. In *The Fireman's Daughter*, an 1852 melodrama with a fireman (not Mose) as hero, good and evil are more clearly class markers than in earlier melodrama. The fireman hero is "low-class, low-comedy," according to Grimsted, and the villain is an aristocrat. "What was being created was a theater that aimed only at the lower classes." Grimsted, *Melodrama Unveiled*, 193.

13. Latta and Latta, *The Origin and Introduction of the Steam Fire Engine*, 15.

14. Lynch, *Volunteer Fire Department*, 12.

15. David Grimsted, "Rioting in Its Jacksonian Setting," *American Historical Review* 77 (April 1972): 365.

16. Laurie, *Working People of Philadelphia*, 58–61, 151–156; Neilly, "The Violent Volunteers," chap. 9; Wilentz, *Chants Democratic*, 258–263. In his recent book *Rioting in America*, Paul Gilje upholds Laurie's vision and suggests that Philadelphia was far from exceptional. "In city after city fire companies ambushed each other and often set fires to attract their opponents." Paul A. Gilje, *Rioting in America* (Bloomington, Ind., 1996), 68–69. See also Paul A. Gilje, *The Road to Mobocracy: Popular Disorder in New York City, 1763–1834* (Chapel Hill, N.C., 1987), 260–264.

17. Of 427 firemen belonging to four fire companies in 1857–1859, I was able to locate 219 in either the city directory of 1858 or in the 1860 census. This sample could be biased in any number of ways: these four fire companies might not be representative of the entire department, and the firemen who showed up in the city directory or the census might be higher-status firemen than those who did not show up. These statistics (like all statistics used in this book) are thus meant to be suggestive rather than conclusive. Firemen drawn from McCreary, *Ancient and Honorable Mechanical Company of Baltimore;* Mechanical Company membership list of 1858, no honorary members included; Pioneer Hook and Ladder Company membership list of 1859, from the Peale Museum Collection, no contributing or honorary members included; New Market roster of 1857, from the Peale Museum Collection, no contributing members included; Deptford Company membership roster of 1858, from the Peale Museum Collection, no contributing members included. Names cross-referenced in Jackson, *Baltimore, Md., 1860 Census Index*, and the 1860 census returns for Baltimore.

18. Forrest, *Official History*, 13; Holloway, *Chief Engineer's Register*, 3.

19. Mechanical Fire Company volume of quarterly meetings, December 7, 1813, in Union Fire Company records, August 3, 1824, vol. 3, MdHS, Manuscripts Division.

20. Albert Dukehart, "Baltimore Reminiscences," *New York Fireman's Journal* 1 (1877): 69; Union Fire Company records, February 10, 1832.

21. Forrest, *Official History*, 67; Baltimore *Sun*, January 16, 1838.

22. Mechanical Fire Company records, December 11, 1834; Union Fire Company records, January 9, 1835.

23. Mechanical Fire Company records, September 15, 1839.

24. Records of the Volunteer Fire Department Standing Committee, 1837, MdHS, Manuscripts Division.

25. Mechanical Company records, August 15, 1840.

26. Ibid., 1834–1840.

27. Ibid., 1837.

28. Mechanical Fire Company ledgers, August 22, 1840.

29. Grimsted, "Rioting in Its Jacksonian Setting," 374; Michael Feldberg, *The Turbulent Era: Riot and Disorder in Jacksonian America* (New York, 1980), 71–72; Cassedy, *Firemen's Record*, 30–31.

30. Baltimore *Sun*, January 20, 1838. On the potent image of the confidence man in middle-class culture, see Halttunen, *Confidence Men and Painted Women*.

31. Mechanical Fire Company ledgers, August 18, 1844.

32. Ibid., August 9, 1841; Jean Baker, *Ambivalent Americans: The Know-Nothing Party in Maryland* (Baltimore, 1977), 121–122.

33. Baltimore *Sun*, July 21, 1843; March 19, April 1, 1844.

34. Mechanical Fire Company ledgers, April 8, 1844; Baltimore American, April 9, 1844.

35. Mechanical Fire Company ledgers, April 13, 1845.

36. Ibid., September 2, 20, 1847.

37. Baltimore *Sun*, September 11, 1847.

38. Ibid., October 28, 1847.

39. Mechanical Fire Company ledgers, December 2, 1847.

40. Ibid., October 22, 1847; Independent Fire Company ledger, September 27, December 10, 1847; Forrest, *Official History*, 77.

41. Baltimore *Sun*, September 23, 1847.

42. Mechanical Fire Company ledgers, November 3, 1840.

43. Feldberg, *The Turbulent Era*, 55–83. Other major "expressive" riots in Baltimore in 1834 included an earlier "first" Bank of Maryland riot in March 1834, and a Whig-Democratic political riot in April of the same year, neither of which involved the fire department. Carl E. Prince, "The Great 'Riot Year': Jacksonian Democracy and Patterns of Violence in 1834," *Journal of the Early Republic* 5(1) (1985): 1–19.

44. Scharf mentions one, between rowdies and the Baltimore *Clipper* in 1848, after the result of the election for sheriff had been ascertained; see *The Chronicles of Baltimore: Being a Complete History of "Baltimore Town" and Baltimore City from the Earliest Period to the Present Time* (Baltimore, 1874), 528.

45. Based on an examination of riot reports in the Baltimore *Sun* from 1834 to 1858.

46. Baltimore *Sun*, February 6, 1849.

47. Ibid., February 12, 1849.

48. Forrest, *Official History*, 67. In 1845 the police cost the city $70,238; in 1850, $110,102; and in 1855 they cost $232,629. Gary Larson Browne, *Baltimore in the Nation* (Chapel Hill, N.C., 1980), 156, 203, 210. On uniforms, see "The Re-Organization of the Police and Night Watch," Baltimore *Sun*, November 29, 1856. The nineteenth-century expansion of police and their duties has been well documented by historians. See Lane, *Policing the City*; Eric Monkkonen, "From Cop History to Social History: The Significance of the Police in American History," *Journal of Social History* 15(4) (1982): 575–591.

49. Baker, *Ambivalent Americans*, 133. Baker points out that the Know-Nothing police stood by passively at election riots.

50. Independent Fire Company ledgers, 1850–1855.

51. Baltimore *Sun*, August 20, 1855.

52. Ibid., September 9, 1856; Cassedy, *Firemen's Record*, 43–45; Scharf, *Chronicles of Baltimore*, 570–571; Baker, *Ambivalent Americans*, 129.

53. Forrest, *Official History*, 78. That, as Forrest claims, "the elections year after year became less and less free from intimidation and terror" cannot be attributed to the firemen.

54. Three excellent studies of Southern honor are Edward L. Ayers, *Vengeance and Justice: Crime and Punishment in the Nineteenth Century American South* (New York, 1984); Kenneth S. Greenberg, *Honor and Slavery: Lies, Duels, Noses, Masks, Dressing as a Woman, Gifts, Strangers, Humanitarianism, Death, Slave Rebellions, the Proslavery Argument, Baseball, Hunting, and Gambling in the Old South* (Princeton, N.J., 1996); Bertram Wyatt-Brown, *Southern Honor: Ethics and Behavior in the Old South* (New York, 1982).

55. Dana, *The Fireman*, 179; Adler, *Yankee Merchants and the Making of the Urban West*, 101–102; Missouri Fire Company records, July 29, 1849, vol. 10, Volunteer Firemen Collection, MoHS. A large number of volunteer firemen in St. Louis had Irish surnames, although it is impossible to say whether these members participated in the riot.

56. Union Fire Company records, May 30, 1845, ibid., vol. 14; Missouri Fire Company records, March 5, 1848.

57. Phoenix Fire Company records, February 10, March 10, 1845; March 9, 1846; March 1, 1848; volume 11; Lynch, *Volunteer Fire Department*, 40.

58. Franklin Fire Company minutes, September 5, 1850, vol. 2, MoHS.

59. Phoenix Fire Company records, January 13, 1845; Laclede Fire Company records, March 11, 1850; both in MoHS.

60. Missouri Fire Company records, March 4, 1852.

61. Ibid., November 16, 1846; March 5, 1848.

62. Ibid., November 18, 1850.

63. Union Fire Company minutes, June 26, 1850.

64. Missouri Fire Company records, October 11, 1856; Franklin Company records, October 11, 1856.

65. Franklin Fire Company records, July 17, 1851; September 26, 1854.

66. St. Louis Firemen's Association minutes, May 8, 21, 23, 1855.

67. Edwards, *History of the Volunteer Fire Department of St. Louis*, 73.

68. Lynch, *Volunteer Fire Department*, 78.

69. Edwards, *History of the Volunteer Fire Department of St. Louis*, 73.

70. *Missouri Democrat*, July 19, 1854.

71. Missouri Fire Company, June 25, 1855; January 3, 18, 1856; Laclede Fire Company Minutes, May 12, 1851.

72. *Mayor's Message*, May 14, 1855.

73. Arlen R. Dykstra, "Rowdyism and Rivalism in the St. Louis Fire Department, 1850–1857," *Missouri Historical Review* 69(1) (1974–1975): 58.

74. On the insecurity of St. Louis transplants, see Adler, *Yankee Merchants and the Making of the Urban West*, 103–109. Christian quote from George Winfred Hervey, *Principles of Courtesy: With Hints and Observations on Manners and Habits* (New York,

1852), 63, quoted in Kasson, *Rudeness and Civility*, 157. Of course, sectional pressures did more harm to the decorum of St. Louis than the firemen ever could, but the firemen made an easy target.

75. Richard L. Bushman, *The Refinement of America: Persons, Houses, Cities* (New York, 1992), 353–401.

76. On women in the streets, see Ryan, *Women in Public*, 64–88; Abelson, *When Ladies Go A-Thieving*, 13–22; Kasson, *Rudeness and Civility*, 128–146. For an excellent discussion of women and the uses of benevolence, see Ginzberg, *Women and the Work of Benevolence*.

77. Augustine E. Costello, *Our Police Protectors: A History of the New York City Police* (Montclair, N.J., 1885), 116, 216, quoted in Ryan, *Women in Public*, 69.

78. Firemen's Association minutes, July 3, 1855.

79. St. Louis Firemen's Fund, *History of the St. Louis Fire Department* (St. Louis, 1914), 168.

80. *Missouri Democrat*, February 21, 1858; Edwards, *History of the Volunteer Fire Department of St. Louis*, 277–279.

81. Edwards, *History of the Volunteer Fire Department of St. Louis*, 73.

82. Scharf, *History of St. Louis*, 796.

83. Lynch, *Volunteer Fire Department*, 91. I was unable to find any account of a riot in 1853 in either the *Missouri Democrat* or the *Missouri Republican*. Edward Edwards believes this riot to be a conflation of the riot of 1849 and some other minor dog-related event, resulting from the general disturbances of the period. Edwards, *History of the Volunteer Fire Department of St. Louis*, 70–71.

84. Lynch, *Volunteer Fire Department of St. Louis*, 11.

85. Ibid., 13; Scharf, *History of St. Louis*, 797; Dorson, "Mose the Far-Famed and World-Renowned," 289.

86. Lynch, *Volunteer Fire Department of St. Louis*, 12.

87. *Fireman's Journal*, August 4, 1855.

88. Statistics on the San Francisco Volunteer Fire Department drawn from a voting roster for the 1860 department election. Of the 859 members of the department entitled to vote, 427 were locatable in either the 1860 census or the 1860 city directory.

89. Ibid.

90. *California Spirit of the Times and Fireman's Journal*, July 21, 1860.

91. Ibid.; Robert S. Lammot, March 2, 1851, in Lammot Family Correspondence, Bancroft Library.

92. *Fireman's Journal*, January 9, February 16, July 12, 1856.

93. Ibid., August 30, September 27, 1856.

94. *San Francisco Bulletin*, September 22, 23, October 2, 1856; *Fireman's Journal*, October 18, 1856.

95. *Fireman's Journal*, August 4, 1855 (emphasis in the original); August 11, 1855; April 19, 1856. Uncooperative crowds were a problem in almost every North American city. One exception was Halifax, where a strong military presence at every fire helped maintain order and assist with firefighting efforts. B.E.S. Rudachyk, "'At the Mercy of the Devouring Element': The Equipment and Organization of the Halifax Fire Establishment, 1830–1850," *Collections of the Royal Nova Scotia Historical Society* 41 (1982): 165–184. In other Canadian cities this was not the case; see Weaver and DeLottinville, "The Conflagration and the City," 427.

96. *Fireman's Journal*, May 26, June 2, 9, 1855. The assailant, hackman John Farrell, was arrested and convicted several weeks later of "imposing on a blind man who had engaged Farrell to drive him to the Franklin House"; June 23, 1855.

97. Ibid., June 9, 1855.

98. Ibid.

99. *Evening Bulletin*, December 8, 9, 1857; May 11, 1858.

100. Ibid., December 8, 1857.

101. Ibid., December 8, 10, 12, 1858.

102. Ibid., May 18, 1858; Dolores Waldorf, "Baltimore Fire Laddie: George Hossefross," *California Historical Society Quarterly* 23 (1944): 69.

103. *Alta California*, August 29, November 23, 1860; *California Spirit of the Times and Fireman's Journal*, September 1, 1860.

104. *Alta California*, November 23, 1860.

105. *California Spirit of the Times and Fireman's Journal*, May 11, 1867.

106. Dorson, "Mose the Far-Famed and World-Renowned," 289.

107. Bowlen, "Firefighters of the Past," 65–66.

108. *Fireman's Journal*, March 15, 1856; *California Spirit of the Times and Fireman's Journal*, January 11, February 15, 1862.

109. *Evening Bulletin*, May 18, 1857.

110. James Boyd Jones, Jr., "Mose the Bowery B'hoy and the Nashville Volunteer Fire Department," *Tennessee Historical Quarterly* 40 (Summer 1981): 174.

111. *California Spirit of the Times and Fireman's Journal*, May 25, 1861.

112. Dorson, "Mose the Far-Famed and World-Renowned," 297; Henry A. Murray, *Lands of the Slave and the Free* (London, 1857), 354–355.

113. Holloway, *Chief Engineer's Register*, 108.

114. Baker, *A Glance at New York*, 32.

Chapter Four
Smoke-Filled Rooms

1. *Letters of Pliny the Council* (Edinburgh, 1807), 2:263, reprinted in the Baltimore *Sun*, August 17, 1849.

2. Philip Hone MS Diary, May 6, 1836, quoted in Stephen F. Ginsberg, "Above the Law: Volunteer Firemen in New York City, 1836–1837," *New York History* 50(2) (1969): 165; Park, *The Cincinnati Equitable Insurance Company*, 96; Firemen in Chicago reportedly engaged in bloc voting to elect mayors in the 1840s. Bushnell, "Chicago's Rowdy Firefighters," 232–241.

3. Pendleton, *Exempt Firemen*, 18.

4. Lyons, *Fire in America!*, 46. For "colorful" accounts of volunteer firefighting that stress famous firefighter membership, see Earnest, *Volunteer Fire Company*; Ditzel, *Fire Engines, Fire Fighters*; Hazen and Hazen, *Keepers of the Flame*.

5. Warner, *Private City*, 93. For other examples of this view, see Katznelson, *City Trenches*, 51; Anderson, "The Development of Municipal Fire Departments in the United States," 336, 343–344; Holzman, *Romance of Firefighting*, 16.

6. William E. Gienapp, "'Politics Seem to Enter into Everything': Political Culture in the North, 1840–1860." In *Essays on American Antebellum Politics, 1840–1860*, edited by Stephen E. Maizlish and John J. Kushma (College Station, Tex., 1982), 43. "Between

1830 and 1860 the number of federal employees increased 3.2 times, whereas the population grew 2.4 times. Inclusion of state government workers would make the difference look more striking"; Louis Hartz, *Economic Policy and Democratic Thought: Pennsylvania, 1776–1860* (Chicago, 1968), 177–178, 314, quoted in Bridges, *A City in the Republic*, 6. Also see Ronald G. Walters, *American Reformers, 1815–1860* (New York, 1978), 6–9, and on political ambivalence among another preeminent association, see Bullock, *Revolutionary Brotherhood*, 225–228.

In stating that firemen felt ambivalent toward party politics I do not mean to suggest that they, or most other Jacksonian Americans, were "detached" from popular politics, as Glenn C. Altschuler and Stuart Blumin have recently argued. Altschuler and Blumin, " 'Where Is the Real America?': Politics and Popular Consciousness in the Antebellum Era," *American Quarterly* 49(2) (1977): 225–267.

7. *Fireman's Journal*, November 3, 1855; October 11, 1856.

8. Knickerbocker Engine Co. No. 5, *Constitution and By-laws of the Knickerbocker Engine Co. Number 5 of San Francisco*, adopted October 17, 1850, revised April 10, 1856 (San Francisco, 1856), article 4, sec. 11; Phoenix Fire Company minutes, 1843–1849; November 10, 17, 1845, MoHS Volunteer Firemen Collection; Edwards, *History of the Volunteer Fire Department of St. Louis*, 123.

9. William Carr Lane was an organizer and member of the second fire company in the city. He held office for seven years in the 1820s, three years in the 1830s, served in the U.S. House of Representatives, and was the governor of New Mexico under President Fillmore (who had been a member of the Eagle Hose Company of Buffalo, New York). He was never defeated in a race for office. Ronald L. Davis, "Community and Conflict in Pioneer Saint Louis, Missouri," *The Western Historical Quarterly* 10 (July 1979): 334–338; Richard C. Wade, *The Urban Frontier: Pioneer Life in Early Pittsburgh, Cincinnati, Lexington, Louisville, and St. Louis* (Cambridge, Mass., 1959), 270–290; Edwards, *History of the Volunteer Fire Department of St. Louis*, 250–251.

10. Although there were two fire engines "with properly organized companies" by 1821, every dwelling and store was still required to keep a fire bucket for self-protection. Firefighting was still the responsibility of the whole community. John Paxton in *The Early Histories of St. Louis*, edited by John Francis McDermott (St. Louis, 1952), 70.

11. Wade, *Urban Frontier*, 277.

12. Edwards, *History of the Volunteer Fire Department of St. Louis*, 27–28.

13. Ibid., 126, 134, 253.

14. Maximilian Reichard, "Urban Politics in Jacksonian St. Louis: Traditional Values in Change and Conflict," *Missouri Historical Review* 70 (April 1976): 258–262; Edwards, *History of the Volunteer Fire Department of St. Louis*, 254.

15. Reichard, "Urban Politics," 263–266; Edwards, *History of the Volunteer Fire Department of St. Louis*, 126–145, 254.

16. Reichard, "Urban Politics," 265.

17. Ibid., 269; John Vollmer Mering, *The Whig Party in Missouri* (Columbia, Mo., 1967), 71–85.

18. Mering, *Whig Party*, 71–85; Edwards, *History of the Volunteer Fire Department of St. Louis*, 111, 241–256.

19. Mering, *Whig Party*, 71–85.

20. With the exception of 1846, when the Native American Party controlled both the City Council and mayor's office. Mering, *Whig Party*, 79.

21. Bridges, *City in the Republic*, 74–75.

22. Ibid., 72-77. Bridges's claim, after a subtle analysis of patrician participation in the companies up until 1845, that "the gang, the militia company, and even the fire company were largely organizations of the working classes," is one of the mysteries that led me to this project.

23. James Neal Primm, *Lion of the Valley* (Boulder, 1981), 123.

24. *Missouri Argus*, April 24, May 8, 1840; Mering, *Whig Party*, 83–85; Lynch, *Volunteer Fire Department*, 100–101; Edwards, *History of the Volunteer Fire Department of St. Louis*, 241–258; Arthur M. Schlesinger, Jr., *The Age of Jackson* (Boston, 1945), 269–305. Bridges agrees that wealthy men in New York were represented in both parties; Bridges, *City in the Republic*, 62–63.

25. Scharf, *History of St. Louis*, vol. 1, 675-677; Edwards, *History of the Volunteer Fire Department of St. Louis*, 111.

26. *Missouri Republican*, April 8, 1845; Edwards, *History of the Volunteer Fire Department of St. Louis*, 31, 252; Mering, *Whig Party*, 76–82.

27. Tom Lynch, quoted in the *National Fireman's Journal* (New York), vol. 2, August 3, 1878.

28. Holt, "Volunteer Fire Fighting," 7, 11; Edwards, *History of the Volunteer Fire Department of St. Louis*, 43; Dykstra, "Rowdyism and Rivalism in the St. Louis Fire Department, 1850–1857," 62.

29. Union Fire Company minutes, May 6, 1840; June 21, August 14, 1845; July 8, December 19, 1846; December 8, 1851; MoHS Volunteer Firemen Collection.

30. Edwards, *History of the Volunteer Fire Department of St. Louis*, 43; Holt, "Volunteer Fire Fighting," 11.

31. William E. Gienapp *The Origins of the Republican Party, 1852–1856* (New York, 1987), 92–101; Michael F. Holt, *Political Crisis of the 1850's* (New York, 1978); *Missouri Democrat* quoted in John C. Schneider, "Riot and Reaction in St. Louis, 1854–1856," *Missouri Historical Review* 68 (January 1974): 172; Mering, *Whig Party*, 79–81.

32. Gienapp, *Origins of the Republican Party*, 92–101; Michael F. Holt, "The Politics of Impatience: The Origins of Know-Nothingism," *Journal of American History* 60 (1973): 309–331; Edwards, *History of the Volunteer Fire Department of St. Louis*, 71, 126–194; Missouri Fire Company minutes, January 8, May 7, 1857, MoHS Volunteer Firemen Collection.

33. Schneider, "Riot," 171–185; *Missouri Republican*, August 9, 10, 1854; *Missouri Democrat*, August 9, 1854; Edwards, *History of the Volunteer Fire Department of St. Louis*, 72.

34. Edwards, *History of the Volunteer Fire Department of St. Louis*, 72, 221–222; *Missouri Democrat*, August 9, 1854; Schneider, "Riot," 178–179.

35. St. Louis Firemen's Association minutes, May 31, 1849–March 14, 1859, MoHS Volunteer Firemen Collection; Dana, *The Fireman*, 176–178; Edwards, *History of the Volunteer Fire Department of St. Louis*, 75.

36. *Daily Missouri Republican*, March 27, 1850; St. Louis Firemen's Association minutes, March 26, 1850.

37. *Missouri Republican*, May 19, 1850; March 3, 1851; St. Louis Firemen's Association minutes, May 23, 1850.

38. Firemen's Association minutes, July 2, 10, 1850.

39. Ibid., January 28, February 7, 24, 1851.

40. St. Louis Fireman's Fund, *History of the St. Louis Fire Department*, 154; Edwards, *History of the Volunteer Fire Department of St. Louis*, 75–77.

41. Edwards, *History of the Volunteer Fire Department of St. Louis*, 76–77, St. Louis Fireman's Fund, *History of the Volunteer Fire Department of St. Louis*, 168.

42. Saint Louis Firemen's Association minutes, July 3, 1855; St. Louis Fireman's Fund, *History of the Volunteer Fire Department of St. Louis*, 168; Bridges, *City in the Republic*, 30–35.

43. St. Louis Fireman's Fund, *History of the Volunteer Fire Department of St. Louis*, 168; Saint Louis Firemen's Association minutes, April 13, 29, 1857. St. Louis's near total economic collapse in 1856 probably helped spur reform impulses. See Adler, *Yankee Merchants and the Making of the Urban West*, 138.

44. William Hyde, "Recollections of St. Louis," in the *Globe Democrat*, January 24, 1892.

45. Edwards, *History of the Volunteer Fire Department of St. Louis*, 42–43; Holt, "Volunteer Fire Fighting," 11.

46. In 1863 a bill to replace the volunteers with a paid department was presented in Sacramento, where it was tabled but not forgotten. The firemen of San Francisco attempted to work out a compromise with a bill preserving some aspects of their organization while handing virtually all control of the department over to the Board of Supervisors. They had little support in the legislature, however, and a paid department was instituted in 1866.

47. The 1856 Hawes, or Consolidation, Act created an extremely powerful, twelve-member elected Board of Supervisors in San Francisco. This board was in charge of allocating all of the city's revenue into its expenditure funds, and then disbursing the funds. This included allocating and distributing the General Fund, or "common services" fund, the source of support for the fire department. This put the expenses of the fire department directly under the control of the supervisors. When the Board of Supervisors came under control of the People's Party, it cut department funding by two-thirds. Terrence J. McDonald, *The Parameters of Urban Fiscal Policy: Socioeconomic Change and Political Culture in San Francisco, 1860–1906* (Berkeley, 1986), 20-22; Lotchin, *San Francisco 1846–1856*, 138.

48. *Evening Bulletin*, March 3, 1857; *Alta California*, February 23, 1857.

49. *Fireman's Journal*, November 29, 1856.

50. McDonald, *Parameters*, 128. For a lengthy discussion of politics and the San Francisco Volunteer Fire Department, see Greenberg, "Cause for Alarm," 88–128.

51. Five firemen were elected on the Democratic ticket to positions in the city government in 1854, including the city treasurer, William McKibbin. In the 1855 elections, seven firemen ran on both the Democratic and Whig tickets. *Fireman's Journal*, June 2, September 1, 1855.

52. *Evening Bulletin*, May 14, 1858.

53. *California Spirit of the Times and Fireman's Journal*, March 27, 1860.

54. Ibid., March 12, 1859. Considering San Francisco's over 50 percent mobility rate in this period, most people would have had more than a reading acquaintance with firemen of other cities. See Waldorf, "Baltimore Fire Laddie," 69.

55. Two examples of the least reputable firemen who were also politicians in San Francisco follow. Charles P. Duane, former head of the department, was exiled in 1856 by the Vigilance Committee. "Dutch Charlie," as he was known, was a hoodlum of the

first order. He was born in Ireland, ran with the machine (fire engine, not political) in New York, held the office of chief engineer in San Francisco from 1853 to 1854, and was later foreman of the Empire Engine Company. In the meantime he excelled at firefighting and athletics. He was frequently cited for bravery at the scene of fires, and once broke the arm of a man who turned in a false alarm.

Duane also invested in shady real estate deals and hurt people. In the words of Kevin Mullen, "his life can be traced by his frequent outbursts of physical violence." Among his more notable exploits: choking and stomping a policeman who foolishly attempted to cite Duane for shooting a dog; shooting an actor in the back at a ball, after the actor accidentally stepped on Duane's foot while dancing; joining with a police officer in the beating of a prisoner in the basement of the jail cell; and assaulting a jury member who had voted to convict him for one of his earlier exploits.

David Scannell also brought negative attention to the San Francisco firemen, even while he was sheriff of San Francisco. Scannell, who was also foreman of a fire company, was once called the "Saul among the prophets of Firemen." A known gambler with a shady past, his election to sheriff in 1855 was greeted with suspicion. While in office he was accused of graft, keeping a gambling den, and of general impudence. Both Duane and Scannell were a source of continuing bad press for the department. Kevin J. Mullen, *Let Justice Be Done: Crime and Politics in Early San Francisco* (Reno, 1989), 199–201, 292; *Alta California*, December 19, 1850; Pendleton, *Exempt Firemen*, 11; *Evening Bulletin*, May 10, 1858; *Herald*, April 29, 1853; *Fireman's Journal*, November 24, 1855.

56. Colson, "The Fire Company Library Associations of Baltimore," 162–163.

57. Starting in 1807, annual allocations were made to each company that submitted vouchers to the mayor for the amount of its expenditures. Extra appropriations were often made to those companies which fell into debt building their engine houses and buying apparatus. When the department was reorganized in 1834 to provide for a representative overseeing committee, the right of appropriation was transferred to the new departmental Standing Committee. The mayor no longer had the power to grant funds to companies. Forrest, *Official History*, 23, 38, 43; records of the Volunteer Fire Department Standing Committee, 1835–1853, MdHs Manuscripts Division.

58. Union Fire Company records, vol. 3, January 31, 1842, MdHs, Manuscripts Division.

59. Baker, *Ambivalent Americans*, 121–122; letter from Baltimore in the *Fireman's Journal*, March 7, 1857; Forrest, *Official History*, 49–50.

60. Although the United and New Market companies were both supporters of the Democratic Party and were willing to unite against the Whigs after Tippecanoe's election, their political allegiances did not prevent them from battling each other on at least three occasions that same year. Either company allegiances to a party were not particularly significant to Baltimore's firemen, or firemen simply enjoyed physical fights too much to resist battling even their allies. In Philadelphia, by contrast, riotous firemen proved amenable to compromise with other similarly aligned fire companies. Common political sympathies formed the basis for a lasting peace between two violent companies in Southwark, while political differences provoked only "uncompromising hostility." Mechanical Fire Company, July 29, 30, August 2, 1840. Philadelphia comparison in Laurie, "Fire Companies and Gangs in Southwark: The 1840's," 79.

61. Browne, *Baltimore in the Nation*, 157, 199.

62. Urban residents in Baltimore and the rest of the nation increasingly expressed

dissatisfaction with both the Democratic and Whig parties in the early 1850s. A perceived absence of party ideology, the growing sectional struggle, and local controversies over education and temperance left Maryland's two-party system vulnerable to attack. The election of the first Know-Nothing mayor and twenty-two Know-Nothing City Council members in 1854 was accomplished through a complex and secret party organization that drew upon popular hostility toward immigration, Catholicism, crime, and the labor stance of the Democratic Party. Baker, *Ambivalent Americans*, 108–151; Douglas Bowers, "Ideology and Political Parties in Maryland, 1851–1856," *Maryland Historical Magazine* 64 (Fall 1969): 197–217.

63. Baker, *Ambivalent Americans*, 128–133; Holloway, *Chief Engineer's Register*, 32–33.

64. *National Fireman's Journal*, vol. 2, April 27, 1878.

Chapter five
Insuring Protection

1. *Fireman's Journal*, May 17, 1856.

2. John S. Law letter, February 1, 1857, in Latta and Latta, *Origin and Introduction of the Steam Fire Engine*, 33.

3. *Alta California*, January 5, 1862; *Report on the Fire Departments of Cincinnati and St. Louis, and the Use of Steam Fire Engines. By Order of the Fire Underwriters of St. Louis* (St. Louis, 1858); *Report of the Special Committee of the Baltimore United Fire Department in Reference to the Funds of Said Department* (Baltimore, 1859); "Report of the Chief Engineer of the Fire Department of St. Louis, to the City Council at their meeting, March 11, 1859," in Latta and Latta, *Origin and Introduction of the Steam Fire Engine*, 18–19.

4. Holloway, *Chief Engineer's Register*, 36.

5. Boston was actually the first to pay its firemen. As early as 1837 the city offered firemen small fees for each fire they put out. Firemen in Boston were not put on salary until the 1850s. Geoffrey Gigierano, "'A Creature of Law:' Cincinnati's Paid Fire Department," *Cincinnati Historical Society Bulletin* 40(2) (1982): 80; John H. White, Jr., "Origins of the Steam Fire Engine," *Technology and Culture* 14(2, part 1) (1973): 166–169; King, *History of the American Steam Fire-Engine*, 13–18.

6. Chief engineer of the Cincinnati Fire Department, quoted in Latta and Latta, *Origin and Introduction of the Steam Fire Engine*, 11; Holloway, *Chief Engineer's Register*, 14.

7. Daniel Defoe described the seventeenth-century firemen in his *Tour through Great Britain* in 1724: "The several insurance offices . . . have each of them a certain sett of men, who they keep in constant pay, and who they furnish with tools proper for the work. . . . These men make it their business to be ready at call, all hours, and night or day, to assist in case of fire; and it must be acknowledged, they are very dexterous, bold, diligent and successful. These they call fire-men, but with an odd kind of contradiction in the title, for they are really most of them water-men." Quoted in Blackstone, *A History of the British Fire Service*. On steam engine development, see Gilbert, *Fire Engines and Other Firefighting Appliances*; Goudsblom, *Fire and Civilization*, 151; Lyons, *Fire in America!*, 9; King, *History of the American Steam Fire-Engine*, 1–3. For most of the eighteenth century, London fire insurance companies funded fire companies. In 1866 the United

Fire Brigade was turned over to London, because the level of protection provided by the insurance companies was insufficient for a city the size of London. Insurance companies continued to contribute to the upkeep of a municipal fire brigade until 1925. Anderson, "The Development of Municipal Fire Departments in the United States," 332–335; Blackstone, *A History of the British Fire Service*, 65–77; Holloway, *London's Noble Fire Brigades*, 18.

8. Ralph Waldo Emerson, *Selected Essays*, edited by Larzer Ziff (New York, 1982). On the rise of the expert system, see Anthony Giddens, *The Consequences of Modernity* (Stanford, Calif., 1990). On the rise of expertise in society, see Bledstein, *The Culture of Professionalism*.

9. Charles Clisby, "Experiencing Fires," in *Fires and Human Behavior*, edited by David Canter (New York, 1980), 325. On the rise of property interests in the 1850s, see Einhorn, *Property Rules*; Carl Smith, *Urban Disorder and the Shape of Belief*, 13; Ginzberg, *Women and the Work of Benevolence*, 174–213.

10. Holloway, *Chief Engineer's Register*, 109–110.

11. Edward Pollock, "Tribute to the Firemen," in the *Fireman's Journal*, September 13, 1856.

12. Holloway, *Chief Engineer's Register*, 108.

13. *California Spirit of the Times and Fireman's Journal*, April 27, 1867.

14. Carl Smith's metaphor for this transformation in Chicago in the later nineteenth century is "fireproofing." In order for Chicago to be made safe from fire, the city needed to be ordered and controlled. "Rebuilding a city that was 'fireproof' would require a wide range of regulation that would extend well beyond more stringent building codes and a better fire department. Any measures that hoped to be effective would have to be based on preserving and protecting a carefully structured social order." Smith, *Urban Disorder and the Shape of Belief*, 63. On the move from volunteerism to order see Smith, ibid., 13; Bledstein, *Culture of Professionalism*, 31–32; Daniel Walker Howe, "Victorian Culture in America," in *Victorian America*, edited by Daniel Howe (Philadelphia, 1976), 18; Blumin, *The Emergence of the Middle Class*, 66–107.

15. Pyne, *Fire in America*, 459; Goudsblom, *Fire and Civilization*, 151.

16. Hazen and Hazen, *Keepers of the Flame*, 132–133.

17. Lynch, *Volunteer Fire Department*, 11; *Missouri Republican*, April 27, 1842; *Alta California*, January 28, 1865. The Scannell presentation was protested by the *Alta California* because Scannell allowed "dangerous" wooden buildings to be constructed by members of his company. Had the insurance agents seen these buildings, a "fireman" wrote to the *Alta*, "Mr. Scannell would surely not have met with the approval of the Insurance Companies by endorsing his official acts, and praying him to accept, as a token of their high regard, that beautiful cane." Letter from "A Fireman," *Alta California*, 1863, in the Wells Fargo Archives.

18. Letter from "An Insurance Agent" to the *Fireman's Journal*, February 9, 1856.

19. "Stimulated by higher and more certain compensation, competition among the fire brigades waxed hot, soon reaching a stage of bloody noses"; quoted in the Insurance Company of North America Collection, *American Fire Marks* (Philadelphia, 1933), 9, and later without attribution by Lyons, *Fire in America*, 25.

20. "Baltimore Equitable Society: Historical Information," distributed by the Baltimore Equitable Society, Baltimore; Holloway, *Chief Engineer's Register*, 120–121.

21. Lynch, *Volunteer Fire Department*, 9, 63; Edwards, *History of the Volunteer Fire*

Department of St. Louis, 217–219; Holt, "Volunteer Fire Fighting in St. Louis, 1818–1859," 9.

22. *Fireman's Journal*, March 28, May 17, 1857.

23. Letter from the chairman of the Association of Insurance Agents to the Chief Engineer's Office, *Fireman's Journal*, May 31, 1856.

24. *Fireman's Journal*, September 22, 1855; February 1, 21, March 28, 1857.

25. Sacramento *State Journal*, February 4, 1857.

26. Letter from "Citizen" to the *Fireman's Journal*, December 24, 1859.

27. *Fireman's Journal*, December 24, 1859; March 3, 1860.

28. Ibid., February 2, 1861 (emphasis in the original).

29. *Alta California*, January 23, 1866. The Board of Supervisors proved willing to shut down two engine houses in 1857, according to James Baumohl, because they were "frightened by the threats of insurance companies to raise premiums or cancel policies due to the department's disarray." Baumohl, "Dashaways and Doctors," 85.

30. *Report of the Fire Departments of Cincinnati and St. Louis*, 1858.

31. Ibid.

32. "A Libel upon the Fire Department," *California Spirit of the Times and Fireman's Journal*, January 26, 1867.

33. Insurance companies were probably guilty of even worse crimes against the fire department. The British traveler Frederick Marryat listed in his four-point tabulation of the principal causes of fires in New York in the 1830's, "4th. Conflagrations of houses not insured, effected by agents employed by the *fire insurance companies*, as a punishment to some and a warning to others, who have neglected to take out policies." Marryat, *A Diary in America*, 38, quoted in Hazen and Hazen, *Keepers of the Flame*, 99–100.

34. By the 1850s, home and business fire insurance had become commonplace in all three of these cities. Not only did numbers of insurance companies increase during this decade, as did the amount of aggregate capital represented in individual companies, but notices of fires in the Baltimore *Sun*, St. Louis *Missouri Republican* or *Missouri Democrat*, and San Francisco *Alta California* or *Evening Bulletin* suggest that at least half of all burned buildings were insured in the 1850s. Generally this point was highlighted in the coverage, naming the company that insured the burned building and the amount for which the building was insured. Based on an examination of reports of fires and advertisements for insurance companies in the *Fireman's Journal*, in Holloway, *Chief Engineer's Register*, as well as the named papers.

35. "Report on the Fire Departments of Cincinnati and St. Louis, and the use of Steam Fire Engines, by order of the Fire Underwriters of St. Louis," quoted in Latta and Latta, *Origin and Introduction of the Steam Fire Engine*, 22.

36. *Fireman's Journal*, April 7, 1855 (emphasis in the original).

37. Arendt, *The Human Condition*, 41.

38. Boruck might have had better luck if he had stuck with a transcendental spring, like that in Emerson's "Over-Soul." Ralph Waldo Emerson, "The Over-Soul," in the *Selected Essays*, 205–224.

39. The aesthetic of the technological sublime, according to John Kassen, "excited ideas of pain and danger." John Kasson, *Civilizing the Machine: Technology and Republican Values in America, 1776–1900* (New York, 1976), 166; Leo Marx, in *The Machine in the Garden: Technology and the Pastoral Ideal in America* (New York, 1964), offers an excellent critique of the ambivalent figure of the machine in nineteenth-century America.

40. King, *History of the American Steam Fire-Engine*, 1–5; White, "Origins of the Steam Fire Engine," 166–167; Earnest, *Volunteer Fire Company*, 108. According to Earnest (p. 109), Braithwaite's engine was a great success when tested in London against hand pumps in 1830, but steamers were not accepted in London until 1858 due to the opposition of fire chiefs in that city. "Opposition came from the retained (U.S. 'on-call') men who received free beer and a few shillings for pumping. They often worked the brakes to the chant of 'Beer-oh, Beer-oh,' and if the supply were slow in coming would simply quit work. Anxious to preserve their pay and their beer, the mob would sometimes cut the hoses of steamers."

41. Shawk is a mysterious character. He was a leading Cincinnati mechanic, like Latta and Miles Greenwood, and became Latta's competitor in steam engine production in the mid-1850s. It is not clear what role he played in the development of Latta's early engines. Although Latta quickly claimed for himself the honor of inventing the "first successful machine," Shawk probably deserves some of the credit. White, "Origins of the Steam Fire Engine," 166–167; King, *History of the American Steam Fire-Engine*, 19.

42. King, *History of the American Steam Fire-Engine*, 16.

43. Alexander Latta letter excerpted in the *Fireman's Journal*, June 9, 1855. The *Journal* responded: "As far as usefulness in case of a great fire is concerned, the stable spoken of is the best place for the steam engine, and the only days she ought to come out are exhibition days and the fourth of July"; Earnest, *Volunteer Fire Company*, 74, 108–109.

44. King, *History of the American Steam Fire-Engine*, 16.

45. Geo. P. Little, *The Fireman's Own Book* (Boston, 1860), 113–114.

46. *California Spirit of the Times and Fireman's Journal*, March 3, 1860; *Missouri Democrat*, January 11, 1858; Baltimore *Sun*, July 11, 1849; *New York Fireman's Journal* 3 (1879): 137.

47. Baltimore *Sun*, April 20, 1849; *Alta California*, April 6, 1854; *California Spirit of the Times and Fireman's Journal*, March 3, 24, April 28, 1860; March 15, 1862.

48. The Fire Annihilator got off to a good start. It won a prize at London's Grand Exhibition in 1851, and received a good review in the *Quarterly Review*. Blackstone, *A History of the British Fire Service*, 144; Baltimore *Sun*, September 6, 1851; Hazen and Hazen, *Keepers of the Flame*, 110.

49. *Alta California*, February 11, 1852.

50. Ibid.

51. Speech by Frank Pixley, in the *Firemen's Procession, on the Second Anniversary of the Organization of the Fire Department of San Francisco, February 22d, 1853*, 10; Blackstone, *A History of the British Fire Service*, 144.

52. Speech by Frank Pixley, in the *Firemen's Procession*, 10.

53. *Alta California*, April 26, 1866.

54. William F. Channing, "The American Fire-Alarm Telegraph," *Ninth Annual Report of the Smithsonian Institution*, March 1855, 147–155; Jon C. Teaford, *The Unheralded Triumph: City Government in America, 1870–1900* (Baltimore, 1984), 242.

55. *Alta California*, January 2, 1865; Joel Tarr, Thomas Finholt, and David Goodman, "The City and the Telegraph: Urban Telecommunications in the Pre-Telephone Era," *Journal of Urban History* 14(1): 38–62. On centralization in the city, see Einhorn, *Property Rules*, 144–187.

56. John F. Kennard and Co., *The American Fire Alarm and Police Telegraph* (Boston, 1864), 9; *New York Fireman's Journal* 2 (1878): 175.

57. Joel Tarr, Thomas Finholt, and David Goodman have argued that volunteer firemen opposed technology in general, and the fire alarm specifically, but this is based on evidence from the turn of the century. In these three cities that is clearly not the case; Tarr et al., "The City and the Telegraph," 60–61; Saint Louis Firemen's Association minutes, July 1, 17, 1856; St. Louis Fireman's Fund, *History of the St. Louis Fire Department*, 173; *Alta California*, November 14, 1863.

58. *Alta California*, November 4, 1863; April 14, 1864; January 2, May 31, 1865; Pioneer Hook and Ladder Company records, June 3, 1858, MdHS, Manuscripts Division; Tarr et al., "The City and the Telegraph," 53. The same ordinance which reorganized the Baltimore Fire Department in 1858 insured the future erection of the telegraph; Baltimore *Sun*, October 25, 1858.

59. Park, *The Cincinnati Equitable Insurance Company*, 97–98.

60. Geo. C. Davis, quoted in Latta and Latta, *Origin and Introduction of the Steam Fire Engine*, 39.

61. Roper, *Handbook of Modern Steam Fire Engines* (Philadelphia, 1876); William C. Lewis, *A Manual for Volunteer or Paid Fire Organizations* (New York, 1872.)

62. Unfortunately there were few such men in America's paid departments as late as 1896, a misfortune attributed by William King to "political influence"; King, *History of the American Steam Fire-Engine*, ix–x.

63. "Professions" as we know them today came into being in the mid-nineteenth century, according to Bledstein. Professional firefighting fit perfectly into this culture. "The culture of professionalism required amateurs to trust in the integrity of trained persons, to respect the moral authority of those whose claim to power lay in the sphere of the sacred and charismatic"; Bledstein, *Culture of Professionalism*, 90.

64. Letter from John S. Law to Latta, 1857, quoted in Latta and Latta, *Origin and Introduction of the Steam Fire Engine*, 33.

65. Park, *The Cincinnati Equitable Insurance Company*, 105.

66. Pioneer Hook and Ladder Collection, March 4, 1858, MdHS, Manuscripts Division; Mechanical Fire Company Records, June 11, September 14, 1858, in ibid.

67. Lynch, *Volunteer Fire Department*, 22; Edwards, *History of the Volunteer Fire Department of St. Louis*, 98–99; St. Louis Fireman's Fund, *History of the St. Louis Fire Department*, 168.

68. *California Spirit of the Times and Fireman's Journal*, February 18, 1860.

69. *Fireman's Journal*, April 21, 1855.

70. *Evening Bulletin*, December 17, 1857; *Fireman's Journal*, April 21, August 11, 1855; *California Spirit of the Times and Fireman's Journal*, April 9, June 11, 25, 1859.

71. *Alta California*, January 10, 1860; *California Spirit of the Times and Fireman's Journal*, January 14, 1860.

72. *California Spirit of the Times and Fireman's Journal*, February 4, 18, 1860.

73. Ibid., March 10, 1860 (emphasis in the original).

74. *Fireman's Friend* article, in *California Spirit of the Times and Fireman's Journal*, June 9, 1860.

75. Scharf, *Chronicles of Baltimore*, 563.

76. King, *History of the American Steam Fire-Engine*, 1–20; Baltimore *Sun*, October 9, 27, November 2, 3, 5, December 14, 19, 1858; Cassedy, *The Firemen's Record*, 49.

77. Baltimore *Sun*, December 19, 1858.

78. Ibid., October 25, November 5, 1858.

79. *Alta California*, July 12, 28, 29, August 31, 1860; *Evening Bulletin* quoted in *Alta California*, July 29, 1858.

80. *Alta California*, September 18, 29, 1860; *California Spirit of the Times and Fireman's Journal*, March 26, 1861.

81. *California Spirit of the Times and Fireman's Journal*, March 26, 1861.

82. Ibid., July 21, December 28, 1861; March 1, 1862.

83. *Evening Bulletin*, February 2, 1863.

84. Ibid., February 19, 1863.

85. Geo. Graham letter, March 17, 1857, in Latta and Latta, *The Origin and Introduction of the Steam Fire Engine*, 44.

86. Report of the Sacramento State Assembly in the *Alta California*, January 23, 1866; "Mayor's Message," Baltimore *Sun*, November 17, 1858.

87. Carl Smith has documented this transition well. Leadership in Chicago switched in the late nineteenth century to the business and professional elite, men who were "modernizers as well as moralizers." These men were more concerned with maintaining a stable workforce than saving the souls of the poor, and they believed in expertise and efficiency. Carl Smith, *Urban Disorder and the Shape of Belief*, 66–69. Also see Kathleen D. McCarthy, *Noblesse Oblige: Charity and Cultural Philanthropy in Chicago, 1849–1929* (Chicago, 1982), 53–72; Ginzberg, *Women and the Work of Benevolence*, 174–213; Leverenz, *Manhood and the American Renaissance*, 137; Bledstein, *Culture of Professionalism*. For a more general view of the fall of public culture in nineteenth-century America, see Richard Sennett, *The Fall of Public Man* (New York, 1978).

88. Alfred D. Chandler, Jr., *The Visible Hand: The Managerial Revolution in American Business* (Cambridge: Mass., 1977), 15–78, 281–283; Robert H. Wiebe, *The Search for Order, 1877–1920* (New York, 1967), 111–127; Paul Starr, *The Social Transformation of American Medicine* (New York, 1982); Blumin, *The Emergence of the Middle Class*, 78–83; Bledstein, *Culture of Professionalism*.

89. Holloway, *Chief Engineer's Register*, 96.

90. Circular distributed by Josiah Quincy to the citizens of Boston, July 4, 1825, quoted in Brayley, *A Complete History of the Boston Fire Department from 1630–1888*, 154–155.

91. *Evening Bulletin*, February 19, 1863; *Alta California*, January 5, 1862.

92. *Alta California*, February 9, 1866.

93. King, *Origins and Introduction of the Steam Fire-Engine*, 6, 19, 29.

94. St. Louis Fireman's Fund, *History of the St. Louis Fire Department*, 171–173.

95. Roper, *Handbook of Modern Steam Fire-Engines*, 94.

96. Holloway, *Chief Engineer's Register*, 12–20, 26–27. Indeed, one historian sees the municipalization of the department as the natural conclusion to the development of a "public order" in Baltimore started by the Democrats and Whigs in the 1840s. Browne, *Baltimore in the Nation*, 110–111.

97. Letter from "Future City," *National Fireman's Journal* (New York), vol. 3 (1879), 6.

98. As an example, see Norman W. Wheeler, *Report of Norman W. Wheeler, Engineer, upon Steam Fire Engines, Fire Extinguishers, etc.* (New York, 1876).

99. Teaford, *Unheralded Triumph*, 198–202; William G. Jordan, *One Hundred Years of Fire Insurance, the Aetna Insurance Company, 1819–1919* (Hartford, 1919), 60; Robert W. D'Ambry, *Pioneers in Protection: The Story of a Century of Fire Insurance Service* (York, Pa., 1953), 23–30.

100. Although destructive fires did decrease in the nineteenth century throughout the world. Frost and Jones, "The Fire Gap and the Greater Durability of Nineteenth-Century Cities," 333–347.

101. Clifford Thomson, ed., *The Fireman's Journal: The Fire Departments of the United States. A series of tables showing the fire equipment of the various cities, towns and villages, altogether with their water supply and other Facilities for extinguishing fires* (New York, 1879), 3–4.

102. Charles Clisby, a senior member of the London Fire Brigade, argued strongly in 1980 that the involvement of "people who have not experienced fires" in fire planning, and especially in "fireproofing" buildings, has resulted in unnecessary casualties. The struggle between the firemen and outside authorities (now more likely to be scientists than insurance agents) has continued to the modern day. "Experiencing fire counts," maintains this fireman. "The firemen should not be blinded with science, nor should his straightforward approach to fire problems be disregarded as unqualified." Clisby, "Experiencing Fires," 323–332.

103. Boruck and the *Spirit of the Times and Underwriter's Journal* were later implicated in the Central Pacific Railway Company federal investigation of 1887. Boruck apparently accepted huge "advertising payments" and was made a commissioner of the railway company by Governor Stanford in return for the editorial support of the paper for the railroad. *Testimony taken by The United States Pacific Railway Commission, appointed Under the Act of Congress Approved March 3, 1887, Entitled "An Act Authorizing an Investigation of the Books, Accounts, and Methods of Railroads Which Have Received Aid From the United States, and For Other Purposes."* Senate Ex. Doc. 51, part 7, vol. 6 (Washington, D.C., 1887), 3421–3429.

Chapter Six
Deluged and Disgraced

1. Capt. W. Barlow, "Burial of the Volunteer Department," a paper delivered before the St. Louis Veteran Volunteer Firemen's Historical Society, June 19, 1890. Quoted in Edwards, *History of the Volunteer Fire Department of St. Louis*, 277.

2. Lynch, *Volunteer Fire Department*, 13.

3. Brayley, *Complete History of the Boston Fire Department*, 112.

4. St. Louis Fireman's Fund, *History of the St. Louis Fire Department*, 170; Lynch, *Volunteer Fire Department*, 13; Murray, *Unheralded Heroes*, 7; *Evening Bulletin*, January 13, 1868; Pendleton, *Exempt Firemen*, 27–28.

5. *Fireman's Journal*, February 9, 1856.

6. Ibid., December 30, 1854, reprinted in Pendleton, *Exempt Firemen*, 49.

7. Ibid., 50.

8. *Alta California*, January 10, 1860; *California Spirit of the Times and Fireman's Journal*, January 14, 1860.

9. Lynch, *Volunteer Fire Department*, 111.

10. Josiah Boyce, "Collecting Volunteer Relics," read to the Veteran Volunteer Firemen's Historical Society, 1890, quoted in Edwards, *History of the Volunteer Fire Department of St. Louis*, 286. Many countries had volunteer firefighting forces in the nineteenth century, some of which offered a model on which the constitutions of American volunteer fire companies were based; Young, *Fires, Fire Engines and Fire Brigades*, 468–489.

Hubert Lussier's work points to some interesting similarities between the function and social significance of French volunteer companies and their American counterparts; Hubert Lussier, *Les Sapeurs-Pomiers au XIXe siècle: Associations volontaires en milieu populaire* (Paris, 1987).

11. Hessians were German mercenaries in the American Revolution. During the Civil War, Confederates used the word as a term of obloquy against Union soldiers.

12. St. Louis Fireman's Fund, *History of the St. Louis Fire Department*, 171; *California Spirit of the Times and Fireman's Journal*, February 23, 1867.

13. Weaver and DeLottinville, "The Conflagration and the City," 428; Holloway, *Chief Engineer's Register*, 75.

14. Letter from Machine, Sacramento, October 9, 1855, *Fireman's Journal*, October 13, 1855.

15. Murray, *Unheralded Heroes*, 4.

16. St. Louis Fireman's Fund, *History of the St. Louis Fire Department*, 171.

17. Lynch, *Volunteer Fire Department*, 112.

18. Edwards, *History of the Volunteer Fire Department of St. Louis*, 278.

19. Letter from John Klumker to the Silsby Manufacturing Company, Silsby Manufacturing Company, *History of the Silsby Steam Fire Engine* (Buffalo, 1881), 133.

20. *Alta California*, January 31, 1865; Lynch, *Volunteer Fire Department*, 12.

21. New Orleans correspondent to the *Fireman's Journal*, January 5, 1856.

22. Mechanical Fire Company register of alarms and fires, 1846–1865, February 22, 1859, MdHS, Manuscripts Division.

23. Ibid., May 5, 1859.

24. *The Constitution and By-Laws of the Board of Relief of the Baltimore United Fire Department* (Baltimore, 1865); Proceedings of the Relief Board of the Baltimore United Fire Department, August 25, 1871, Enoch Pratt Free Library, Baltimore Manuscripts Collection.

25. *Report of the Special Committee of the Baltimore United Fire Department in Reference to the Funds of Said Department* (Baltimore, 1859) (emphasis in the original).

26. Edwards, *History of the Volunteer Fire Department of St. Louis*, 233–238, 282–287; Veteran Firemen's Association of the City of New York, *Souvenir of the Transcontinental Excursion from New York to San Francisco, September 1887* (New York, 1887); *California Spirit of the Times and Fireman's Journal*, February 23, 1867; Pendleton, *Exempt Firemen*, 4, 20–21. For a period in the 1890s, San Francisco provided a total sum of $12,000 a year to the aged volunteers.

27. Edwards, *History of the Volunteer Fire Department of St. Louis*, 282–287.

28. Young, *Fires, Fire Engines, Fire Brigades*, 485 (emphasis in the original).

29. Letter from "Insurance" to the *National Fireman's Journal* 2 (1878): 399; Silsby Manufacturing Company, *History of the Silsby Steam Fire Engine*, 137.

30. The paid department was far from the desired moral environment hoped for in San Francisco. The *Evening Bulletin* opposed allowing clerks to work for the new fire department because to do so would mean "removing young men of ability out of the business of life and training them for bummers." Full-time firemen in San Francisco made forty dollars a month, extra or call-men made twenty. *Evening Bulletin*, January 13, 1867; Forrest, *Official History*, 108; Lewis, *A Manual for Volunteer or Paid Fire Organizations*, 40.

31. "Chief Whitney's Annual Report," printed in the *California Spirit of the Times and Fireman's Journal*, October 19, 1867; Forrest, *Official History*, 108.

32. "Chief Whitney's Annual Report," *California Spirit of the Times and Fireman's Journal*, October 19, 1867.

33. For three somewhat different views on the impact of this transformation, see Paul Johnson, *A Shopkeeper's Millennium*, 38–61; Daniel T. Rodgers, *The Work Ethic in Industrial America, 1850–1920* (Chicago, 1979), 65–124; Ross, *Workers on the Edge*, 94–140.

34. Paid department composition computed in Baumohl, "Dashaways and Doctors," 166; Lynch, *Volunteer Fire Department*, 13.

35. Seven paid firemen, of 37 firemen locatable in the census, were foreign born (four in Ireland). This is not a large sample of the 129 paid firemen. While this works out to 19 percent foreign born, I believe that the paid department was far more consistently native born than this statistic would indicate. While studying the census returns for Baltimore, I twice happened upon firehouses where all firemen identified themselves as born in Maryland. Statistics on class are drawn from both the census returns and the city directory of 1858 and constitute a much larger sample: 78 of 129 firemen. Paid department membership list in Holloway, *Chief Engineer's Register*, 71–74. List cross-referenced with William H. Boyd, *Baltimore City Directory*, 1858; Jackson, *Baltimore, Md., 1860 Census Index*, and the 1860 census returns for Baltimore.

36. When the Cincinnati department raised salaries in 1873 and prohibited the paid firemen from holding other jobs, many firemen quit for their more lucrative occupations. Gigiernano, "'A Creature of Law,'" 80; Anderson, "The Development of Municipal Fire Departments in the United States," 349.

37. Letter from "Gray Shirt" to the *New York Fireman's Journal* 2 (1878): 357; letter from "Insurance" to the *National Fireman's Journal* 2 (1878): 399; Robert Dickson et al., *An Impending Crisis; San Francisco's Danger by Reason of Being Unprepared to Cope with an Ordinary Conflagration* (San Francisco, 1889); Forrest, *Official History*, 110–111.

38. *Report upon the National Convention of Chief Engineers of Fire Departments, Held in Baltimore, in October 1873* (Providence, 1874), 5; Dickson et al., *An Impending Crisis, 4; Evening Bulletin*, April 5, 1871; Forrest, *Official History*, 106.

39. Lewis, *A Manual for Volunteer or Paid Fire Organizations*, 40.

40. McDonald, *Parameters of Urban Fiscal Policy*, 143 ff.

41. Browne, *Baltimore in the Nation*, 210–211; Holloway, *Chief Engineer's Register*, 9–10; Forrest, *Official History*, 104; Murray, *Unheralded Heroes*, 10; *National Fireman's Journal* 3 (1878): 170.

42. Cassedy, *Fireman's Record*, 49; *California Spirit of the Times and Fireman's Journal*, October 19, 1867; correspondent for a London daily paper, quoted in Young, *Fires, Fire Engines, and Fire Brigades*, 486.

43. That professional firefighters distanced the public from their actions fits the pattern of human interaction in expert systems outlined by Anthony Giddens in *The Consequences of Modernity* (pp. 85–86). Trust can only be maintained if the public is kept from the "backstage."

44. Even Marcus Boruck came to call the paid department of San Francisco "Our Pet." *California Spirit of the Times and Fireman's Journal*, June 1, 1867.

45. Baltimore *Clipper*, July 6, 1859.

46. Edwards, *History of the Volunteer Fire Department of St. Louis*, 100.

47. Incendiary fires in San Francisco did $477,000 of damage in the first seven months of 1867; *Evening Bulletin*, January 13, 1868.

48. Frost and Jones, "The Fire Gap," 341; *Alta California*, February 9, 1866; Latta and Latta, *Origin and Introduction of the Steam Fire Engine*, 19; *California Spirit of the Times and Fireman's Journal*, February 23, 1867; Forrest, *Official History*, 100; Cassedy, *Firemen's Record*, 67; Teaford, *Unheralded Triumph*, 243–245.

49. *Missouri Republican*, September 15, 1859.

Conclusion
One Last Eulogy

1. Perkins, "Volunteer Fire Departments: Community Integration, Autonomy and Survival," 342–348; Anderson, "The Development of Municipal Fire Departments in the United States," 359. Reading's Volunteer Fire Department, formed in 1773, is the oldest active volunteer fire department in the United States; Federal Writer's Project, *Reading's Volunteer Fire Department: Its History and Traditions* (Philadelphia: William Penn Association, 1938), 1–4.

2. Quote in Katznelson, *City Trenches*, 18

3. *California Spirit of the Times and Fireman's Journal*, January 14, 1860.

4. Michel Foucault, *Discipline and Punish: The Birth of the Prison* (New York, 1979), 26–27.

BIBLIOGRAPHY

SPECIAL COLLECTIONS

Bancroft Library, University of California at Berkeley

Bancroft Scraps, San Francisco Fire Department Volunteers, 1850–1860
Bowlen, Frederick J. "Firefighters of the Past: A History of the Old Volunteer Fire Department of San Francisco from 1849–1866" (unpublished manuscript)
"By-Laws of the St. Francis, Lafayette, Volunteer, Knickerbocker, Young America Companies, Laws of the Fire Department, 1858; German Mutual Fire Insurance Company By-Laws"
"Complementary Dinner Given by the Howard Engine Company #3"
"Constitution et Reglement Interieur de la Compagnie," Lafayette Fire Company, 1854
"Constitution and By-Laws of the St. Francis Ladder Company," 1856, 1857
"Exempt Fire Company By-Laws"
"Howard Engine Company #3, Constitution and By-Laws," 1857
"Laws of the Fire Department of San Francisco," 1858, 1863
"Notice to Form a Fire Company," 1849
Pamphlet boxes on materials on fire and fire prevention
"San Francisco Constitution and By-Laws," Young America Engine Company #13, 1856
"San Francisco Empire Engine Company #1, Code of Laws," 1850
Weed, Samuel Richards. "My Early Experiences and Recollections of the Great Fires and First Fire Department in San Francisco." Paper presented at the Annual Meeting of the Pacific Coast Underwriters' Association, San Francisco, January 14, 1908

Enoch Pratt Free Library, Baltimore

"Constitution and By-Laws of the Patapsco Fire Company of Baltimore," 1824
Proceedings of the Relief Board of the Baltimore United Fire Department
Recordbook of the Washington Hose Company of Baltimore

Maryland Historical Society (MdHS)

MS. 101 Baltimore United Fire Company, 1834–1865
MS. 354 Federal Fire Company, 1799–1822
MS. 358 Unidentified Fire Company Book
MS. 373 Friendship Fire Company, 1798–1822
MS. 478 Independent Fire Company, 1823–1853
MS. 584 Mechanical Fire Company, 1769–1789, 1804–1860
MS. 662 Pioneer Hook and Ladder, 1851–1863
MS. 856 Union Fire Company, 1782–1865
MS. 2488 Ancient and Honorable Mechanical Company, 1837–1979
Fire Insurance Company Records

Missouri Historical Society (MoHS)

D. N. Burgoyne Papers
St. Louis Volunteer Firemen Collection

The Peale Museum, Baltimore:
Baltimore Volunteer Fire Company Membership Rosters

Deptford Fire Company, 1858
Howard Fire Company, 1854
Independent Fire Company, 1838, 1856
Liberty Fire Company, 1852
Mechanical Fire Company, 1834
New Market Fire Company, 1814, 1848, 1857
Patapsco Fire Company, 1849
Pioneer Fire Company, 1859
Vigilant Fire Company, 1811

Wells Fargo Archives, San Francisco

Newspaper clippings

NEWSPAPERS

Baltimore *American*
Baltimore *Sun*
California Spirit of the Times and Fireman's Journal, San Francisco
California Spirit of the Times and Underwriters Journal, San Francisco
Daily Alta California, San Francisco
Fireman's Almanac 1860–1861, New York
Fireman's Journal, San Francisco
Missouri Democrat
Missouri Republican
National Fireman's Journal, New York, 1877–1886
The *Pickwickian*, New York, 1856
Sacramento *State Journal*
San Francisco *Evening Bulletin*

WEB SITES

Inter-University Consortium for Political and Social Research. Study 00003: Historical Demographic, Economic and Social Data: U.S., 1790–1970 (Ann Arbor: ICPSR): http://icg.fas.harvard.edu/cgi-bin/brown/newCensus.pl

PUBLISHED PRIMARY SOURCES

Baker, Benjamin A. *A Glance at New York: A Local Drama in Two Acts*. New York: S. French, 1857.

Beecher, Catherine. *Treatise on Domestic Economy for the Use of Young Ladies at Home and at School*. Boston: T. H. Webb and Co., 1843.

Beecher, Catherine, and Harriet Beecher Stowe. *American Woman's Home*. Hartford: Stowe Day Foundation, 1869; reprinted 1991.

Boyd, William H. *The Baltimore City Directory*. Baltimore: Richard Edwards and William H. Boyd, Publishers, 1858.

Chevalier, Michel. *Society, Manners, and Politics in the United States*. Boston: Weeks, Jordan and Co., 1839.

The Constitution and By-Laws of the Board of Relief of the Baltimore United Fire Department. Baltimore, 1865.

The Constitution and By-Laws of the Fire Department of the City of New York; to which are added The Act of Incorporation, and the Laws of the Corporation and State Relating to Fires. New York: Vanderpool and Cole, 1826.

Dana, David D. *The Fireman: The Fire Departments of the United States, With a Full Account of All Large Fires, Statistics of Losses and Expenses, Theaters Destroyed by Fire, and Accidents, Anecdotes, and Incidents*. Boston: James French and Company, 1858.

Dickson, Robert, Chas. A. Laton, et al. *An Impending Crisis; San Francisco's Danger by Reason of Being Unprepared to Cope with an Ordinary Conflagration*. San Francisco: Underwriters' Fire Patrol, 1889.

Downing, Andrew Jackson. *The Architecture of Country Houses*. New York: D. Appleton, 1850.

Dwight, Theodore. *The Father's Book*. Springfield, Mass.: G and C Merriam, 1834.

Emerson, Ralph Waldo. *Selected Essays*. Ed. Larzer Ziff. New York: Penguin Classics, 1982.

"Fires in Our City—the Annihilator." *Scientific American* 9(19): 1854.

Gilbert, Louis N. *The Centennial History of the Eagle Fire Company of New York, 1806–1906*. New York, 1906.

Hall, John B. *The Fireman's Own Book: Containing Accounts of Fires Throughout the United States, As Well as Other Countries; Remarkable Escapes From the Devouring Element; Heroic Conduct of Firemen in Cases of Danger; Means of Extinguishing Fires; Accounts of Firemen Who Have Lost Their Lives While on Duty; Together with Facts, Incidents and Suggestions, Interesting and Valuable to Firemen and Citizens Generally*. New York, Philadelphia, Boston, 1850.

Hartley, David. *Proposals for the Security of Spectators in Any Public Theater Against Fire*. London, 1792.

Hesiod. *Theogony*. Baltimore: Johns Hopkins University Press, 1983.

Holloway, Charles T., ed. *The Chief Engineer's Register and Insurance Advertiser, containing a Full Account of the Organization of the Baltimore City Fire Department, also The Laws of the State of Maryland and the Ordinances of the City of Baltimore etc*. Baltimore: Steam Press, 1860.

Johnson, Samuel D. *The Fireman. A Drama, in Three Acts*. Boston: William V. Spencer, 1856.

Kennard, John F., and Co. *The American Fire Alarm and Police Telegraph*. Boston, 1864.

Lakin, James. *The Baltimore Directory and Register, for 1814–1815*. Baltimore: J. C. Reilly, 1814.

Latta, Alexander Bonner, and E. Latta, *The Origin and Introduction of the Steam Fire Engine Together with the Results of the Use of Them in Cincinnati, St. Louis and Louisville, For One Year, also, Showing the Effect on Insurance Companies, etc*. Cincinnati: Moore, Wilstach, Keys and Co, 1860.

Little, Geo. P. *The Fireman's Own Book*. Boston: Dillingham and Bragg, 1860.

Matchett, Richard. *Matchett's Baltimore Director*. Baltimore: Director's Office, 1837 and 1855.

Murray, Henry A. *Lands of the Slave and the Free, or, Cuba, the United States, and Canada*. London, 1857.

An Ordinance to Establish a Fire Department . . . Published by Order of the Common Council, November 23, 1857. Brooklyn: L. Darbee and Son, 1857.

Piatt, Donn. *Some Historical Notes Concerning the Cincinnati Fire Department*. Cincinnati, n.d.

Proceedings of the Committee of Safety: Appointed by The Public Meeting of Citizens, on the Subject of Fires; Held at the Merchants Exchange, January 31, 1840. New York: Coolidge and Lambert, 1840.

Report of the Committee on a Paid Fire Department made to Common Council, May 5, 1859. Philadelphia, 1859.

Report on the Fire Departments of Cincinnati and St. Louis, and the Use of Steam Fire Engines. By Order of the Fire Underwriters of St. Louis. St. Louis: George Knapp and Co., 1858.

Report upon the National Convention of Chief Engineers of Fire Departments, Held in Baltimore, in October 1873. Providence: Hammond, Angell and Co., 1874.

Report of the Special Committee of the Baltimore United Fire Department in Reference to the Funds of Said Department. Baltimore: James Young, 1859.

Second Anniversary of the Organization of the Fire Department of San Francisco, 1853, Programme of the Procession; Address; Treasurer's Annual Report of the S.F. F. Department Charitable Fund and List of Officers and Members of the San Francisco Fire Department. San Francisco, 1853.

Soule, Frank, John H. Gihon, and James Nisbet. *The Annals of San Francisco; Containing a Summary of the History of the First Discovery, Settlement, Progress and Present Condition of California, and a Complete History of all the Important Events Connected with Its Great City: to which are added, Biographical Memoirs of Some Prominent Citizens*. New York: D. Appleton, 1855.

Testimony taken by The United States Pacific Railway Commission, appointed Under the Act of Congress, Approved March 3, 1887, Entitled "An Act Authorizing an Investigation of the Books, Accounts, and Methods of Railroads Which Have Received Aid From the United States, and for Other Purposes." Senate Ex. Doc. 51, part 7, vol. 6. Washington, D.C.: Government Printing Office, 1887.

Thomson, Clifford, ed. *The Fireman's Journal: The Fire Departments of the United States. A series of tables showing the fire equipment of the various cities, towns and villages, altogether with their water supply and other Facilities for extinguishing fires*. New York: Fireman's Journal, 1879.

Tocqueville, Alexis de. *Democracy in America*. The Henry Reeve Text as Revised by Francis Bowen and Further Corrected by Phillips Bradley. Abridged with an Introduction by Thomas Bender. New York: Modern Library, 1981.

Trollope, Frances. *Domestic Manners of the Americans*. New York: Vintage, 1948.

Veteran Firemen's Association of the City of New York. *Souvenir of the Transcontinental Excursion from New York to San Francisco*, September 1887. New York, 1887.

Young, Charles F. T. *Fires, Fire Engines and Fire Brigades*. London: Lockwood and Co., 1866.

Secondary Sources

Books

Abelson, Elaine S. *When Ladies Go A-Theiving: Middle-Class Shoplifters in the Victorian Department Store*. New York: Oxford University Press, 1989.

Adler, Jeffrey Scott. *Yankee Merchants and the Making of the Urban West: The Rise and Fall of Antebellum St. Louis*. Cambridge, U.K.: Cambridge University Press, 1991.

Arendt, Hannah. *The Human Condition*. Chicago: University of Chicago Press, 1958.

Asbury, Herbert. *Ye Olde Fire Laddies*. New York: Knopf, 1930.

Ayers, Edward L. *Vengeance and Justice: Crime and Punishment in the Nineteenth-Century American South*. New York: Oxford, 1984.

Bachelard, Gaston. *The Psychoanalysis of Fire*. Trans. Alan C. M. Ross. Boston: Beacon Press, 1964.

Baker, Jean H. *Ambivalent Americans: The Know-Nothing Party in Maryland*. Baltimore: Johns Hopkins University Press, 1977.

Baym, Nina. *Novels, Readers and Reviewers: Responses to Fiction in Antebellum America*. Ithaca, N.Y.: Cornell University Press, 1984.

Blackstone, Geoffrey Vaughan. *A History of the British Fire Service*. London: Routledge, 1957.

Bledstein, Burton J. *The Culture of Professionalism: The Middle Class and the Development of Higher Education in America*. New York: Norton, 1976.

Blumin, Stuart M. *The Emergence of the Middle Class: Social Experience in the American City, 1760–1900*. New York: Cambridge University Press, 1989.

Bourdieu, Pierre. *Distinction: A Social Critique of the Judgment of Taste*. Trans. Richard Nice. Cambridge, Mass.: Harvard University Press, 1984.

Boyer, Paul. *Urban Masses and Moral Order in America, 1820–1920*. Cambridge, Mass.: Harvard University Press, 1978.

Brayley, Arthur Wellington. *A Complete History of the Boston Fire Department from 1630–1888*. Boston: John Dale and Company, 1889.

Bridges, Amy. *A City in the Republic: Antebellum New York and the Origins of Machine Politics*. Cambridge, U.K.: Cambridge University Press, 1984.

Brinckloe, William Draper. *The Volunteer Fire Company*. Boston: National Fire Company, 1934.

Brown, Gillian. *Domestic Individualism: Imagining Self in Nineteenth-Century America*. Berkeley: University of California Press, 1990.

Browne, Gary Lawson. *Baltimore in the Nation, 1789–1861*. Chapel Hill: University of North Carolina Press, 1980.

Bryan, J. L. *Smoke as a Determinent of Human Behavior in Fire Situations*. Report from Fire Protection Curriculum, College of Engineering, University of Maryland, College Park (mimeo).

Bullock, Steven C. *Revolutionary Brotherhood: Freemasonry and the Transformation of the American Social Order, 1730–1840*. Chapel Hill: University of North Carolina Press, 1996.

Burdett, Charles A. *The Gloucester Fire Department; Its History and Work From 1793 to 1893*. Gloucester, Mass.: Steam Fire Association, 1892.

Burger, Jim. *In Service: A Documentary History of the Baltimore City Fire Department*. Baltimore: Paradigm Books, 1976.

Bushman, Richard L. *The Refinement of America: Persons, Houses, Cities*. New York: Knopf, 1992.

Calhoun, Craig, ed. *Habermas and the Public Sphere*. Cambridge, Mass.: MIT Press, 1992.

Cannon, Donald J. *Heritage of Flames*. New York: Doubleday, 1977.

Carnes, Mark C. "Middle-Class Men and the Solace of Fraternal Ritual." In Mark C. Carnes and Clyde Griffen, eds., *Meanings for Manhood: Constructions of Masculinity in Victorian America*. Chicago: University of Chicago Press, 1990, 37–52.

———. *Secret Ritual and Manhood in Victorian America*. New Haven: Yale University Press, 1989.

Cassedy, J. Albert. *The Firemen's Record*. Baltimore: Wm. Day and Co., 1891.

Champlin, Henry L. *The American Firemen*. Chelsea, Mass: H. L. Champlin, 1880.

Chandler, Alfred D., Jr. *The Visible Hand: The Managerial Revolution in American Business*. Cambridge, Mass.: Harvard University Press, 1977.

Clement, Patricia Ferguson. *Welfare and the Poor in the Nineteenth-Century City: Philadelphia, 1800–1854*. Rutherford, N.J.: Fairleigh Dickenson University Press, 1985.

Clisby, Charles. "Experiencing Fires." In David Canter, ed., *Fires and Human Behavior*. New York: John Wiley and Sons, 1980, 323–332.

Cmiel, Kenneth. *Democratic Eloquence: The Fight over Popular Speech in Nineteenth-Century America*. New York: William Morrow and Co., 1990.

Costello, Augustine F. *Our Firemen: A History of the New York Fire Department*. New York, 1887.

Cott, Nancy. *The Bonds of Womanhood: 'Woman's Sphere' in New England, 1780–1835*. New Haven: Yale University Press, 1977.

Cronon, William. *Changes in the Land: Indians, Colonists, and the Ecology of New England*. New York: Hill and Wang, 1983.

———. *Nature's Metropolis: Chicago and the Great West*. New York: Norton, 1991.

D'Ambry, Robert W. *Pioneers in Protection: The Story of a Century of Fire Insurance Service*. York, Pa.: Farmers Fire Insurance Company, 1953.

Davis, Susan. *Parades and Power: Street Theater in Nineteenth-Century Philadelphia*. Berkeley: University of California Press, 1986.

Decker, Peter R. *Fortunes and Failures: White-Collar Mobility in Nineteenth-Century San Francisco*. Cambridge, Mass.: Harvard University Press, 1978.

Dilts, Bryan Lee, ed. *1860 California Census Index*. Salt Lake City: Index Publishers, 1984.

Ditzel, Paul. *Fire Engines, Fire Fighters*. New York: Crown, 1976.

Douglas, Ann. *The Feminization of American Culture*. New York: Knopf, 1977.

Earnest, Ernest. *The Volunteer Fire Company, Past and Present*. New York: Stein and Day, 1979.

Easterbrook, H. H. *History of the Somerville Fire Department from 1842–1892*. Boston: Robinson Printing Co., 1893.

Edwards, Edward. *History of the Volunteer Fire Department of St. Louis*. St. Louis, 1906.

Einhorn, Robin L. *Property Rules: Political Economy in Chicago, 1833–1872*. Chicago: University of Chicago Press, 1991.

Ellis, Leonard Bolles. *History of the Fire Department of the City of New Bedford, Massachusetts, 1772–1890*. New Bedford, 1890.

Ethington, Philip J. *The Public City: The Political Construction of Urban Life in San Francisco, 1850–1900*. New York: Cambridge University Press, 1994.

Federal Writer's Project. *Reading's Volunteer Fire Department: Its History and Traditions*. Philadelphia: William Penn Association, 1938.

Feldberg, Michael. *The Turbulent Era: Riot and Disorder in Jacksonian America*. New York: Oxford University Press, 1980.

Forrest, Clarence H. *Official History of the Fire Department of the City of Baltimore*. Baltimore: Williams and Wilkins Co. Press, 1898.

Foucault, Michel. *Discipline and Punish: The Birth of the Prison*. New York: Vintage Books, 1979.

———. *History of Sexuality*. Vol. 1: *An Introduction*. New York: Vintage Books, 1990.

Franchot, Jenny. *Roads to Rome: The Antebellum Protestant Encounter with Catholicism*. Berkeley: University of California Press, 1994.

Frisch, Michael H. *Town into City: Springfield, Massachusetts, and the Meaning of Community, 1840–1880*. Cambridge, Mass.: Harvard University Press, 1972.

Gagey, Edmond M. *The San Francisco Stage: A History*. Westport, Conn.: Greenwood Press, 1950.

Giddens, Anthony. *The Consequences of Modernity*. Stanford, Calif.: Stanford University Press, 1990.

Gienapp, William E. *The Origins of the Republican Party, 1852–1856*. New York: Oxford University Press, 1987.

———. "'Politics Seem to Enter into Everything': Political Culture in the North, 1840–1860." In Stephen E. Maizlish and John J. Kushma, eds., *Essays on American Antebellum Politics, 1840–1860*. College Station: Texas A & M University Press, 1982, 15–69.

Gilbert, Keith Reginald. *Fire Engines and Other Firefighting Appliances*. London: H.M.S.O., 1966.

Gilje, Paul A. *The Road to Mobocracy: Popular Disorder in New York City, 1763–1834*. Chapel Hill: University of North Carolina Press, 1987.

———. *Rioting in America*. Bloomington: Indiana University Press, 1996.

Ginzberg, Lori D. *Women and the Work of Benevolence: Morality, Politics and Class in the Nineteenth-Century United States*. New Haven: Yale University Press, 1990.

Gorn, Elliot J. *The Manly Art: Bare-Knuckle Prize Fighting in America*. Ithaca, N.Y.: Cornell University Press, 1986.

Goudsblom, Johan. *Fire and Civilization*. New York: Penguin, 1992.

Greenberg, Kenneth S. *Honor and Slavery: Lies, Duels, Noses, Masks, Dressing as a Woman, Gifts, Strangers, Humanitarianism, Death, Slave Rebellions, the Proslavery Argument, Baseball, Hunting, and Gambling in the Old South*. Princeton, N.J.: Princeton University Press, 1996.

Griffen, Clyde. "Reconstructing Masculinity from the Evangelical Revival to the Wanings of Progressivism: A Speculative Synthesis." In Mark C. Carnes and Clyde Griffen, eds., *Meanings for Manhood: Constructions of Masculinity in Victorian America*. Chicago: University of Chicago Press, 1990, 183–205.

Grimsted, David. *Melodrama Unveiled: American Theater and Culture, 1800–1850*. Berkeley: University of California Press, 1987.

Habermas, Jurgen. *The Structural Transformation of the Public Sphere: An Inquiry into a Category of Bourgeois Society*. Trans. Thomas Berger and Frederick Lawrence. Cambridge, Mass.: MIT Press, 1989.

Halsted, John B. *Romanticism*. New York: Harper and Row, 1969.

Halttunen, Karen. *Confidence Men and Painted Women: A Study of Middle-Class Culture in America, 1830–1870*. New Haven: Yale University Press, 1982.

Hamer, David. *New Towns in the New World: Images and Perceptions of the Nineteenth-Century Urban Frontier*. New York: Columbia University Press, 1990.

Hartt, Frederick. *History of Italian Renaissance Art*. New York: Harry Abrams and Co., 1969.

Hartz, Louis. *Economic Policy and Democratic Thought: Pennsylvania, 1776–1860*. Chicago: Quadrangle Books, 1968.

Hazen, Margaret Hindle, and Robert M. Hazen. *Keepers of the Flame: The Role of Fire in American Culture, 1775–1925*. Princeton, N.J.: Princeton University Press, 1992.

Holdredge, Helen. *Firebelle Lillie: The Life and Times of Lillie Hitchcock Coit of San Francisco*. New York: Meredith Press, 1967.

Holloway, Sally. *London's Noble Fire Brigades, 1833–1904*. London: Cassell, 1973.

Holt, Michael F. *Political Crisis of the 1850's*. New York: John Wiley and Sons, 1978.

Holzman, Robert, S. *The Romance of Firefighting*. New York: Bonanza Books, 1956.

Howe, Daniel Walker. "Victorian Culture in America." In Daniel D. Howe, ed., *Victorian America*. Philadelphia: University of Pennsylvania Press, 1976.

Insurance Company of North America Collection. *American Fire Marks*. Philadelphia: Insurance Company of North America, 1933.

Jackson, Ronald Vern. *Baltimore, Md., 1860 Census Index*. Salt Lake City: Accelerated Indexing Systems, 1988.

Johnson, David R. "Police and Fire Protection." In Mary Kupiec Cayton et al., *The Encyclopedia of American Social History*, 3 vols. New York: Charles Scribner and Sons, 1992, 3: 2167–2174.

———. *Policing the Urban Underworld: The Impact of Crime on the Development of the American Police, 1800–1877*. Philadelphia: Temple University Press, 1979.

Johnson, Paul E. *A Shopkeeper's Millennium: Society and Revivals in Rochester, New York, 1815–1837*. New York: Hill and Wang, 1987.

Johnson, Paul E., and Sean Wilentz. *The Kingdom of Matthias*. New York: Oxford University Press, 1994.

Jordan, William G. *One Hundred Years of Fire Insurance: The Aetna Insurance Company, 1819–1919*. Hartford: Aetna Insurance Company, 1919.

Kasson, John. *Civilizing the Machine: Technology and Republican Values in America, 1776–1900*. New York: Penguin Books, 1976.

———. *Rudeness and Civility: Manners in Nineteenth-Century Urban America*. New York: Hill and Wang, 1990.

Katznelson, Ira. *City Trenches: Urban Politics and the Patterning of Class in the United States*. New York: Pantheon Books, 1981.

Kerber, Linda. *Women of the Republic: Intellect and Ideology in Revolutionary America*. Chapel Hill: University of North Carolina Press, 1980.

Kett, Joseph. *Rites of Passage: Adolescence in America, 1790 to the Present*. New York: Basic Books, 1977.

King, William T. *History of the American Steam Fire-Engine*. Boston: William King, 1896.

Kohl, Lawrence Frederick. *The Politics of Individualism: Parties and the American Character in the Jacksonian Era*. New York: Oxford University Press, 1989.

Lane, Roger. *Policing the City: Boston, 1822–1885*. New York: Atheneum, 1975.

———. *Violent Death in the City: Suicide, Accident and Murder in Nineteenth-Century Philadelphia*. Cambridge, Mass: Harvard University Press, 1979.

Larson, Lawrence H. *The Urban West at the End of the Frontier*. Lawrence: University of Kansas Press, 1978.

Laurie, Bruce. "Fire Companies and Gangs in Southwark: The 1840's." In Allen F. Davis and Mark H. Haller, eds., *The Peoples of Philadelphia: A History of Ethnic Groups and Lower Class Life, 1790–1940*. Philadelphia: Temple University Press, 1973, 71–88.

———. *Working People of Philadelphia, 1800–1850*. Philadelphia: Temple University Press, 1980.

Leverenz, David. *Manhood and the American Renaissance*. Ithaca, N.Y.: Cornell University Press, 1989.

Levine, Lawrence W. *Highbrow/Lowbrow: The Emergence of Cultural Hierarchy in America*. Cambridge, Mass.: Harvard University Press, 1988.

Lewis, Jan. "Mother's Love: The Construction of an Emotion in Nineteenth-Century America." In Andrew E. Barnes and Peter N. Stearns, eds., *Social History and Issues in Human Consciousness: Some Interdisciplinary Connections*. New York: New York University Press, 1989.

Lewis, William C. *A Manual for Volunteer or Paid Fire Organizations*. New York: William C. Lewis, 1872.

Lipsitz, George. *The Sidewalks of St. Louis: Places, People and Politics in an American City*. Columbia: University of Missouri Press, 1991.

Lotchin, Roger. *San Francisco 1846–1856: From Hamlet to City*. New York: Oxford University Press, 1974.

Lussier, Hubert. *Les Sapeurs-Pomiers au XIXe siecle: Associations volontaires en milieu populaire*. Paris: A.R.F.-Editions/L'Harmattan, 1987.

Lynch, Thomas R. *The Volunteer Fire Department of St. Louis, 1819–1859*. St. Louis: R. Ennis, 1880.

Lyons, Paul Robert. *Fire in America!* Boston: National Fire Protection Association, 1976.

Macleod, David I. *Building Character in the American Boy: The Boy Scouts, YMCA, and Their Forerunners, 1870–1920*. Madison: University of Wisconsin Press, 1983.

Maguire, Henry. "Disembodiment and Corporeality in Byzantine Images of the Saints." In *Iconography at the Crossroads*. Papers from the Colloquium Sponsored by the Index of Christian Art, Princeton University, March 23-24, 1990. Princeton, N.J.: Princeton University, Department of Art and Archaeology, 1993, 75–90.

Marx, Leo. *The Machine in the Garden: Technology and the Pastoral Ideal in America*. New York: Oxford University Press, 1964.

McCarthy, Kathleen D. *Noblesse Oblige: Charity and Cultural Philanthropy in Chicago, 1849–1929*. Chicago: University of Chicago Press, 1982.

McCoy, Drew R. *The Elusive Republic: Political Economy in Jeffersonian America*. Chapel Hill: University of North Carolina Press, 1980.

McCreary, George W. *The Ancient and Honorable Mechanical Company of Baltimore*. Baltimore: Kohn and Pollock, 1901.

McDermott, John Francis, ed. *The Early Histories of St. Louis*. St. Louis: St. Louis Historical Documents Foundation, 1952.

McDonald, Terrence J. *The Parameters of Urban Fiscal Policy: Socioeconomic Change and Political Culture in San Francisco, 1860–1906*. Berkeley: University of California Press, 1986.

Mering, John Vollmer. *The Whig Party in Missouri*. Columbia: University of Missouri Press, 1967.

Monkkonen, Eric H. *America Becomes Urban: The Development of U.S. Cities and Towns, 1780–1980*. Berkeley: University of California Press, 1990.

———. *Police in Urban America, 1860–1920*. Cambridge, U.K.: Cambridge University Press, 1981.

Moore, Albert C. *Iconography of Religions: An Introduction*. Philadelphia: Fortress Press, 1977.

Mullen, Kevin J. *Let Justice Be Done: Crime and Politics in Early San Francisco*. Reno: University of Nevada Press, 1989.

Murray, William A. *The Unheralded Heroes of Baltimore's Big Blazes*. Baltimore: John Schmitz and Sons, 1969.

Muśee Rath. *Les Icones dans les collections suisses*. Berne: Editions Bentelli S.A., 1968.

Novak, Barbara. *Nature and Culture: American Landscape Painting, 1825–1875*. New York: Oxford University Press, 1980.

Olsen, Sherry H. *Baltimore: The Building of an American City*. Baltimore: Johns Hopkins University Press, 1985.

Park, Clyde W. *The Cincinnati Equitable Insurance Company*. Cincinnati: Cincinnati Equitable Insurance Co., 1954.

Pendleton, Harry C. *The Exempt Firemen of San Francisco*. San Francisco: Commercial Publishing Company, 1900.

Peters, Harry T. *Currier and Ives, Printmakers to the American People*. New York: Doubleday, 1942.

Pliny the Younger. *Letters of Pliny the Council*. Edinburgh: J. Ballantyne for W. J. and J. Richardson, 1807.

Pratt, John Lowell, ed. *Currier and Ives, Chronicles of America*. Maplewood, N.J.: Hammond, 1968.

Primm, James Neal. *Lion of the Valley*. Boulder: Pruett, 1981.

Pyne, Stephen J. *Fire in America: A Cultural History of Wildland and Rural Fire*. Princeton, N.J.: Princeton University Press, 1982.

Rawls, Walton. *The Great Book of Currier and Ives' America*. New York: Abbeville, 1979.

Reminiscences of Past Members of the Worcester Fire Society. Worcester, Mass.: Printed for the Society, 1874.

Reynolds, David S. *Walt Whitman's America*. New York: Knopf, 1995.

Rice, David, and Tamara Talbot. *Icons*. Dublin: National Gallery of Ireland, 1968.

Riess, Stephen A. "The City." In Mary Kupiec Cayton et, al. *The Encyclopedia of American Social History*, 3 vols. New York: Charles Scribner and Sons, 1992, 2: 1259–1275.

Rodgers, Daniel T. *The Work Ethic in Industrial America, 1850–1920*. Chicago: University of Chicago Press, 1979.

Roper, Stephen. *Handbook of Modern Steam Fire-Engines*. Philadelphia: Claxton, Remsen and Haffelfinger, 1876.

Rorabaugh, W. J. *The Alcoholic Republic: An American Tradition*. New York: Oxford University Press, 1979.

Rose, Anne C. *Voices of the Marketplace: American Thought and Culture, 1830–1860*. New York: Twayne, 1995.

Ross, Steven J. *Workers on the Edge: Work, Leisure, and Politics in Industrializing Cincinnati, 1788–1890*. New York: Columbia University Press, 1985.

Rotundo, Anthony. *American Manhood: Transformations in Masculinity from the Revolution to the Modern Era*. New York: Basic Books, 1993.

Ryan, Mary P. *Cradle of the Middle Class: The Family in Oneida County, New York, 1790–1865*. Cambridge, U.K.: Cambridge University Press, 1981.

———. *Women in Public: Between Banners and Ballots, 1825–1880*. Baltimore: Johns Hopkins University Press, 1990.

St. Louis Fire Department. *Justifiably Proud*. Marcelline, Mo.: Walsworth Printing Company, 1977.

St. Louis Firemen's Fund. *History of the St. Louis Fire Department*. St. Louis: Central Publishing Company, 1914.

Scharf, John Thomas. *The Chronicles of Baltimore: Being a Complete History of "Baltimore Town" and Baltimore City from the Earliest Period to the Present Time*. Baltimore: Turnbull Brothers, 1874.

———. *History of St. Louis City and County from the Earliest Period to the Present Day, including Biographical Sketches of Representative Men*. Philadelphia: Louis H. Evarts, 1883.

Schlesinger, Arthur M., Jr. *The Age of Jackson*. Boston: Little, Brown and Co., 1945.

Sennett, Richard. *The Fall of Public Man*. New York: Random House, 1978.

Sheldon, George W. *The Story of the Volunteer Fire Department of the City of New York*. New York: Harper and Brothers, 1882.

Silsby Manufacturing Company. *History of the Silsby Steam Fire Engine*. Buffalo: Gries and Co., 1881.

Simkin, Colin, ed. *Currier and Ives' America*. New York: Crown, 1952.

Sklar, Katherine Kish. *Catherine Beecher: A Study in American Domesticity*. New Haven: Yale University Press, 1973.

Skocpol, Theda. *Protecting Soldiers and Mothers: The Political Origins of Social Policy in the United States*. Cambridge, Mass.: Harvard University Press, 1992.

Smith, Carl. *Urban Disorder and the Shape of Belief*. Chicago: University of Chicago Press, 1995.

Smith, Dennis. *Dennis Smith's History of Firefighting in America: 300 Years of Courage*. New York: Dial Press, 1978.

Stansell, Christine. *City of Women: Sex and Class in New York, 1789–1860*. Urbana: University of Illinois Press, 1987.

Starr, Paul. *The Social Transformation of American Medicine*. New York: Basic Books, 1982.

Stellman, Louis J. *Sam Brannan: Builder of San Francisco*. New York: Exposition Press, 1953.

Stevens, Walter B. *St. Louis: The Fourth City, 1764–1909*. St. Louis: S. J. Clarke Publishing Co., 1909.

Tagg, John. *The Burden of Representation: Essays on Photographies and Histories*. Amherst: University of Massachusetts Press, 1988.

Teaford, Jon C. *The Municipal Revolution in America: Origins of Modern Urban Government, 1650–1825*. Chicago: University of Chicago Press, 1975.

———. *The Unheralded Triumph: City Government in America, 1870–1900*. Baltimore: Johns Hopkins University Press, 1984.

Thernstrom, Stephan. *The Other Bostonians: Poverty and Progress in the American Metropolis, 1880–1970*. Cambridge, Mass.: Harvard University Press, 1973.

Tyrrell, Ian R. *Sobering Up: From Temperance to Prohibition in Antebellum America, 1800–1860*. Westport, Conn.: Greenwood Press, 1979.

Veblen, Thorstein. *The Theory of the Leisure Class: An Economic Study of Institutions*. New York: Viking, [1899] 1931.

Wade, Richard C. *The Urban Frontier: Pioneer Life in Early Pittsburgh, Cincinnati, Lexington, Louisville, and St. Louis*. Cambridge, Mass.: Harvard University Press, 1959.

Walters, Ronald G. *American Reformers, 1815–1860*. New York: Hill and Wang, 1978.

Warner, Sam Bass, Jr. *The Private City: Philadelphia in Three Periods of Its Growth*. Philadelphia: University of Pennsylvania Press, 1968.

Wheeler, Norman W. *Report of Norman W. Wheeler, Engineer, upon Steam Fire Engines, Fire Extinguishers, etc.* New York: New York Underwriters Agency, 1876.

White, Charles E. *The Providence Fireman*. Providence: E. L. Freeman and Son, 1886.

Wiebe, Robert H. *The Search for Order, 1877–1920*. New York: Hill and Wang, 1967.

Wilentz, Sean. *Chants Democratic: New York City and the Rise of the American Working Class*. New York: Oxford University Press, 1984.

Williams, Walter. *The State of Missouri, an Autobiography*. Columbia, Mo.: E. W. Stephens, 1904.

Wolf, Bryan Jay. *Romantic Re-Vision: Culture and Consciousness in Nineteenth-Century American Painting and Literature*. Chicago: University of Chicago Press, 1982.

Wood, Gordon S. *The Creation of the American Republic, 1776–1787*. New York: W. W. Norton and Co., 1969.

Wood, Peter G. "A Survey of Behavior in Fires." In David Canter, ed., *Fires and Human Behavior*. New York: John Wiley and Son, 1980.

Wright, Conrad Edict. *The Transformation of Charity in Postrevolutionary New England* Boston: Northeastern University Press. 1992.

Wright, Gwendolyn. *Building the Dream: A Social History of Housing in America*. New York: MIT Press, 1983.

Wyatt-Brown, Bertram. *Southern Honor: Ethics and Behavior in the Old South*. New York: Oxford. 1982.

Zurier, Rebecca. *The American Firehouse: An Architectural and Social History*. New York: Abbeville, 1982.

Periodicals

Altschuler, Glenn, and Stuart Blumin, "Where is the Real America?': Politics and Popular Consciousness in the Antebellum Era," *American Quarterly* 49(2) (1997): 225–267.

Anderson, Annelise Graebner. "The Development of Municipal Fire Departments in the United States," *Journal of Libertarian Studies* 3(3) (1979): 331–359.

Bloch, Ruth H. "American Feminine Ideals in Transition: The Rise of the Moral Mother, 1785–1815," *Feminist Studies* 4 (1978).

———. "The Gendered Meanings of Virtue in Revolutionary America," *Signs* 13(1) (1987): 37–58.

Bowers, Douglas. "Ideology and Political Parties in Maryland, 1851–1856," *Maryland Historical Magazine* 64 (Fall 1969): 197–217.

Bushnell, George D. "Chicago's Rowdy Firefighters," *Chicago History* 2(4) (1973): 232–241.

Caric, Ric Northrup. "Blustering Brags, Dueling Inventors, and Corn-Square Geniuses: Processes of Recognition among Philadelphia Artisans, 1785–1825," *American Journal of Semiotics*, forthcoming.

Channing, William F. "The American Fire-Alarm Telegraph," *Ninth Annual Report of the Smithsonian Institution*, March 1855, 147–155.

Colson, John Calvin. "The Fire Company Library Associations of Baltimore," *Journal of Library History* 21(1) (1986): 158–176.

Cooper, Robyn. "The Fireman: Immaculate Manhood," *Journal of Popular Culture* 24(4) (Spring 1995): 138–170.

Davis, Ronald L. F. "Community and Conflict in Pioneer Saint Louis, Missouri," *Western Historical Quarterly* 10 (July 1979): 337–355.

Dorson, Richard M. "Mose the Far-Famed and World-Renowned," *American Literature* 15(3) (November 1943): 288–300.

Doyle, Don H. "The Social Functions of Voluntary Associations in a Nineteenth-Century American Town," *Social Science History* 1 (Spring 1977): 338–343.

Dykstra, Arlen R. "Rowdyism and Rivalism in the St. Louis Fire Department, 1850–1857," *Missouri Historical Review* 69(1) (1974–1975): 49–64.

Engerman, Stanley. "Up or Out: Social and Geographical Mobility in the United States," *Journal of Interdisciplinary History* 3 (Winter 1975): 469–489.

Ethington, Philip J. "Vigilantes and the Police: The Creation of a Professional Police Bureaucracy in San Francisco, 1847–1900," *Journal of Social History* 21(2) (Winter 1987): 197–228.

Frost, L. E., and E. L. Jones. "The Fire Gap and the Greater Durability of Nineteenth-Century Cities," *Planning Perspectives* 4 (1989): 333–347.

Gigierano, Geoffrey. " 'A Creature of Law': Cincinnati's Paid Fire Department," *Cincinnati Historical Society Bulletin* 40(2) (1982): 78–99.

Ginsberg, Stephen F. "Above the Law: Volunteer Firemen in New York City, 1836–1837," *New York History* 50(2) (1969): 165–186.

Gorn, Elliot. " 'Good-Bye Boys, I Die a True American': Homicide, Nativism, and Working-Class Culture in Antebellum New York City," *Journal of American History* 74(2) (1987): 388–410.

Grimsted, David. "Rioting in Its Jacksonian Setting," *American Historical Review* 77 (April 1972): 365–397.

Holt, Glen E. "Volunteer Fire Fighting in St. Louis, 1818–1859," *Gateway Heritage* 4(3) (Winter 1983–1984): 2–13.

Holt, Michael F. "The Politics of Impatience: The Origins of Know-Nothingism," *Journal of American History* 60 (1973): 309–331.

Jones, James Boyd, Jr. "Mose the Bowery B'hoy and the Nashville Volunteer Fire Department, 1849–1860," *Tennessee Historical Quarterly* 40(2) (1981): 170–181.

Kingsdale, Jon. " 'The Poor-Man's Club': Social Functions of the Urban Saloon, Working Class," *American Quarterly* 25 (October 1973): 472–489.

Kloppenberg, James T. "The Virtues of Liberalism: Christianity, Republicanism, and Ethics in Early American Political Discourse," *Journal of American History* 74(1) (June 1978): 9–13.

Knobel, Dale T. "A Vocabulary of Ethnic Perception: Content Analysis of the American Stage Irishman, 1820–1860," *Journal of American Studies* (Great Britain) 15(1) (1981): 45–71.

Lampe, Anthony B. "St. Louis Volunteer Fire Department, 1820–1850: A Study in the Volunteer Age," *Missouri Historical Review* 62(3) (1967–1968): 235–259.

MacMullen, Jerry. "The Company of Hooks and Ladders," *Westways*, May 1962, 14–16.

Merish, Lori " 'The Hand of Refined Taste' in the Frontier Landscape: Caroline Kirkland's *A New Home, Who'll Follow?* and the Feminization of American Consumerism," *American Quarterly* 45(4) (December 1993): 485–523.

Monkkonen, Eric H. "From Cop History to Social History: The Significance of the Police in American History," *Journal of Social History* 15(4) (1982): 575–591.

Perkins, Kenneth B. "Volunteer Fire Departments: Community Integration, Autonomy and Survival," *Human Organization* 46(4) (1987): 342–348.

Prince, Carl E. "The Great 'Riot Year': Jacksonian Democracy and Patterns of Violence in 1834," *Journal of the Early Republic* 5(1) (1985): 1–19.

Pyne, Stephen J. "Firestick History," *Journal of American History* 76 (March 1990): 1132–1141.

Reichard, Maximilian. "Urban Politics in Jacksonian St. Louis: Traditional Values in Change and Conflict," *Missouri Historical Review* 70 (April 1976): 259–271.

Rodgers, Daniel T. "Republicanism: The Career of a Concept," *Journal of American History* 79(1) (June 1992): 11–38.

Rotundo, Anthony E. "Body and Soul: Changing Ideals of American Middle-Class Manhood, 1770–1920," *Journal of Social History* 16(4) (1883): 23–38.

Rudachyk, B.E.S. " 'At the Mercy of the Devouring Element': The Equipment and Organization of the Halifax Fire Establishment, 1830–1850," *Collections of the Royal Nova Scotia Historical Society* 41 (1982): 165–184.

Schneider, John C. "Riot and Reaction in St. Louis, 1854–1856," *Missouri Historical Review* 68 (January 1974): 171–185.

Smith-Rosenberg, Caroll. "The Female World of Love and Ritual: Relations between Women in Nineteenth-Century America," *Signs* 1 (1975): 1–29.

Snyder, Katherine V. " 'Luxurious Bachlerdom': Domesticity, Consumer Culture, and Single Manhood in 1890s New York," unpublished paper delivered at the Organization of American Historians Annual Meeting, March 1996.

Tarr, Joel A., Thomas Finholt, and David Goodman. "The City and the Telegraph: Urban Telecommunications in the Pre-Telephone Era," *Journal of Urban History* 14(1): 38–80.

Vole, Robert, "When Men Were Men and Firemen," *American History Illustrated* 17(3) (1982): 33–35.

Waldorf, Dolores. "Baltimore Fire Laddie: George H. Hossefross," *California Historical Society Quarterly* 23(1): 69–77.

Weaver, John C., and Peter DeLottinville. "The Conflagration and the City: Disaster and Progress in British North America during the Nineteenth Century," *Social History* (Canada) 13(26) (1980): 417–449.

White, John H., Jr. "Origins of the Steam Fire Engine," *Technology and Culture* 14(2, part 1) (1973): 166–169.

Dissertations

Baumohl, James Andrew. "Dashaways and Doctors: The Treatment of Habitual Drunkards in San Francisco from the Gold Rush to Prohibition." Ph.D. dissertation, School of Social Welfare, University of California at Berkeley, 1986.

Calhoun, Richard B. "From Community to Metropolis: Fire Protection in New York City, 1790–1875." Ph.D. dissertation, Columbia University, 1973.

Cannon, Donald James "The Fire Department of the City of New York, 1835–1898: A Study of Institutional Adaptability." Ph.D. dissertation, Fordham University, 1976.

Ginzberg, Stephen F. "The History of Fire Protection in New York City, 1800–1842." Ph.D. dissertation, New York University, 1968.

Greenberg, Amy S. "Cause for Alarm: The Volunteer Fire Department in the Nineteenth-Century City." Ph.D. dissertation, Harvard University, 1995.

Kiefer, Kathleen J. "A History of the Cincinnati Fire Department in the Nineteenth Century." M.A. thesis, University of Cincinnati, 1967.

Lampe, Anthony B. "St. Louis Volunteer Fire Department, 1820–1850: A Study of the Volunteer Age." Ph.D. dissertation, St. Louis University, 1966.

McNally, Vincent Paul. "A Most Dangerous and Noble Calling: The Development, Organization and Operation of the American Volunteer Fire Service," vols. 1 and 2. Ph.D. dissertation, Temple University, 1979.

Neilly, Andrew. "Violent Volunteers: A History of the Volunteer Fire Department of Philadelphia, 1736–1871." Ph.D. dissertation, University of Pennsylvania, 1959.

Olson, Audrey Louise. "St. Louis Germans, 1850–1920: The Nature of an Immigrant Community and Its Relation to the Assimilation Process." Ph.D. dissertation, University of Kansas, 1970.

INDEX